WAR

An Illustrated History

JEREMY BLACK

SUTTON PUBLISHING

First published in 2003 by
Sutton Publishing Limited · Phoenix Mill
Thrupp · Stroud · Gloucestershire · GL5 2BU

British Library Cataloguing in Publication Data
A catalogue record for this book is available from the British Library.

ISBN 0-7509-2407-1

For Judith and Max King

Typeset in 11/15pt New Baskerville.
Typesetting and origination by
Sutton Publishing Limited.
Printed and bound in England by
J.H. Haynes & Co. Ltd, Sparkford.

CONTENTS

PREFACE

There are essentially two different ways to write history. One is to present it as a seamless whole, with the historian passing on knowledge and analysis as they must be. The second is to present to the reader the problems of understanding and explaining the past, making it clear that there is not one correct answer or approach, but rather a number of possible 'takes' on the past. In popular works, the former approach is adopted, largely, it appears, because of a view that readers do not wish to be introduced to problems.

In my view, this is unsatisfactory. First, for intellectual reasons, as there is no single history to be told. Second, because I believe that it is inappropriate for historians to talk down to their readers, imagining that people who can face the complexities of living, working and thinking in modern societies cannot grasp the complexities of analysing the past and would not be interested in doing so.

It is now far harder than it was a few years ago to write a history of war, illustrated or otherwise. There is one major reason: it is no longer satisfactory to take simply a Western approach to the subject, and to see the history of war essentially in terms of the development of European military systems and their spread and impact round the world. That this is the established approach can be clearly seen. *The Cambridge Illustrated History of Warfare* (1995), a first-rate work edited by Geoffrey Parker, has on the title page the addition 'The Triumph of the West' and accepts that it is 'open to the charge of Eurocentrism'. *The Oxford Illustrated History of Modern War* (1997), edited by Charles Townshend, adopts a similar approach, essentially by defining modern war as Western warfare.

Reader expectation, marketing pressures, the availability of sources, and linguistic limitations all combine to push in the same direction, but I have tried in this work to devote more space to non-Western warfare than is customary. This serves two purposes. First, it throws much light on important aspects of military history, and, second, it offers a new context within which to judge Western developments. However, the broader geographical range exacerbates the standard authorial problems of choice of emphasis, balance between description and analysis, and deciding how best to explain change. Doubtless all these problems will emerge in the text that follows. In order to cover non-Western developments, it is necessary to mention more names and dates than some readers will be comfortable with, but it is important to introduce those interested in the history of war to the range and variety of military developments in the past. Hopefully, readers will be excited to be introduced to some subjects and areas that are new to them and will welcome the challenge of deciding how best they would have organised this topic. I would be very glad to hear from them.

I would like to thank the students I have taught at Exeter on undergraduate and postgraduate courses on the history of war for providing much of the stimulus to face this question. While writing this book, I benefited from the opportunity to develop ideas presented by lecturing to the Triangle Institute for Security Studies, the Near-East–South Asia Center for Strategic Studies, and the Oxford Conference in Education, as well as at Georgetown, High Point and Rutgers Universities, the Universities of Delaware, Maryland, North Carolina, and Tennessee, and for the United States Naval War College, College of Continuing Education, Strategy and Policy Division at Annapolis, Washington and Naples. Comments on earlier drafts by Simon Barton, David Braund, Richard Connell, John France, David Gates, Jan Glete, David Graff, Stewart Lone, Peter Lorge, Stephen Mitchell, Stephen Morillo, Michael Prestwich, John Rich and Everett Wheeler were most useful, but they are not responsible for such errors as remain. I would like to thank Christopher Feeney for commissioning this book and Paul Ingrams for proving an exemplary copy editor. It is a great pleasure to dedicate it to old friends.

Picture Credits

References are to page numbers.

Ancient Art and Architecture Library: front endpaper, 31, 34, 35, 55, 62, 63, 66, 75, 107

Ann Ronan Picture Library: back endpaper, 1, 12, 14, 42, 79, 68, 69, 100, 111, 132, 133, 138, 167, 170, 177, 178

Ann S. K. Brown: 95

Archive für Kunst: 9, 10, 11, 54, 82, 98, 99, 106, 126, 131, 135, 139

Bibliothèque nationale: 39

Liverpool Museum: 69

Salisbury District Council: 46

Topham Picture Point: 173, 174, 214, 215

Trip and Art Directors: 15, 19, 47, 50, 51, 58, 87, 103

INTRODUCTION

What is the history of war? I know from teaching students and talking with others from a wide range of backgrounds that war today is generally seen as organised conflict waged by armed forces, and that the emphasis in any discussion, either of why one side prevailed or of how change occurred, is on weaponry. Indeed, mechanisation plays a major role in the modern concept of war. There is a focus on the capabilities of particular weapons and weapons systems, and a belief that progress stems from their improvement. This stress on the material culture of war can also be seen with discussion of earlier eras. Thus, with, for example, the Iron Age replacing the Bronze Age, the emphasis is on how the superior cutting power of iron and the relative ease of making iron weapons led to a change in civilisations.

Weaponry is certainly important, but, as we know from observing modern conflicts, such as the Vietnam War and the Russian attempt to dominate Afghanistan, it is not always the best armed that prevail. Indeed, war, seen as an attempt to impose will, involves more than victory in battle.

Yet to focus solely on battle for a moment, there is another problem stemming from the Western perception, namely the assumption that the 'face of battle', the essentials of war, are in some fashion timeless, as they involve men being willing to undergo the trial of combat. In practice, the understanding of loss and suffering, at both the level of ordinary soldiers and that of societies as a whole, is far more culturally conditioned than any emphasis on the sameness of battle might suggest. At the crudest of levels, the willingness to suffer losses varies, and this helps to determine both military success and differences in combat across the world in any one period. To contrast the willingness of the Western powers to suffer heavy losses in the two World Wars, especially the First, with their reluctance to do so subsequently, and also the different attitudes towards casualties of the Americans and the North Vietnamese in the Vietnam War, is to be aware of a situation that has a wider historical resonance. It is far from clear that variations and changes in these 'cultural' factors should play a smaller role in the history of war than weaponry. Morale remains the single most important factor in war.

The same is true of organisational issues: how troops were organised on the battlefield, the nature of force structures, and the organisation of societies for conflict. Instead of assuming that these were driven by weaponry, specifically how best to use weapons, and maybe also how to move and supply them, it is necessary to appreciate the autonomous character of organisational factors and their close linkage with social patterns and developments. A parallel case can be made with the causes of war. Looked at differently, armies and navies are organisations with objectives, and, in assessing their capability and effectiveness, it is necessary to consider how these objectives changed, and how far such changes created pressures for adaptation. In short, a demand-led account has to be set alongside the more familiar supply-side assessment that presents improvements in weaponry or increases in numbers without considering the wider context.

Territorial aggrandisement was an important theme in warfare, as was a related interest in preventing threatening developments in international relations. These encouraged an emphasis on particular types of force structure and military doctrine. But force was also frequently used to contain or suppress domestic disaffection, and this led to different requirements. It is necessary to move away from the notion of war as essentially a struggle between organised regular forces. Instead, it is pertinent to emphasise the role of irregular forces in warfare. Terrorism and guerrilla activities should be included in the discussion of military history.

Note on Dating

CE (Common Era) and BCE (Before Common Era) are used throughout this book. Those not familiar with the terms may read them as 'AD' and 'BC'.

1

UNTIL THE CREATION OF THE ISLAMIC WORLD

Any periodisation in military history is at once open to question. In this book, we depart from the standard Classical, Medieval, Early Modern, Late Modern divisions organised round events in European history, such as the onset of the Italian Wars in 1494, or the end of the Napoleonic Wars with the defeat of Napoleon at Waterloo in 1815, and, instead, search for periods of division first defined in terms of major developments in relations between parts of the world that stemmed from war, and, subsequently, in centuries, with the focus within them on these relations. The first section of this book thus closes with the movements of peoples that put pressure on settled societies in the fourth, fifth and sixth centuries CE, culminating with the dramatic expansion of Islamic power that created a new world from the Atlantic to central Asia, a span of power that had not been matched by the great empires of antiquity, such as those of Macedonia under Alexander the Great, Han China or imperial Rome. Within this period, war was framed by the natural and human environment.

Fighting is not some result of the corruption of humankind by society: it is integral to human society. From the outset, humans competed with other animals, and fed and protected themselves as a result of these struggles. There was far less contrast between this and fighting other humans than in modern culture. Instead, the pattern in long-standing modern hunter-gatherer societies, such as those in Amazonia and New Guinea, indicates a situation that was formerly far more common. For example, among the Native population of North America, there appears to have been no sharp distinction between raiding other human groups and hunting animals. The two activities merged. In part, this may be because non-tribal members were not viewed as human beings, or at least as full persons. Although the context was very different, the treatment of enemies as beasts or as subhuman can also be seen in the case of some conflict by modern and earlier states. Sometimes the raising of this threshold is a necessary precursor to war. To return to the Natives of North America, it is very difficult to define what war meant to them. Instead, there was both 'public' warfare, in

Arch of Titus on the Forum in Rome. The commemoration of victory provides important clues to armies and warmaking in the ancient world, although it is also necessary to note the extent to which conventions about contents affected presentation. An inside relief shows the booty taken by Titus after the fall of Jerusalem on 8 September 70 CE. The Jewish revolt, which broke out in 66 CE, was a major challenge to the Roman position in the Middle East.

the form of conflict between tribes, and 'private' warfare, raids with no particular sanction, often designed to prove manhood, as well as hunting.

Around the globe, hunter-gatherers became more successful and more dominant in the animal world in the prehistoric period. They made more successful weapons, especially composite tools – points and blades mounted in wood or bone hafts – which were developed in areas of early settlement, such as Israel, about 45,000 BCE. Bows and arrows, harpoons, and spear throwers were used in Europe from about 35,000 BCE, and Clovis points, made by chipping rocks into sharp, flat shapes in order to produce large stone points able to pierce the hides of mammoths, in North America from about 10,000 BCE. In some coastal areas, humans used boats, and the earliest evidence of their use relates to the migration from south-east Asia to Australia about 60,000 years ago.

Humans also had important physiological and social advantages over animals. They could perspire and move at the same time, a major advantage in both pursuit and flight. Their ability to communicate through language was also significant, as was being able to organise into groups, an important ability in hunting herds of megafauna (mastodons and mammoths). Learning processes helped to ensure that innovations spread and were improved. Humans were also able to develop their tools, testing the opportunities presented by stone, wood, bone, hide, antler, fire and clay to create weapons, shelters, and pottery. About 10,000 BCE, the Japanese, for example, began to use bows and arrows, which gave greater range and penetrative power than the spears and axes hitherto thrown at animals. Spears and arrows were originally stone-tipped.

The improvement in temperature at the close of the Ice Age further enhanced the situation for humans: the animals they hunted became more plentiful as it became warmer. Some animals also fell victim to humans: the megafauna were wiped out – in Europe by about 10,000 BCE and North America by about 9000 BCE – and humans were able to dominate the other animals. Some animals were domesticated, the first – dogs, in the Middle East – in about 11,000 BCE, while humans were increasingly able to confront other carnivores, such as bears and wolves, and to reduce the competition they posed for food as well as their threat to humans. The greater numbers of humans made possible by improved temperatures helped in raising their capability.

So also did the development of agriculture, as humans moved from harvesting wild cereals, which they did in the Middle East from at least 17,000 BCE, to cultivating crops. This became large-scale in western Asia and north China by about 7000 BCE, in Egypt by 6000 BCE, and in northern India and central Europe by 5000 BCE. The spread of agriculture accentuated the development of permanent settlements and led to important innovations in irrigation and in the processing and storage of food. Metalworking and trade both became important, as food surpluses made it possible for some workers to specialise in other tasks. This led to urbanisation, with cities, such as Uruk in Mesopotamia, developing from about 3500 BCE.

Economic development was linked to growing social organisation, not least the emergence of a powerful élite that provided political direction. States followed,

Narmer uniting the towns along the lower Nile in about 3,100 BCE. Control and clashing interests encouraged the walling of settlements and large-scale conflict. In the north China plain in the third millennium BCE, walled settlements and metal weapons appeared.

At the same time, it is difficult to assess patterns of causation and change in the development of warfare. Archaeological evidence of conflict consists of weapons, defences and marks on human skeletons. This evidence is valuable, but does not explain the motives for conflict. Skeletal remains showing violence as a cause of death may indicate war, but may also indicate murder or feud. There has been debate about the propensity of early peoples for conflict, and about the extent to which this conflict was unlimited. Debate has focused on whether early warfare contained important limiting 'ritual' and symbolic elements.

The impact of the natural and human environment on warfare over subsequent millennia is apparent in a number of ways. For example, the possibilities that the horse brought for operational and tactical flexibility were denied to societies, such as those in the Americas and Australasia, that lacked the horse. The horse was the fundamental technology affecting patterns of warfare. Once horses were domesticated, a range of possibilities opened up to their riders for making military use of them. Long before the coming of stirrups, most of these possibilities had already been explored with success: the Scythians were feared archers and the Sarmatians had heavy cavalry.

More generally, the natural environment shaped force structures, military opportunities, and the way in which war was waged. Warfare was different in the tropical forested regions of Kerala in southern India and in south-east Asia, in which elephants were used, from the situation further north, in much of India and in China, in both of which, particularly in the plains of northern India and northern China, cavalry could play a major role, and thus lessen the impact of elephants. As far as naval power and conflict were concerned, there were also major differences framed by the natural environment. Inland seas, such as the Baltic, Black and Mediterranean, lacked the tidal range of oceans. Furthermore, the presence or absence of islands where water could be taken on was important to naval operations. There was also a major difference between coastlines that provided anchorages and supplies, and those that did not.

The human environment, more specifically the density of population and the nature of its economic, social and political organisation also greatly affected force structures and warfare. The natural and human environments combined to ensure a variety of military systems. The creation and development of specialised forces – those trained regulars under the control of 'states' that engage most attention in military history – for long occurred against the background of a world in which there was a general lack of such specialisation. Furthermore, such forces were also less frequently under 'state' control than today, because some units were mercenary bands prepared to change allegiance.

The paucity of state-directed regular forces, a very definite contrast to the last hundred years, owed much to the absence of powerful sovereign authority across much of the world. Instead, it is commonly more appropriate to think of tribal and feudal organisation, rather than a state-centric system. This, and the resulting diversity in the political background to military activity, was evidence of the vitality of different traditions, rather than an anachronistic and doomed resistance to the diffusion of a progressive model. In other words, 'best practice' varied, and was largely set by natural and human environments, rather than being some unitary concept dictated by weaponry and doctrine.

Diversity owed much to the environment: to the interaction of military capability and activity with environmental constraints and opportunities. This interaction was itself dynamic. Climate, vegetation and animal populations could, and did, change. For example, the domestication and use of horses spread. However, there were still constraints: horses could not be used in some areas, such as the tsetse-fly belt of Africa or the mountainous terrain of Norway; whereas in others, such as Hungary and Mongolia, cavalry could operate easily. When, in the First World War, horses were used in heavily infected areas in East Africa, the 'equine wastage' rate was 100 per cent per month.

In areas of developed state power, such as China, the Achaemenid Persian empire (c. 550–c. 330 BCE), and in republican and, even more so, in imperial Rome, state-controlled forces had a long history; whereas, elsewhere, they were created, or imposed, far more recently. Some early military powers could wield strong forces. Thanks to imperial power, the relatively low productivity of pre-nineteenth-century agrarian economies was not incompatible with large forces, while the constraints that primitive control and command technology and practices placed on centralisation did not prevent a considerable measure of organisational alignment over large areas, as in the case of the Inca empire in South America in the fifteenth century.

The size of some of these forces could be considerable. In China, in the Warring States period (403–221 BCE), improved weapons and the use of mass infantry formations led to some of the largest military engagements yet recorded, although the reliability of the literary sources that record very large armies and high casualties is in question. The legions (citizen regulars) of the Roman army at the beginning of the second century CE contained about 160,000 men, although there were also about 220,000 men in auxiliary regiments, as well as naval forces and tribal semi-irregulars. The Byzantine (Eastern Roman) empire had a total army size of about a third of a million in the mid-sixth century. There was also a navy. The army of Song China was maybe 1.25 million men strong by 1041.

These forces were based on sophisticated and wide-ranging systems for raising and supporting troops. Thus, in the Achaemenid Persian empire, land was granted in return for military service, graded as horse-land, bow-land and chariot-land according to what had to be provided. The information was recorded in a census maintained by army scribes. When personal service was not required, a tax had to be paid in silver, which thus gave the government the ability to move resources more easily. These resources could be employed to pay mercenaries and helped ensure that large armies could be fielded by the Persians, as in the unsuccessful invasions of Greece that were stopped by defeats at Marathon (490 BCE), Salamis (480 BCE) and Plataea (479 BCE). In 490, the Persian expeditionary force was less than 30,000 men strong, but for the Plataea campaign the Persians had about 200,000 men.

The situation in such empires was different to tribal warfare societies, where force was an expression of collective social power, rather than the authority of the state; although, in most states, warfare and force were also expressions of collective social power. The strength of states and cultures was indicated by the ability of many to survive conquest by tribal warfare societies. For example, conquests of China were not followed by the destruction of its society and culture. Instead, 'barbarian' conquerors, such as the Manchu in the seventeenth century, acculturated to the China they conquered. It can be argued that the Romans (who were not a tribal power) at least partially acculturated to the Greeks they conquered.

In states, notions and practices of service, duty and discipline combined in order to make military specialisation and hierarchy possible and effective. In tribal societies, in contrast, this process was challenged by customs and ideas that were more contractual and, in some respects, egalitarian. There was a conditionality of military behaviour in the steppe tribes of central Asia or the Native peoples of North America that was very different to patterns of military control in societies such as Ming China (1368–1644 CE) that had a more authoritarian political ideology and practice. Native American use of weapons and tactics allowed for more autonomy on the part of individual warriors than was the case with Chinese soldiers, although it is important not to underrate the role of organised tactics and discipline among Native Americans, certainly by the eighteenth century. More generally, the extent to which it is helpful to differentiate between state and pre-state warfare is a matter of debate.

The complex relationship and frequent conflict between settled states and native peoples (a distinction that is not always easy to draw) was not the sole dynamic in war and military organisation. There was also warfare between states. This was particularly intense in the Middle East where a number of cultures clashed from soon after the development of cities. Mesopotamia and Egypt supported a series of states, each of which sought to defeat local rivals and then to expand. The first empire in western Asia was founded in about 2300 BCE by Sargon, who united the city states of Sumer (southern Mesopotamia) and conquered neighbouring regions including Elam (south-west Persia) and south-eastern Anatolia. The empire collapsed, in large part due to an extended drought, and the Gutians took advantage of the resulting disorder. An empire based on the city of Ur followed (the Ur III Empire, *c.* 2111–*c.* 2004 BCE), and, later, the Babylonian empire of Hammurabi.

In the fifteenth century BCE, an expanding Egypt challenged the Mitanni empire of Mesopotamia for dominance of the region west of Mesopotamia proper, the climax being the dramatic, daring victory of Thutmosis III of Egypt over a Syrian coalition at

Megiddo in about 1460 BCE. In the thirteenth century, however, Egypt had to give ground before a revitalised and expanding Hittite kingdom (based in Anatolia) that asserted its dominance in the Syrian region. There was another climax of sorts at Kadesh in about 1285 BCE, where Rameses II narrowly escaped defeat, despite his propagandist claim of victory. In about 1260, the two powers negotiated a treaty acknowledging Hittite expansion and establishing a zone of influence for the two kingdoms in the Syrian region. Further east, the Hittites had destroyed Babylon in a raid in 1596 BCE.

Both the Egyptians and the Hittites used bronze weapons. The Hittites' precocious but very limited use of iron was not a significant factor at this stage. The Assyrians were the first to make systematic use of iron in military technology. The Egyptians also made good use of the bow. This itself was not a static weapon. The composite bow, in which the stave of wood is laminated, was first attested in the West in Mesopotamia in about 2200 BCE. Compound bows, made of more than one piece of wood glued together, a technique that provided greater force, followed. The combination of the compound bow with the light, two-wheeled chariot, beginning in the seventeenth century BCE in Egypt and the Middle East, has been seen by some commentators as a tactical revolution that ushered in mass confrontations of chariots carrying archers in the Later Bronze Age; although, at the same time, it is important to avoid a weapons-based determinism.

Egyptian forces were able to operate not only north into the Levant but also south into Nubia, which was conquered on several occasions, including in about 1965 BCE and *c.* 1492–1471 BCE, with the frontier established at the 4th Cataract on the Nile in *c.* 1446 BCE. The Egyptian army developed during the period. Impressions can be gained from temple carvings. These show a use of bowmen mounted on chariots as well as of infantry using swords, battle-axes and other cutting and hitting weapons.

Meanwhile, new weapons were developing in other areas, frequently as a result of their spread from regions in which they were already in use. Thus, in the Aegean, the spear began to be used in about 2000 BCE, while the sword developed during the Bronze Age, eventually becoming both a cutting and a thrusting weapon. Chariots were prominent in the Near East in the Middle and Late Bronze Age, while in Iron Age Britain (700 BCE – 50 CE), the powerful were buried with their chariot and spear. In China, the use of chariots, composite bows, and bronze-tipped spears and halberds developed in the second millennium BCE. In Japan, where bows played a major role, the compound bow was in use by about 300 BCE.

The Hittite empire disintegrated following attacks by the mysterious 'Sea Peoples' at the end of the Bronze Age in about 1200 BCE. This was an aspect of a more widespread collapse, also seen in the fall of Mycenaean Greece, Troy, and the Syrian and Canaanite cities, that appears to have been triggered partly by invaders and rebels, and the resulting crises in international trade and political control. This collapse marked the end of the Bronze Age and the entry of iron weapons.

A series of other empires based on conquest subsequently developed. The Kushites expanded north along the Nile valley into Egypt, all of which they controlled from the late eighth century BCE, and south into the central Sudan. The Assyrian empire, founded in 950 BCE, and greatly strengthened under Assurnasipal II (r. 883–859 BCE), conquered not only Mesopotamia, where Babylon was destroyed in 689 BCE, and Phoenicia – the coast of modern Lebanon – but also Egypt, creating the first empire to span from the Persian Gulf to the Nile: Memphis was captured in 671 BCE and Thebes in 663 BCE. The Assyrians had a large, well-organised army that was effective in both campaign and battle, and were particularly good with both siegecraft and cavalry. Assyrian military success came partly from their use of iron weapons (they were one of the first cultures to make the transition from bronze) and from their great ability to supply horses, on which their cavalry and prominent chariot corps depended. They had the first real cavalry and were notable for the first effective use of an army integrated with all arms. Success in siegecraft ensured that Assyrian advances, whether or not they led to battle, could not be resisted by remaining behind walls, as was often the case in warfare.

There was an element of holy war in Assyrian campaigning as they saw themselves spreading the domain and worship of their god Ashur. Their terroristic style of rule,

Charioteer and Horse. Stone panel from the palace of Sargon II (745–705 BCE). Assyrian power spread under Sargon, with gains in Palestine, where the kingdom of Israel was conquered in 722–4 BCE, and Persia. The ability to supply horses, on which their cavalry and prominent chariot corps depended, was important to Assyrian success. They had the first real cavalry. (*Heritage Image Partnership*)

Assyrian storming of an Egyptian city, from the military campaign of Assurbanipal against Egypt. His father, Esarhaddon (r. 680–69 BCE), the son of Sennacherib, conquered northern Egypt in 671–69 BCE. Assurbanipal campaigned further up the Nile, destroying Thebes in 663 BCE. Stone relief from the palace in Nineveh, showing archers playing a role for both attackers and defenders. *(British Museum)*

Siege of the Jewish-held town of Lachish by Sennacherib, 701 BCE. Sennacherib (r. 704–681 BCE), the son of Sargon II, was an active ruler who destroyed Babylon in 689 and, in 701, unsuccessfully attacked Judah, the southerly of the two Jewish kingdoms, which had a capital at Jerusalem.

Assyrian troops pursuing Arabs *c.* 645 BCE. Stone panel from the North Palace of Ashurbanipal in Nineveh. Cavalry, using spears or bows, camel-borne archers, infantry and charioteers are all depicted. The mobile Arabs posed a challenge to the control of neighbouring areas by established states.

Assyrian archers. Bronze mountings from the door of the palace at Balawat (Yeni-Assur), Iraq, built under Salmaneser III, 859–824 BCE. *(Istanbul Archaeological Museum)*

Assyrian assault on city with battering ram. Prominent role of archers on both sides. Success in siegecraft ensured that Assyrian advances could not be resisted simply by remaining behind walls. *(British Museum)*

Assyrian troops from the period of Tiglathpileser III (744–727 BCE).

which involved mass killings, torture and deportation, failed, however, because it bred hatred that fostered rebellions. The debilitating attempt to take and hold Egypt, the rebellion of the Babylonians, and the rise of the neighbouring Medes, who aligned with Babylon to destroy the Assyrian capital Nineveh in 612 BCE, were responsible for the downfall of Assyria. Seven years later, the armies of Babylonia and Media defeated those of Assyria and Egypt at Carchemish.

The subsequent Babylonian empire under Nebuchadnezzar II reached to Palestine, where Jerusalem was destroyed in 587 BCE, but it was overthrown in 539 BCE by a far more wide-ranging empire, that of the Persians under Cyrus the Great (r. 559–30). He had already defeated Croesus, King of Lydia in 547–546 BCE, allegedly in part by using camels to disconcert the opposing cavalry, extending his power to the Aegean. Cyrus was to be killed by the nomadic Massagetae when he campaigned into central Asia in 530 BCE, but his successor, Cambyses II, conquered Egypt in 525 BCE. The Persians were particularly effective in cavalry warfare and were also successful in siegecraft, a necessary skill if permanent gains were to be sought.

To continue the familiar account entails discussing the warfare of Greece and its neighbours. This leads to a stress on the Greek innovation of the citizen hoplite soldier fighting in phalanx formations in pitched battles that helped settle disputes between Greek city states speedily so that agricultural life could be resumed. City states, with their distinctive citizen militias, undermine any straight polarity between tribal warfare societies and imperial states. This leads to a focus on the Persian failure to conquer Greece in 490 and 480–479. Thereafter, first Sparta, and then Athens, formed leagues of cities (in Athens's case based on naval power), but were unable to convert these into durable empires. The attention then shifts to the rise of Macedon. The autonomy of the Greek city states was lost at the hands of the Macedonians with their larger phalanx and heavy cavalry, the key victory being Philip II's triumph at Chaeronea in 338 over Thebes and Athens. His unity of purpose triumphed over the squabbling Greeks. Philip's son Alexander the Great conquered the Persian empire from 334 BCE to his death in 323. The wars of Alexander's successors in the Hellenistic period produced from c. 280 BCE a *de facto* balance of power between the successor kingdoms of Macedon (ruled by the Antigonids), Syria, including Iraq and Persia (Seleucids) and Egypt (Ptolemies), that was only disrupted by the incursion of Rome in 200 BCE, immediately following their defeat of Hannibal. Hellenistic warfare was characterised by the development of tendencies seen in Alexander's campaigning, including the much greater use of siege warfare. Hellenistic armies relied on the different resource bases of the particular kingdoms, although their cores fought in a similar style. The familiar approach would culminate in the rise of Rome, not least its eventually successful struggle with Carthage for dominance of the middle and western Mediterranean in

Alexander the Great defeating the Persians under Darius III at the battle of Issus (333 BCE), as depicted in a first-century (CE) Roman mosaic. This battle opened the way for Alexander to advance into Phoenicia, Palestine and Egypt, before he returned to Syria and turned east to defeat Darius at Gaugamela (331 BCE) near Nineveh, the decisive defeat of the Persian army.

the Punic Wars (264–241 BCE, 218–202 BCE, and 149–146 BCE), and its conquest of Macedon and the Ptolemaic empire in Egypt.

These conflicts were indeed important, and provide a rich diet of famous generals and battles, such as Alexander's victories at Issus (333 BCE) and Gaugamela (331 BCE), and Hannibal's over the Romans at Trasimene (217 BCE) and Cannae (216 BCE), each of the battles won against larger armies. In addition, it is possible to recapture in some detail the organisation, tactics and weaponry of the Roman army and this encourages attention, not least because the military history of so much of the ancient world is obscure in comparison, including that of settled societies such as Phoenicia. Furthermore, Greece, Macedon and, even more, Rome helped frame the subsequent military imagination of Europeans; although the claim that Greek hoplites pioneered the Western way of war is overblown. Latin texts, such as those of Vegetius, were seen as providing valuable guides, and practices allegedly modelled on those of Rome enjoyed considerable prestige. This can be seen, for example, in sixteenth-century interest in Classical models, in Marshal Saxe's idea in the 1730s and 1740s of reviving the legion, as well as in Napoleon's search for iconographical validation in terms of Roman models, and in the German search, in their planning for what was to be the First World War, for a battle of annihilation to match Hannibal's success over the

Hadrian's Wall. By the early years of the second century CE, the Romans had abandoned their occupation of southern and central Scotland. Instead, they developed a frontier at the narrowest part of the island, the Tyne–Solway line. This was consolidated by the construction of Hadrian's Wall from about 122.

Water Trough and Watchtower, Hadrian's Wall.

Romans at Cannae. Ironically, like Hannibal, the Germans in the twentieth century proved adept at winning battles while losing the war.

The Romans were particularly impressive, not only for the training and discipline that enabled them to march at a formidable rate, to deploy in a variety of planned formations, to perform complex manoeuvres on the battlefield and to manoeuvre effectively there, but also for the range of physical and military environments that they mastered; although in that, as in roadbuilding, they had been anticipated to a certain extent by the Persians. Having unified Italy, in campaigning that also entailed resistance to Celtic attack from the north, and to invasion in 280 BCE by Pyrrhus, King of Epirus in Greece, whose army included elephants, the Romans eventually triumphed in the Punic Wars, wide-ranging struggles that involved conflict in Italy, Sicily, Spain and North Africa – where, in 202 BCE, Scipio won a decisive victory over Hannibal at Zama. In the First Punic War, the Romans benefited from superior resources, and in the Second from the combination of greater manpower and Hannibal's strategic mistakes.

Warfare with Carthage had obliged the Romans to build a fleet in the First Punic War in order to contest the waters off Sicily, although, in general, in the ancient world, naval power was mainly logistical and used for the projection of land forces. The adaptability shown in building up the navy, with the Romans literally copying the design of Carthaginian ships, was also shown in other aspects of Roman military development, including incorporating the infantry organisation of the Sammites, borrowing the javelins and sword types used by their enemies, and adopting Hannibal's infantry and cavalry tactics. The large size of the army of republican Rome derived from their organisation of the peoples of Italy into various citizen and allied statuses, all of which were required to serve in the Roman army. Like the Han, the Romans believed in a mass army based on the adult males of the farming population. This provided huge reserves of manpower for use against Carthage.

Having defeated Hannibal, the Roman legionaries, with their short stabbing iron sword, heavy javelin and shield, fighting together shoulder-to-shoulder, were involved in conflict in Greece and further east. Rome became the leading power in the eastern Mediterranean, thanks to their ability to defeat the Macedonian phalanx of spearmen at Cynoscephalae (197 BCE) and, especially, Pydna (168 BCE). However, these battles were close-run things and it is unclear that the Roman legion was superior to the phalanx. Polybius's claim to this effect was largely Roman propaganda aimed at discouraging further Greek revolts. The Greeks argued that the Romans had been lucky. In practice, the Romans had superior manpower, resources, willpower and organisation. It is noteworthy that legions changed to a phalanx formation in the late empire, largely in a response to barbarian cavalry and to a decline in the quality of manpower.

In the first century BCE, Mithridates, King of Pontus, the leading power in Anatolia, was defeated, while Julius Caesar conquered Gaul (France), and Egypt was annexed. In the following century, most of Britain, and much of the northern Balkans, were conquered, Dacia (modern Romania), followed in 101–6 CE; although the defeat of the Emperor Augustus's army in Germany in 9 CE was a severe blow that encouraged caution on that frontier. Successive campaigns showed the range of Roman power and its offensive capability. For example, a stone bridge was built across the Danube to support operations in Dacia. In 116 CE, the Emperor Trajan (r. 98–117) advanced as far as the Persian Gulf, having overcome Armenia and Parthia, but he was soon faced by serious revolts. Southern Mesopotamia was held only till 117, when a Parthian client king was installed.

Trajan's Parthian war demonstrated Rome's offensive capability, but also its lack of staying power east of the Euphrates. The war exposed Rome's over-extension, and also showed the limits of Roman expansion. Trajan's successor, Hadrian (r. 117–38), abandoned Trajan's Mesopotamian conquests and shifted to a policy of consolidation and fixed, defensive frontiers, with large legionary forces in permanent garrisons on or close to the frontier. Eastern wars required a build-up of forces from the other frontiers, especially the Danube and the Rhine. In addition, between the mid-70s CE and the mid-second century, there was a permanent shift in the distribution of legions, particularly from the Rhine to the Danube and the Eastern provinces. Hence the limits on Roman manpower exposed Rome's weakness to war on two fronts, which events were to force on them in the third century CE. There was no adequate strategic reserve until Constantine created a field army in the early fourth century.

Military history understood as a record of campaigns and sieges is of only limited value in this period – not so much because of the nature of the available sources, but because many societies appear to have put the emphasis less on battle than on raids. Furthermore, it is necessary to emphasise the military challenge posed to the empires that tend to form the building blocks of military history by peoples that are less well known. In China, for example, the Zhou dynasty (c. 1050–256 BCE), originally a frontier power to the west, that had overthrown the Shang dynasty (c. 1600–c. 1050 BCE), was, in turn, attacked by border people, especially the Di and the Xianyun from the bend in the Yellow River to the north-west. Chariots played a major role in conflict in this period. Their use had spread to China from central Asia in about 1200 BCE and, thereafter, chariot-borne nobles played a crucial part in battle. This was a type of warfare centred on a social élite.

There was a marked change in the character of Chinese warfare during the Warring States period (403–221 BCE), in which warring regional lords ignored and finally overthrew the weak power of the Zhou. These lords became in effect independent. The most successful of these dynasties in the end was the Qin, who, in 221–206 BCE, ruled in all of China after a major series of conquests by King Zheng (r. 247–210 BCE) in 230–221 BCE. Zheng took a new title, First Emperor, for himself. Disciplined mass armies of infantry and cavalry came to dominate conflict in China, and new weapons, for example, in the fourth century, the crossbow, were introduced. The scale of conflict grew, a development that drew on organisational strength, and led, in the fourth and third centuries, to the development of military treatises, for example those of Sunzi and Sun Bin. The rise of mass armies, a product of population growth and the introduction of conscription, ensured that chariots no longer played an important role. With iron weapons, infantry became more effective; but it was also necessary to develop iron casting. Much of the Chinese infantry was armed with spears. Cavalry was introduced from the fourth century, as the northern state of Jin responded to the horsemen of non-Chinese peoples to the north. Siege warfare developed with the use of siege towers and stone-throwing catapults (both also used by the Romans) against cities protected by thick earth walls.

This period suggests that institutions, not technology, drove change in Chinese military history. The first element of the Warring States's 'military revolution' to appear was conscription of mass infantry armies, and these were the result of developments in administrative technique and in the extension of state authority over rural populations. Use of iron weapons on a large scale, and the introduction of the crossbow, came later. When gunpowder weapons subsequently appeared they did not transform warfare in China to anywhere near the extent they did in Europe.

Han China, Terracotta army (*above and opposite*). In silent testimony to power, thousands of life-size terracotta soldiers and horses were buried near the tomb of King Zheng (r. 247–10 BCE) who conquered much of China in 230–221 BCE and took the title First Emperor. The power of the Qin dynasty was extended south of the Yangtze in the 220s and to the South China Sea in 209 BCE.

The marked growth of Chinese power under the Qin in the third century BCE, with major extensions of territorial control (it far exceeded the Shang and the Zhou, both loose hegemonies limited to north China), brought new external opponents, especially among the nomadic steppe people to the north. The Qin and their predecessors in the Warring States period built a series of walls, including the Long Walls of Wei, Zhao and Yan (c. 353–290 BCE), which testified to the sense of challenge from the nomadic people in the arid steppe north of China, and their well-trained mounted archers. They also indicated the organisational powers at the disposal of the major states.

The Qin empire was overly dependent on the character of the emperor. Zheng's death was followed by conflict in the ruling family, military disaffection and popular uprisings. The eventual civil war was won by Gaozu, who took the title King of Han. The Han dynasty (206 BCE–220 CE), built a new Great Wall to prevent attack from the north, and also established a system of garrisons to provide cohesion to their far-flung empire, which eventually extended into Korea, Vietnam and central Asia. Similarities between the military arrangements of the Roman and Han empires included sophisticated logistical systems, and the use both of military colonies and of non-native or imperial troops.

The Han were challenged by the Xiongnu confederation of nomadic tribes, which was unified in 210–209 BCE, and was the first empire to control all of Mongolia. The Xiongnu, whose relationship with the Huns is controversial, were a formidable threat. The Han responded not only with walls but also with large-scale offensives during the years 201–200 BCE (a disaster that ended with the army encircled and the Emperor suing for peace) and 129–87 BCE, that of 97 BCE involving the use of about 210,000 troops. To confront the Xiongnu, the Han had to build up their cavalry, while chariots ceased to play a role. Much of this cavalry was made up of allied forces, while reliance on conscription to raise a mass army was replaced by the build-up of a smaller professional force. The tension between the two has frequently played a role in military history.

However, the campaigns launched by Emperor Wu, the 'Martial Emperor', who replaced the payment of subsidies by a policy of repeated offensives, failed. Advancing into the vast distances to the north, the Han found it difficult to engage their opponents, and were soon obliged to retreat as supplies ran out. A few victories in battle could not compensate for the heavy costs in manpower and money, and the campaigning was unable to destroy the coherence of the Xiongnu, although the establishment of garrisons and colonists in Gansu helped sever links between the Xiongnu and the Qiang of Tibet.

The policy of advancing into Xiongnu territory was finally discarded and replaced by a defensive strategy. Eventually, peace was negotiated on the basis of ostensible tribute by the Xiongnu and more than ample gifts from the Han, the latter a heavy and continuing charge on imperial resources. In large part in order to strengthen China against the Xiongnu, by gaining both allies and horses, the Han extended their military power into central Asia, forcing Ferghana in 101 BCE to acknowledge Chinese overlordship. Another army was sent beyond the Pamirs in 97 CE in order to maintain this hegemony. The Han also extended their power to the south, taking control of the kingdom of Southern Yue after 137 BCE and defeating the Dian of Yunnan in 109 BCE, making them a tributary state, and suppressing subsequent rebellions. The Qin presence in the south was expanded and consolidated, and this secured a southward migration of settlers that was of great importance in the reshaping of China.

The Xiongnu empire collapsed between 60 and 53 BCE, more through political instability and regionalism than Chinese pressure, and the southern shanyu (branch) of the Xiongnu became Chinese clients in 52 BCE. The elimination of the northern shanyu by a Han expeditionary force in 36 BCE again brought most of the Xiongnu under one leader (the southern shanyu). During the reign of the usurper Wang Mang (r. 9–25 CE), war again broke out between China and the Xiongnu. The Xiongnu had the upper hand until 46 CE, when a succession struggle among them produced a second north–south split. The Southern Xiongnu became subsidised 'tributary' clients of the restored Han empire in 50 CE, while sporadic hostilities continued between China and the Northern Xiongnu, with the Han using the Southern against the North Xiongnu.

In both Han China and imperial Rome, although central government sought to monopolise force and to ensure a demilitarised interior, there was an ambiguous relationship with the power of the socially privileged, many of whom sought to control forces of their own. China was repeatedly to suffer from the problems created by the rise of internal disorder and the failure of central government to suppress it. Furthermore, in both China and Rome, the government's desire to monopolise force and to insist on strict central control, still faced the organisational problem of controlling frontier units. Their regional commanders could launch bids for power, as in the Roman empire in 68–9 CE, when the Emperor Nero's unpopularity and then death led four commanders to seize their opportunity. The struggle was eventually won by Vespasian, who was backed originally by the legions in Syria and, subsequently and crucially, also by those on the Danube; his last rival, Vitellius, had been backed by those on the Rhine frontier. In such struggles between Roman generals, legionaries fought in symmetrical conflict with similarly armed forces. Generalship and political skills, which often amounted to bribery, were crucial for success in these conflicts.

Weaponry varied greatly between the regular forces of the empires of this period. Han Chinese troops relied on crossbows, halberds and spears. In contrast, the well-trained, equipped, motivated and disciplined Roman legionary infantry used a short sword (*gladius*) and javelin under the Republic and until the second century CE. The longer sword (*spatha*) was predominant in the Late empire, and the auxiliary cavalry was already using it in the first century CE. Round shields replaced rectangular in the third century. The first known unit of heavily armed cavalry in the army dates from the early second century. The craft and engineering skills of the legionaries provided Rome with a valuable additional capability in military engineering. The Roman army also had artillery – bolt-shooting catapults and stone-throwing machines.

In both the Roman and the Achaemenid Persian empires, imperial control was fostered by the deployment of troops in garrisons from different ethnic groups to those of the area in question. In the Roman empire, these ethnic groups were integrated in Roman-style forces, and ethnic characteristics were subordinated to an imperial Roman ethos. The creation of military colonies, which stabilised control, was also important.

Much of the success of China and Rome rested on their ability to co-opt assistance from neighbouring 'barbarians'. These brought valuable skills with horse and/or bow, the Romans, for example, benefiting from Syrian archers and Gallic, German (especially Batavian), and Moorish (Mauri) cavalry. The Batavians and Mauri were particularly prized. Much of the technical terminology of Roman cavalry manoeuvres was Celtic; similarly, Egypt benefited from Kushite archers. In addition, after the first century CE, the bulk of the legionaries (regulars) ceased to be Italians. Even in the first century, much of the recruiting in Italy occurred among the mixed Italian-Celtic population of northern Italy, especially the Po River valley region. The co-option of 'barbarians' became more marked in the Roman empire as the demilitarisation of the interior became more pronounced. The role of these 'barbarians' ensures that any account of later Roman (third and fourth century CE) or Chinese imperial military organisation that offers a systematic description of the core regulars is only partial. Indeed, both imperial powers deployed armies that were, in effect, coalition forces.

Such co-option could be structured essentially in two ways. It was possible to equip, train and organise ancillary units in the same fashion as the core regulars, or to leave them to fight in a 'native' fashion. Both methods were followed by imperial powers, such as the Romans. The net effect was a composite army, and such an organisation has been more common in military history than is generally allowed. The composite nature of large forces stemmed from the coordination of different arms. In imperial Rome, the native auxiliary units provided light cavalry and light infantry to assist the heavy infantry of the core Roman units. Granted citizenship on retirement, the auxiliaries also strengthened Rome politically.

Cooperation with 'barbarians' rested not so much on bureaucratic organisation as on a careful politics of mutual advantage and an ability to create a sense of identification. Chinese relations with nomadic and semi-nomadic peoples of the steppe combined military force with a variety of diplomatic procedures, including *jimi* or 'loose rein', which permitted the incorporation of 'barbarian' groups into the Chinese realm. Their chiefs were given Chinese administrative titles, but continued to rule over their own people in traditional fashion. This could assist the policies of divide and rule that were important to the Chinese influence in the steppes.

The frequent combination of 'native' cavalry and 'core' infantry bridged divides that were at once environmental, sociological and political. This bridging complemented the symbiotic combination of pastoralism and settled agriculture that was so important to the economies of the pre-industrial world, although the barbarian ancillary forces used by Rome in the fourth and fifth centuries CE were predominantly from agricultural communities (Goths, Alemanni, etc.) and not from the nomadic Huns, who were less numerous in the ancillary forces.

Indian civilisations also faced attack from the north. Sanskrit-speaking Aryan invaders spread across northern India from about 1500 BCE, and this may have caused the overthrow of the Harappan culture of the cities of the Indus. Over a millennium later, peoples from central Asia invaded India: the Northern Shakas, the Yuezhi, the Scythians under pressure from the Yuezhi and after defeat by the Parthians, and the Shakas under pressure from the Scythians. In the first century CE, the Kushans and Shakas launched invasions. However, the precise identity of these groups and their relations with each other are an ethnographical nightmare. The chronology of early Indian history, especially about the early Kushan, is very uncertain.

Further west, empires based in Persia faced a series of attacks from the north. Thus, the Parni, a Scythian nomadic tribe, invaded the Seleucid empire that had emerged from the eastern conquests of Alexander the Great in about 280 BCE, creating the Parthian state in about 240 BCE and conquering Mesopotamia a century later. Parthia was to be a bitter enemy of the Romans, inflicting a particularly heavy defeat at Carrhae in 53 BCE. The Parthian horse archers were an effective foe. Prior to conquest by Rome, Macedon, to the north of Greece, was itself under pressure from Thrace, while Egypt frequently clashed with the Nubians to the south of Upper Egypt.

Thus, the major series of attacks between 250 CE and 500 CE that attract considerable attention as the 'barbarian' invasions that destroyed or weakened the empires in Eurasia, bringing down the Roman empire, were, in fact, another stage in a long-standing series of struggles and complex diplomacy between such empires and tribes; although the political distinction of empires and tribes was not always clear-cut, while not all the frontiers of the 'settled world' were under such pressure. That of Egypt was peaceful from 21 BCE until 249 CE. The states in the New World faced no such crisis.

The invasions in Eurasia were aspects of major migrations. In Europe, there was a difference between the Germanic invasions which resulted in settlement, and the invasions of the Huns and Avars that were horse-based and not accompanied by settlement on any scale: one theory being that they had to take the horses back to the central Asian plains or Hungary to find enough grass for them. There are great problems in knowing how far these invasions were just a matter of relatively small numbers of a well-armed élite moving in, or whether they were genuine movements of peoples.

Some of the invasions were mounted by cavalry, which is often held to have become more effective as a result of the development of the stirrup in central Asia, the region where the horse had first been domesticated. The genesis of the stirrup was a long one. It is possible that the Scythians used leather loops in the fourth century BCE, although these may simply have been to help in mounting. They were not, therefore, able to provide a better fighting platform. The latter was offered by the use of rigid metal stirrups, which provided stability in motion, helping in both shock action and with firing or throwing projectiles from horseback; in other words assisting both heavy and light cavalry. These actions did not depend on stirrups, but stirrups helped make them more effective. The earliest Chinese figurine with two stirrups probably dates from about 322 CE. It is important not to exaggerate the impact of stirrups, as the horse had been used effectively in warfare long before they were developed. Stirrups were an improvement, but an incremental one. Furthermore, their use diffused slowly. Stirrups provided a small advantage to cavalry facing other cavalry that lacked them. They made less of a difference to cavalry fighting infantry. It is important to focus on the effectiveness brought by the techniques of cavalry use, which were by-products of nomadic lifestyle, not the technology of the stirrup, in judging the capabilities of steppe forces against sedentary foes. Aside from stirrups and saddles, cavalry also benefited from the adoption of more effective edged weapons and from heavy armour. This ensured that shock, mobility and firepower were all possible.

The Japanese first encountered cavalry when they invaded Korea and fought the kingdom of Kogúryó in about 400 CE. It proved a rude shock. Prior to that, horses had been used in Japan for food, religious ceremonies and work. By 650 CE, mounted archery was well developed in Japan, although the infantry, who used swords and spears, remained important. Japanese horses were fairly small and cavalry shock attack did not become significant.

Not all 'barbarians' employed cavalry. The Angles, Jutes, Saxons, Scots and Picts who attacked Roman and post-Roman Britain fought mostly on foot and the first four crucially depended on seapower. The Germans who defeated the Romans in the Teutoburger Forest in 9 CE, destroying three legions and forcing the Romans to pull their frontier back to the Rhine, were infantry. Most of the German tribes were chiefly infantry, although the Goths, who in the late second and third centuries spent time in southern Russia, acculturated with the Iranian Sarmatians, especially the Alans, and had a definite cavalry aspect.

Many of the most effective raiders and conquerors were horsemen. In China, after four decades of conflict between rival generals initially given command in order to suppress rebellions, the Han emperor was forced to abdicate by one of the generals in 220 CE. Rival claimants led to the age of the Three Kingdoms (220–265 CE). The Wei, the most populous kingdom and that with the largest army, defeated its rival in Sichuan in 263, but in 265 the Wei emperor was forced to abdicate by the son of the victorious general. The new Western Jin dynasty reunited China by force but was unable to impose central control. The power of imperial princes combined with disputes over the succession to lead to civil war in 291–305 CE. This made Jin rule vulnerable. The Northern Xiongnu had collapsed in the 80s CE under pressure from the Xianbei, another steppe people from the Mongolian–Manchurian borderland. Part of the Northern Xiongnu fled west in 91, while another part had already defected to the Southern Xiongnu to dwell along the Chinese border. Between that time and the beginning of the fourth century, the Chinese government resettled many tens of thousands of Xiongnu in the interior of the empire, in what is now the central part of Shanxi province. By 300 these Xiongnu were largely sedentary, and certainly not nomadic; their élites were to a considerable extent sinicised. It was these Xiongnu who ravaged to the gates of the Western Jin capital Luoyang in 308 and 309, storming it in 311, and wrecking what had been the largest city in east Asia. The Xiongnu were effective cavalrymen, using both the light cavalry employed by other steppe peoples, and a heavy cavalry armed with spear, sword and shield able to close with infantry. Northern China splintered into what was known as the 'Sixteen Kingdoms' (304–439), encouraging flight south across the Yangzi where a Jin prince ruled from Nanjing, beginning what became known as the Eastern Jin dynasty (317–420). This was followed by the Song, Qi, Liang and Chen, the Southern dynasties (420–589), each founded by generals. Force was crucial to power, and warlords vied for regional control.

Further north, the Xiongnu were succeeded by Turkic peoples, especially the Tuoba clan of the Xianbei, who invaded north China in the late fourth century and overran much of it by 500 CE, establishing the (Northern) Wei dynasty (439–534). The Wei benefited from their control of the steppe which ensured plentiful horses and therefore more cavalry than their opponents. The Wei were also good at winning support from other groups, including from the far more numerous Chinese whom they ruled. Chinese administrative practices were adopted, and the Emperor Xiaowen (r. 471–99) created a hybrid regime, with its capital at Luoyang and a sinicisation of the Tuoba élite.

This, however, was unacceptable to many of their soldiers, who were not sinicised, and led in 524 to rebellion and then civil war. The Northern Wei state in north China split into eastern and western halves in the 530s. The west, now known as Northern Zhou, conquered Sichuan in 553 and the east (Northern Qi) in 577, reuniting the northern part of China under a single regime. The ruling family of Northern Zhou was toppled by Yang Jian, a general who founded the Sui dynasty in 581. The Sui (581–617) went on to conquer the south in 588–9. Armies from the steppe were able to deploy large numbers of skilled cavalry, but those from further south had access to fewer horses and therefore lacked the mobility and offensive shock power of the northerners. The infantry forces from the south also faced logistical problems. Both Chinese cavalry and infantry used crossbows. This encouraged the cavalry to use armour.

Prior to the Song dynasty, who united China in the late tenth century, the tendency in China was to build fleets on an ad hoc basis, rather than to maintain a strong fleet in being. The 'navy' frequently devoted more of its attention to major inland waterways (especially the Yangzi river) than to the coast. Control of the Yangzi was bitterly contested by large fleets during the Sui reunification of the country.

Much of India had been united in the fourth century CE by the Gupta dynasty, but it also was put under great pressure by central Asian peoples. The White Huns (Hephthalites) launched a major attack in 480, following up with more wide-ranging advances in the 500s and 510s. These greatly weakened Gupta power, preparing the way for division among a large number of regional powers until the thirteenth century. The Huns also pressed on Persia where the Sassanian empire had overthrown that of Parthia in about 226 CE. Major invasions were launched in the 350s and 400s. Nevertheless, this empire survived attack until the sixth century. Earlier it had proved a formidable foe for the Romans, deploying both heavily armed and light cavalry and drawing on an extensive infrastructure of roads and bridges. The Sassanians had invaded and destabilised the eastern portion of the Roman empire in the third century, and were responsible for the defeat, capture or death of four Roman emperors.

In the fourth and fifth centuries, the eastern Roman empire, with its capital at Constantinople, successfully resisted attack by 'barbarians', but the western empire eventually succumbed to a series of attacks, Rome being sacked by the Visigoths under Alaric in 410 and the last western emperor being deposed in 476.

Nevertheless, the 'barbarian' invasions were a protracted process and, for a long time, the Romans were successful in recovering from attack. The Marcomanni and Quadi invaded northern Italy and the Costoboci the Balkans in 170 CE, the Moors following in southern Spain the next year. Vigorous campaigning, especially on the Danube frontier, remedied the situation over the following decade. The major attacks launched by the Goths and others from the 240s to 270s, which included the defeat and killing of the Emperor Decius by the Goths at Abrittus in 251, and the sacking of Athens by the Herulians in 268, were brought to an end by a series of Roman victories, especially by Gallienus at Naissus in 268. The frontier was stabilised, although Dacia was abandoned, probably in 270.

The Roman empire was also far from static politically. The Emperor Diocletian (r. 284–305) increased the size of the army by a third to maybe 400,000 troops, and introduced a policy of co-opting colleagues in order to provide leadership. Despite an unstable interlude in 306–12, this introduced a period of relative political stability that lasted until the mid-fifth century. The centre of power moved to the new capital of Byzantium (later Constantinople), founded by Constantine I in 330. However, the permanent division of the empire into eastern and western realms left the less wealthy and populous west to face greater frontier pressures, while the more populous east faced fewer. Mistrust between the two helped prevent the east from supporting the west. Under pressure from the Huns, the Visigoths became troublesome in the late fourth century, defeating and killing the Emperor Valens at Adrianople in 378 and invading Italy in 401.

The invasions were a complex process as some of the resistance was mounted by similar peoples. Germans made up much of the Roman field army in the fourth and, even more so, fifth centuries; the extent to which the Romans maintained their traditional formation of one main battle line, with the infantry in the centre flanked by cavalry, and a reserve in the rear, is unclear. Late Roman infantry was probably deployed as a phalanx. The sophisticated infantry tactics of the Republic (described in Polybius, Livy and Caesar, although still imperfectly understood) had long been abandoned. The Late Roman army was not the same tactically, organisationally or ethnically as the armies of the Republic and the Early empire.

A shift in strategy also had serious consequences, especially when linked to political instability. The policy of strong frontier defence based on permanent border garrisons was abandoned in favour of a defence in depth, relying on mobile field armies, whose ostensible purpose was to move out to meet invaders, but whose primary function became the protection of the emperor from internal rivals. The result was to leave provinces susceptible to invasion.

Both Rome and Han China in the end relied heavily on 'barbarian' mercenaries, seeking to counter the threat from the 'barbarians' by borrowing from them; thus, in part, the process of defeat was a matter of these auxiliaries getting out of control – for example, in Britain. In turn, 'barbarian' kingdoms with their tribal forces found themselves threatened by successors. Thus, Odoacer, who deposed the last Roman emperor in the West, in turn lost Italy in 488–92 to Theodoric, King of the Ostrogoths; while the Franks defeated the Visigoths at Vouillé in 507 and occupied south-west France.

Under the Emperor Justinian I (r. 527–65) and his general Belisarius, the eastern Romans retook Italy in 535–55, a valuable indication of their vitality, which extended also to reconquering the Vandal kingdom in North Africa (533) and the south coast of Visigothic Spain (554). This campaigning reflected the flexibility and range of the Byzantine system. Amphibious capability was a prerequisite; siegecraft a necessary skill, as with the capture of Palermo (535) and Ravenna (539), while victory in battle required an ability to gain the initiative and to maintain the pressure, as shown by that over the Vandals at Tricamerum (533), a struggle decided by Byzantine cavalry charges.

Similarly, in China, civil wars and/or 'barbarian' invasions were countered by restorations of authority, for example by Li Yuan (r. 618–26), the founder of the Tang dynasty, although here the 'barbarians' did not have an impact on Chinese culture and consciousness comparable to that on the western Roman empire. Li Yuan forced an end to the rebellion and civil conflict that had brought down the Sui. The Tang dynasty (618–907) sought to resume traditional Chinese patterns of statebuilding, and their monarchy was more centralised and bureaucratic than those in Western Europe. As a result, China was better integrated politically and economically than Europe. The army was used to check external challenges. The Ruanruan (Avars), who had been a threat from the steppe in the sixth century, were followed by Turks. Traditional Chinese methods – trying to divide the tribes, to win them by trade, tribute and diplomacy, and to fortify against them – were followed in 630 by a successful campaign which won control of the Ordos and south-western Mongolia – the Tang benefited from their ability to emulate the operational behaviour and cavalry forces of their opponents, with their emphasis on speed and surprise – and then, in the 640s and 650s, by joint (Chinese and tribal allies) expeditions into central Asia. Military protectorates over Ferghana and Sogdiana were established in 659.

The value of Chinese military methods was also shown in Korea in 663. The Korean peninsula was divided between three states: Koguryo, Paekche, and Silla. Tang China, supported by Silla, was attempting to subdue Koguryo and Paekche and Japan sent a force to succour its ally Paekche. It was defeated at the Paekch'on river: the Chinese army was more numerous and proved more adept at large-scale warfare. Relying far more on the prowess of individual warriors, the Japanese were heavily defeated. From the west, the Tang dynasty faced another challenge as Tibet was unified in about 600 CE and began a period of rapid expansion linked with other peoples to the west of China, especially the Qiang. The Tibetan empire, which also extended into northern India, remained powerful until it fell in 842.

There were also new challenges in Europe. In Italy, Byzantine power faced a new 'barbarian' people, the Lombards, who invaded in 568, and had overrun much of Italy by 751. The eastern empire was also put under pressure from Sassanian Persia, which conquered Syria in 611 and Egypt in 616, although the conquerors were pushed back, the Sassanians being defeated by the Emperor Heraclius in 628 and Egypt being regained in 629. At a smaller scale, opposition to the Angles and Saxons by the Britons was long-lasting, but the invaders had won control of England apart from Cornwall and the Lake District by the close of the seventh century.

The most effective of the invasions of the Classical world were mounted by Arabs converted to the new religion of Islam. Launched by Muhammad, this rapidly involved conflict with the paganism that prevailed in most of Arabia. Muhammad defeated opposing forces in 624 and 627 and captured Mecca in 630. His successors, known as Caliphs, Abu Bakr (r. 632–4), 'Umar (r. 634–44) and 'Uthman (r. 644–58), presided over a tremendous expansionism that involved the defeat of Byzantium and the overthrow of Sassanian Persia. First, Arabia was united. Then, the Byzantines were defeated at Yarmuk and the Persians at Al Qadisiya, both probably in 636, in part due to the impact of the Arab archers; although the nature of the surviving sources is such that it is difficult to make comments about force structure or size, weapons and tactics. Syria and Mesopotamia were conquered by the Arabs, followed, in 639–41, by Egypt: victory at Heliopolis (640) was followed by the fall of Memphis (641) and Alexandria (641). The Byzantine defenders of Egypt, only 25–30,000 strong, were poorly commanded and many of the local levies were of low quality. But the invading army was smaller – only about 15,500 strong. The dynamic of the Byzantine defensive position had been wrecked by the loss of Syria, as that ensured that the other regions were unable to support one another.

The Arabs also advanced into Persia, routing the Sassanians at Nehavend (642), and capturing Merv (650), Herat (650) and Balkh (652). Other Arab forces advanced into Anatolia in 644 and across North Africa, capturing Tripoli in 647. Cyprus was attacked two years later. With them, the Arabs brought the bridle and stirrup to North Africa, which helped to make their cavalry particularly effective. More generally, the Arab forces appear to have benefited from mobility and morale, rather than numbers. Their ability to win over non-Arab troops was important, particularly during the conquest of Iraq. This capability not only brought more manpower, but also useful new military techniques.

Islam helped to give this series of attacks greater cohesion than those of other 'barbarian' invaders, although the caliphate was disputed from the 650s. Nevertheless, under the Umayyad caliphs (661–750), the process of expansion continued. The remainder of the coast of North Africa was overrun and, in 711, the Berber general Tariq led his men across the Strait of Gibraltar. The Visigoths were defeated at Rio Barbete and most of Iberia was conquered. This was not the end of Arab advances: in 720, the Pyrenees were crossed and Narbonne was captured, Toulouse following in 732. At the other extreme of Islamic power, there was expansion to the Indus and the Aral Sea, and Transoxiana was overrun.

There were checks. Sieges of Constantinople in 668–75 and 716–18 crucially failed; otherwise the Byzantine collapse that came in the fifteenth century would have done so far earlier. In addition, the Arab advance was stopped at Covadonga in northern Spain in 718 and Poitiers in France in 732, in the latter case by Charles Martel. Abd ar-Rachman, Governor of Spain, had invaded Aquitaine with considerable success, defeating the local forces, but, on 25 October 732, his advance on Tours was stopped by a Frankish infantry phalanx at the battle of Poitiers. The Franks were harried by Muslim arrows, but, when the Muslims closed to attack, they suffered heavy losses, including their commander, at the hands of their opponents' effective short-sword and spear combination. The Muslims fell back, never to repeat their advance so far north.

Yet the Arab armies had brought a major change to Eurasia, and one that was to be of lasting impact. As a final sign of the range of their power, in 751, near Atlakh on the Talas river near Lake Balkhash, an Arab army under Ziyad bin Salih, Governor of Samarkand, defeated a Chinese counterpart under Gao Xianzhi, helping to ensure that the expansion of the Tang dynasty into western Turkestan was halted and, instead, driving forward a process of Islamicisation in central Asia. The battle was decided when an allied contingent of Qarluq Turks defected to Ziyad bin Salih. Gao's army was badly defeated in what was to be the sole major battle between Chinese and Arab armies, as the Arabs made no effort to press east into the Tarim Basin and Xinjiang.

The previous year, as a reminder of the variety of commitments, at Tell Kushaf in Iraq (battle of the Zab), Umayyad power was overcome by the outnumbered Abbasids, who claimed descent from the uncle of Muhammad. The latter dismounted, forming a spear-wall from behind which archers fired. Disunity ruined the Umayyad response, emphasising the importance of cohesion. The role of infantry tactics in the battle was characteristic of much early Islamic warfare, and serves as a reminder of the extent to which it should not be seen solely in terms of cavalry. Equally, the latter was not solely light cavalry; for example, the Khurasaniya, on whom the Abbasid caliphs (750–1258) relied, were heavy cavalry, equipped with armour, and armed not with bows but with curved swords, clubs and axes. At the same time, the Abbasid army also included infantry.

The impact of the Muslim advances was to be a lasting one, helping to mould the modern world. It was a cultural as much as a military advance, and, in that, can be compared to the Roman conquest of much (but by no means all) of its empire. Some Muslim lands would pass under non-Muslim control, especially under that of European colonial rulers from the mid-nineteenth century, but Islamicisation was reversed in relatively few areas, principally Iberia, Sicily, Israel and the Volga valley. Instead, as the post-Soviet history of central Asia from the 1990s indicated, the extent of control won by the Arabs in the seventh and eighth centuries established an important and lasting cultural realm.

2

FROM THE EIGHTH CENTURY TO THE FIFTEENTH

The impact of European warfare on the world as a whole has been exaggerated in most histories of war. It is also inappropriate to treat European developments as the model for those elsewhere in the world. Viewed in a world perspective, the most impressive force in this period, in terms of territory and people conquered, was not the feudal cavalry of Europe, but the light cavalry of the Mongols, who, in the thirteenth century, overran not only China but also the Abbasid Caliphate of Persia. Mongol forces advanced as far as Poland, Hungary, Serbia, Syria, Pagan (Burma), Java and Japan. Affected by a subsistence crisis in the steppe that in part arose from a temperature drop that affected grass growth, the Mongols under Chinggis (Genghis, c. 1162–1227) looted large parts of the world of settled agriculture.

Their success offers an important indication of military capability in this period. The Mongols used cavalry, specifically mounted archers, to provide both mobility and firepower. The main weapon was the bow and arrow, and skill in employing it was tactically crucial. They employed short stirrups, which had a major advantage over long stirrups for accurate fire as the rider's torso was free of the horse's jostlings, while his legs acted as shock absorbers. The use of short stirrups required greater ability as a rider as it was easier to be unhorsed. However, the use of these stirrups helped provide a steady firing platform, although skill was also requisite in order to shoot arrows from the saddle in any direction and also when riding fast. Standing in the stirrups provided more accuracy than bareback riding or the use of cavalry saddles. A Song general noted of the Mongols, 'It is their custom when they gallop to stand semi-erect in the stirrup rather than to sit down.' Aside from skill in riding, they also benefited from the hardiness of the horses they used. The Mongols were also adept at cavalry tactics, such as feigned retreats, and at seizing and using the tempo of battle. Cavalry was crucial to the envelopments that characterised many of their battles.

Fighting skill alone did not suffice. Chinggis, who was named Khan, or overlord, of the Mongols in 1206, restructured their army, discarding tribal units in favour of a decimal hierarchy: Mongol forces were divided into multiples of ten, which provided

Mongol hunters in a forest, thirteenth century. The skilled archery and horsemanship crucial to Mongol military success was developed thanks to long practice from childhood, not least in hunting. In battle, the main weapon was bows and arrows, and skill in using arrows was tactically crucial. This was true of conflict with non-Mongols, and also in inter-Mongol battles, such as that at Herat in 1240.

an important degree of coherence. Commanders were selected by Chinggis, and replaced when he chose. The Mongols planned their expeditions carefully, the plans including obtaining food and timing.

As with other successful steppe peoples, such as the Khitans and the Jurchens, Mongol military skill depended in part on making a transition to city-taking conflict. To move from raiding and victory in battle to seizing territory required an ability to capture fortified positions. In large part, this meant expertise in siege warfare, which the Mongols acquired in the numerous campaigns required to conquer the Jurchen Jin empire of northern China (itself the creation, in the 1120s, of earlier invaders from the steppe) and the Song empire of southern China, campaigns that represented the most impressive use of force in the medieval period: the division of China also helped. The Mongols employed a variety of techniques to seize the major Chinese cities, including blockade and bombardment. The lengthy nature of the sieges, especially of Kaifeng in 1232–3 and Xiangyang, key to control of the Yangzi, in 1268–73, was possible only because of Mongol organisation and persistence. Their ability to elicit and coerce support was also important in these campaigns, because non-Mongols provided the siege engineers and much of the infantry for Mongol armies. Chinese catapult experts were helpful against cities. Similarly, the Mongols developed a navy, that was effective against the Song in the 1270s, from captured Chinese maritime resources.

The Mongol ethos was also important. If opponents refused to accept terms, the Mongols employed terror, slaughtering people, burning cities and ravaging lands in order to intimidate them. *The History of the World-Conqueror* by Ata-Malik Juvaini, a Mongol official but also an orthodox Muslim, explained Chinggis (Genghis) Khan's attack on Muhammad II, Khwarazm Shah, the ruler of Persia, in 1219, in part as revenge for the execution of Mongol envoys, but also as a scourge from God: 'He is the Avenger, and the glittering sword of the Tatar was the instrument of His severity.' The news of the execution 'had such an effect upon the Khan's mind that the control of repose and tranquillity was removed, and the whirlwind of anger cast dust into the eyes of patience and clemency while the fire of wrath flared up with such a flame that it drove the water from his eyes and could be quenched only by the shedding of blood'. Juvaini was not present, but such an explanation appeared plausible to him and was the one he thought it appropriate to spread. When Baghdad, the capital of the Abbasid caliphate, fell in 1258 to Chinggis's grandson, Hülegü, reputedly hundreds of thousands were slaughtered.

Success also helped the Mongols, at least initially, to maintain cohesion as well as to win support from other steppe peoples. Khitans helped against the Jurchens. Conquest brought the support of subject people. By 1236, another grandson, Batu, was reputedly able to lead 120,000 men west against the Volga Bulgars and Russians. The army that invaded Syria in 1260 included Armenians, Georgians and Rum Seljuks.

The Mongols took on a large number of opponents in very different military circumstances, a far more challenging task than operating within essentially one military environment. Their conquest of other empires which encompassed both steppe and cities was impressive. The Xixia empire to the north-west of China was attacked in 1209–10, its capital, Ningxia, being flooded when Chinggis dammed the Yellow river. The Jurchens were attacked in 1211, their capital, Beijing, sacked in 1215, and the Jurchens driven south of the Yellow river, where they were crushed in 1234. The Kara Khitai empire north and north-west of Tibet was successfully invaded in 1218, Bukhara falling in 1219 and Samarkand in 1220.

Mongol forces also operated far to the west. In 1221–2, one force advanced from Persia across the Caucasus and invaded the Crimea, before defeating the Russians at the Kalka river north of the Sea of Azov, returning home in 1223. Batu overran the Volga Bulgars and then the Russian principalities before defeating the Alans, crossing the Dnieper (Kiev fell in 1240), and, in 1241, advancing across the frozen Vistula. That year, a Polish-German army was defeated at Liegnitz, while the Hungarians were defeated at Mohi. At Liegnitz, the horns of the more numerous Mongol deployment outflanked the Poles who were hit hard by archers from the flank, while, at Mohi, the Mongols turned the unprotected Hungarian left and, under pressure from front and flank, the densely bunched Hungarians, who had lost tactical flexibility, were defeated with heavy casualties.

In 1242, the Mongols only turned back in Europe when news arrived that the Great Khan Ögödei had died. In 1243, another far-ranging Mongol force invaded Anatolia, defeating the forces of the Seljuk Sultanate of Rum, which then accepted vassalage. In 1259, Hülegü crossed the Euphrates, invading Syria the following year and capturing Aleppo and Damascus. To provide some idea of their range, other Mongol forces had advanced on Daluo in Annam (modern Vietnam), in 1257, while in 1258–9 another force, 40,000 strong under the Mongol Khan Möngke (r. 1251–9), besieged the Song fortress of Hezhou, albeit unsuccessfully: it did not surrender until 1279.

Mongol power did find its bounds. After Liegnitz and Mohi, many cities fell, including both Buda and Esztergom (Gran), but others, including Olomouc and Brno, successfully resisted, while the Mongols decided that it was not worth seriously attacking others, including Split. The Mongol invasion of the Dalmatian Alps was not particularly successful as cavalry could achieve little in the mountainous terrain.

There were more serious problems for the Mongols in the Middle East. The forces remaining in Syria when Hülegü left in 1260 were enveloped and defeated by the more numerous Egyptian-based Mamluks at Ain Jalut south-east of Nazareth. This broke the impression of Mongol invincibility, and was followed by the Mamluks taking over Syria; although in practice the Mongols were already over-extended. Combined with the defeat of another Mongol expedition by the Mamluks near Homs in 1281, this ensured that the Mongols would not extend their power into Egypt. Although a Mongol force was victorious at Wadi al-Khazindar near Homs in 1299 (the Mongol archers shot many of the charging Mamluks), it could not sustain the offensive, departing in 1300, and the last Mongol attack, that of 1312–13, was unsuccessful. The Mamluks were a formidable opponent with considerable military skills. The Mongols suffered in the region from the lack of adequate pasture for the large forces they required to defeat the Mamluks, who were, individually, stronger warriors. They had larger horses and could therefore be better equipped; although this interpretation has been queried by scholarship proposing that fighting methods and quality made less difference than the following sentences suggest. The Mongols mostly had just a bow and an axe, while the Mamluks had, in addition, it has been argued, armour, shields, lances and swords. Weapons manufacture was well developed in Egypt, while the Mamluks used 'shower-shooting': rapidly firing up to five arrows held in the hand at the same time. The Mongols lacked this high-speed archery, and also lacked armour.

Battle of Leignitz. In 1241, about 30,000 Mongols invaded Poland, crossing the frozen Vistula, sacking Cracow in February, and pressing on into Silesia where they routed a German-Polish army. The illustration indicates the Mongol advantage in archery, but not the skill of their tactics: the horns of the Mongol deployment outflanked their opponents.

As the pasture in Syria could only support limited forces in the summer (when it does not rain there), the Mongols could not deploy the overwhelming force necessary to offset Mamluk fighting advantages.

Large-scale Mongol attacks on Japan from Korea (which had surrendered in 1231, and, after fresh resistance had been overcome, 1258), failed in 1274 and 1281, in large part because of storms. In 1274, the Mongols landed and fought the Japanese, but the gale that dispersed their fleet ended the invasion; the 'divine winds' (*kamikaze*) of 1281 had a similar effect after sea battles in Hakata Bay. The Mongol raid on Java in 1292–3 also testified to the development of Mongol naval power in east Asian waters, but it had no lasting impact.

Furthermore, Mongol successes were sometimes only obtained after many years campaigning. It was difficult to translate successful advances into lasting control when campaigning in south-west China. In southern China, having held off the Jurchen Jin of northern China, in part by warfare but more commonly by annual tributary payments, the Song resisted the Mongols from 1234 until 1279, although offensives were not continuous. Mountain fortresses played a major role in the resistance. They were also important in Korean resistance to Mongol invasions in 1252 and 1254. Islands, mountains, rivers, and forests all posed a problem for cavalry forces used to open plains, not, barring islands, an insurmountable problem, but one that lessened their effectiveness. Nevertheless, the Mongols under another of Chinggis's grandsons, Khubilai (r. 1260–94), were the first steppe force to conquer China south of the Yangzi. Their slaughter of the population of Changzhou discouraged resistance.

Like many other external forces, the Mongols had an impact on military developments elsewhere, although the extent of this impact is unclear. In Japan, they presented the samurai with an enemy that relied on more sophisticated tactics and used both novel forms of familiar weaponry, such as swords, bows and armour, and completely unknown weapons, such as exploding shells. The invasions appear to have triggered changes in Japan: in styles of armour better suited to fighting on foot; in weapons, with swords now having shorter, heavier blades, and in tactics, such as the use of more coordinated infantry movements. All these changes were beginning to show during the fourteenth century, but it is difficult to assess whether they were mostly the result of autonomous internal developments, or more likely caused by the Mongol experience and the resulting diffusion and emulation of techniques and tactics.

The Mongol inheritance was divided into four khanates – the Empire of the Great Khan, the Khanate of the Golden Horde, the Chagatai Khanate and the Il-Khanate. These were far-flung empires, especially the first, which united China, included the Mongol homeland, and held sway over Korea, Tibet and much of south-east Asia, where Mongol invading forces had penetrated to Pagan, the capital of the Burmese state. Khubilai moved the capital to Beijing in 1264. However, the Mongols failed to maintain their cohesion or dynamic. Inter-Mongol warfare played a major role in defining the borders of the khanates: Khubilai, for instance, fought the Chagatai Khanate. The fourteenth century was an age of decline, in part because of conflict within the ruling élite. Having effectively controlled or threatened much of Eurasia, the withdrawal and decay of the Mongols offers an appropriate starting point for the subsequent military history of much of Eurasia.

This was particularly apparent in China, where rebellions against Mongol rule in southern China led to the establishment of the Ming dynasty by Zhu Yuanzhang in 1368 after the Mongol emperor had fled from Beijing ahead of the approaching army sent north from Zhu's headquarters at Nanjing. At the other end of the central Asian world, Mamai of the Golden Horde was defeated at Kulikovo in 1380 by an army commanded by Grand Prince Dmitrii Donskoi of Muscovy. The Il-Khanate, established by the Mongols in Persia, fell into division in the mid-fourteenth century.

Instead, a new force emerged in the person of Timur the Lame (1336–1405; later called Tamerlaine), who claimed descent from Chinggis and modelled himself on the Mongols. Having gained control of Transoxiana, where his capital was at Samarkand, Timur conquered Herat in 1381 before turning on Persia. He attacked the Mongol Khanate of the Golden Horde in 1388–91 and 1395, sacking their capital New Sarai on the Volga in the latter year after he had won a major victory in the Terek valley. In 1398, Timur advanced across the Hindu Kush into India, where he sacked Delhi, following with a march west that took him to the capture of Aleppo in 1400 and Damascus and Baghdad in 1401. In 1402, with rumours circulating of his plans for global conquest, Timur turned against the Ottoman Turks, defeating them at Ankara on 28 July. Although up to 3 million troops allegedly took part, according to one participant, it is more likely that about 20,000 men fought on each side. After a long struggle, Timur's army, which was mostly cavalry, was victorious: much of the Ottoman cavalry defected or abandoned the field, a product of Timur's pre-battle propaganda offensive; the Ottoman infantry was finally broken, and the sultan, Bayezid I, was captured.

Timur stayed in Anatolia for a year after his victory inflicting terrible devastation and restoring lands conquered by the Ottomans to their previous emirs. He also advanced to the Aegean, storming the stronghold of the crusading Knights of St John at Smyrna in 1402. He then marched east, with the Ottomans, now divided by rivalry between Bayazid's competing sons, no longer a threat to his position. Instead, Timur's support was sought by numerous rulers, including the Sultan of Cairo and Christian European powers. At the time of his death in 1405, Timur was planning to invade China.

Timur's attacks were all characterised by careful planning, including thorough reconnaissance. His forces were highly organised and well disciplined, and this helped him execute such methods as rapidly changing the direction of march.

These were not just predatory raids. Supplies were raised on the march, but, rather than simple devastation, efforts were made to use existing structures by levying tribute on the basis of lists of businesses and tax registers. In captured cities there was a systematic attempt to seize goods, not disorganised plunder. Indeed, Timur preferred to persuade cities to surrender and then pay ransom. He only stormed cities when this failed, but, when he did so, he used brutal force towards the inhabitants in order to deter other cities from resistance, most vividly by erecting pyramids from the skulls of the slaughtered – possibly 70,000 people when a rising at Isfahan was suppressed in 1388. In these cases, the few who were not killed were treated as slaves and marched to Transoxiana, many dying on the way.

The two great nomadic empires of Chinggis and Timur, and their light cavalry armed with compound bows, had been exceptionally successful in extending their sway, not least because China, Europe and the states of south and south-western Asia really had no answer to the sort of power they deployed. The empires had more organisation than is often appreciated. But they lacked the density of resources and the expertise that the Europeans began to command from the fifteenth century. The political decay of these empires – brought about through lack of legitimating principles, succession struggles, lack of a common ethnic base, and geographical challenges, rather than military limitations or failure – provided openings for other powers. Timur, in particular, failed to plan for the future.

Far-flung empires were not created by cavalry only: in South America, the successive empires of the Andean coast, such as the Tiahuanaco and Huari (c. 500–700 CE), the Chimú empire (c. 700–1475 CE), and the Inca empire (1438–1532 CE) also showed what could be achieved by infantry-based empires. These empires relied on the organisation of society in the interests of rulers with sacral powers. The Incas conquered Chimú and spread their power into modern Ecuador and central Chile, although their technology was unsophisticated. Their counterpart in central Mexico was the Aztec empire, which gained control of much of the region in a series of campaigns in the fifteenth century, although they also made adroit use of alliances. Like the Incas, the Aztecs were highly militaristic. Huitzilipochtli, the god of war, was a major force in their religion.

There were no empires, however, across most of the Americas. Instead, population densities were low and both settlement and authority were dispersed. That did not mean that there were no wars or conquests: in northern Canada, the Dorset culture of the Palaeo-Eskimos of the eastern Arctic was overwhelmed from about 1000 by the Thule people of northern Alaska, whose kayaks, float harpoons and sinew-backed bows made them more effective hunters of whales. On land, the Thule gained mobility from dogsleds. The Dorset people were killed or assimilated. Further south, in southern Ontario, where it was possible to cultivate crops, the spread of settlement led by 800 to the construction of villages protected by palisades, and, eventually, by double palisades. These agricultural societies fought; in about 1300, the Pickering people conquered the Glen Meyer, while, in the fifteenth century, the Huron conquered the St Lawrence Iroquois.

Far more powerful empires emerged in Africa. In the valley of the Niger, the kingdom of Ghana, destroyed by the Berber Almoravids in 1076, who created a far-flung empire that stretched into Spain, was succeeded in the thirteenth century by the Malinke empire of Mali. As in Asia, pastoralists pressed when they could on settled peoples. Thus, also in the thirteenth century, the Banu Marin advanced from the fringes of the Sahara to overrun Morocco, conquering Fez in 1248 and Marrakesh in 1269. Abu'l-Hasan, the 'Black Sultan' (r. 1331–51) of the Marinid dynasty overran the

Or estoit agrant merueille la cite de
sur et moult endenne. Vlpins qui mott
furt deslois ifutiez, sicom len dit. liroumein
iennozerent moult quant ilozent laseingno

Bombarding Nicaea with the heads of captured Turks during the First Crusade. This was the first major city under Muslim rule encountered on the Crusade. The garrison surrendered to the Byzantine Emperor in 1097 when the arrival of Byzantine ships cut supply links across the lake by the city. The Crusaders were furious, not least because they had been thwarted of their hopes of pillage.

Maghrib, capturing Tlemcen in 1337 and Tunis in 1347, but found it impossible to defeat the Christians in Spain when he invaded in 1340.

Different types of forces operated in northern Africa. Whereas the Fatimids successfully invaded Egypt from Tunisia in 969 with an army largely of black slave infantry from the western Sudan, the Christians of Nubia used horse archers to preserve their independence from Egypt until the late thirteenth century.

Compared to the range and sway of the great Asian conquerors, their European counterparts were insignificant. On the global scale, Europe's impact was limited. The Russian principalities were unable to prevail against the powers to their east, ultimately the Khanate of the Golden Horde, had to pay tribute, and found themselves the victims of slave raiding. The Norwegian Vikings reached Iceland in about 860, Greenland in 986, and Newfoundland and the coast of North America in about 1000, but were unable to develop this route. Instead, the settlements in Greenland and America were abandoned. In Greenland, the Vikings fell victim to remoteness, the impact of a deteriorating climate on an already harsh environment and, probably, the resistance of the local Palaeo-Eskimos.

In the Near East, the Byzantine empire regained the initiative from the Muslims in the late tenth century. Crete was recaptured in 960–1 after expeditions in 911 and 949 had failed. The Byzantine fleet was able to transport an expeditionary force and then keep it supplied while the capital was besieged over the winter. On land, Antioch fell after a long siege in 969 and Beirut was stormed in 975. However, the Byzantine position in Asia Minor fell victim to the Seljuk Turks in the late eleventh century, especially after the emperor, Romanos IV Diogenes, was defeated at Manzikert in 1071 as a result of the collapse of the army's coherence. Antioch fell to the Seljuks in 1084.

This led to an appeal for Western European support, which resulted in the Crusades. However, the major effort to recapture and hold the Holy Land ultimately completely failed and, in the event, the Crusaders played a smaller part in the power politics of west Asia than the successive Islamic empires. Proclaimed by Pope Urban II in 1095, the First Crusade fought its way across Anatolia in 1097 and captured Antioch after a long siege in 1098, before storming Jerusalem in July 1099. This Crusade involved not only sieges, including Nicea in 1097, but also battles, such as Dorylaeum against the Seljuks in 1097, and Ascalon against a Fatimid relief army from Egypt in August 1099. An ability to succeed in both modes was crucial in the establishment of the initial Crusader presence. By 1143, this had been greatly expanded – not least as the coastline was taken. This owed much to Crusader success in siegecraft, but also to the potency of the heavy cavalry charge, for example in the defeat of the Damascus forces at Marj as-Suffar in 1126. However, the Second Crusade failed when it attacked Damascus in 1148, and the Muslim response became stronger. Already, in 1119, when Roger, Prince of Antioch attacked a far larger army under Il-Ghazi at the Field of Blood, the Crusader force was destroyed.

The regent of Mosul, Zangi, captured the county of Edessa from the Crusaders in 1144, while Raymond of Antioch was totally defeated at Fons Muratus in 1149. The

Kurdish general, Saladin (1138–93), was able to take over both Egypt and Syria and then defeat the Crusaders at Hattin (1187), capturing Acre and Jerusalem in the aftermath of his victory. At Hattin, the heavily outnumbered forces of the kingdom of Jerusalem were also outgeneralled, advancing in the July heat under the fire of mounted archers. The Christians were surrounded and defeated. The destruction of the field army left most of the fortress garrisons in too weak a position to hold out. Jerusalem surrendered after its walls were undermined and breached. The fate of the fortresses indicated some of the weaknesses of castles, specifically the danger of denuding them of troops in order to create a field army and the psychological effects of the defeat of such an army. Yet, at the same time, castles were a potent display of power and an impressive force-multiplier and, for these reasons, many were built by the Crusaders. With the development of the concentric plan from the late 1160s, castle design in the Holy Land advanced more rapidly than in Western Europe, but the challenge the Crusaders faced was more serious. Indeed, better Muslim siege techniques led the Crusaders to adopt the new plan.

Light cavalry were very numerous in Islamic armies of the period. Those who were horse archers provided Islamic commanders with a resource their Crusader opponents lacked: the Crusaders did develop a light cavalry, but not on the same scale. There were heavy horses in Islamic armies as well. During the First Crusade, the Crusaders encountered Agulani (probably drawn from Persia) with armour of plates of iron, which also covered the horses: heavier than anything seen in Western Europe. They were exceptional, but well-armoured men were essential to close with the enemy and, by the time of Saladin, there were large numbers of *ghulam* (military slaves), which played a major role in his victories. Infantry never enjoyed great prominence in the Islamic armies the Crusaders faced: in the Middle East, they were too vulnerable to cavalry, though useful at sieges. Saladin seems to have left his infantry to besiege Tiberias while he engaged the Crusaders at Hattin. The expansion of Saladin's power was not restricted to the Near East. His brother, Turan Shah, overran Hejaz and Yemen and moved up the Nile into Nubia, while one of Saladin's generals advanced across North Africa to Gabes (in modern Tunisia).

Christian efforts to repair the disaster of Hattin led to important successes, including the capture of Acre in 1191 by Richard I of England and Philip Augustus of France, the leaders of the Third Crusade. However, the Mamluks (soldier-slaves), who seized power in Egypt in 1250, defeating the Syrians in 1251 and the Mongols in 1260, were able to mop-up the remaining Christian positions: Haifa in 1265, the major fortress of Krak des Chevaliers in 1271, Tripoli in 1289, and, at last, Acre, which fell in 1291 to a determined assault, after the defences had been weakened by mining and stone-throwing siege-engines. The Crusaders suffered from a lack of sufficient manpower, as well as from serious divisions. They did not compare to the threat posed to the Muslim states by the Mongols. The wealth of Egypt enabled the Mamluks to develop a well-equipped and well-trained standing army. They combined the virtues of heavy cavalry and heavy horses with effective archery from the saddle: weight and firepower.

Council of Acre and Siege of Damascus, 1148. At the Council, the Crusaders of the Second Crusade and King Baldwin III of Jerusalem agreed on a joint attack on Damascus, which had already been unsuccessfully attacked by the (unnumbered) crusade of 1128–9. In July 1148, the attacks on Damascus from, first, the south-west and then the east failed, and the Second Crusade, originally intended to recapture Edessa (lost in 1144), came to an ignominious end.

The Crusaders were also unsuccessful in North Africa. Louis IX of France invaded Egypt in 1249, captured the port of Damietta and advanced on Cairo. However, defeat in 1250 of the vanguard at Mansurak and the capture of the retreating and disease-ridden French army under Louis when it was surrounded near Sharamsah led to the disastrous failure of the expedition. In 1270, Louis tried again, this time at Tunis, but disease wrecked the expedition and Louis died.

The Christians were more successful in the Mediterranean and Iberia, where their successes amounted to a substantial expansion of Christian Europe. A series of islands that had been conquered by the Muslims were regained, including Crete in 961 and Sicily in 1093, while Muslim bases on the northern shore of the Mediterranean were recaptured: Bari in 871 and Fraxinetum in southern France in 972. Greater Christian maritime effectiveness in the Mediterranean was crucial to the ability to project power in the Crusades, and to the development of European trading systems centred on the Italian cities of Pisa, Genoa, and, most successfully, Venice. Genoa and, even more, Venice used their naval and financial strength to become important territorial powers in the eastern Mediterranean profiting, in particular, from Byzantine weakness from 1204. A series of island possessions and mainland bases were crucial adjuncts to their naval capability. In turn, trade financed naval power.

In Iberia, over six hundred years of struggle was required to destroy Muslim power. The *reconquista* gathered pace in the late eleventh century, with Toledo captured in 1085. The Muslims mounted a powerful response, particularly under the Almoravids, but in 1147 Lisbon was captured, and in 1212, at the battle of Las Navas de Tolosa, the Christians, under Alfonso VIII of Castille, won a major victory. In the aftermath, much of southern Spain fell over the following fifty years: Cordova in 1236, Seville in 1248 and Cadiz in 1262. The Moors were restricted to the kingdom of Granada.

These were impressive gains that, in part, reflected the impact of the Christian heavy cavalry. Indeed, high regard for these horsemen led to the hire of some of them by Muslim factions competing in North Africa. However, the extent of the shift towards Christian Europe has to be qualified, not least because, in the Balkans, the Ottomans made even greater gains in the fourteenth and fifteenth centuries, especially after the defeat of the allied Balkan army at Kosovo in 1389. In the aftermath of this victory, the Ottomans reduced Serbia to vassalage, helped by a further victory at Nicopolis in 1396. In this second battle, French Crusaders advanced through the Ottoman infantry, but were driven back by the Ottoman cavalry reserve. The Wallachians and Transylvanians on the Crusader flanks fled, and the defeat was a heavy blow to the attempt to hold back the Ottomans. Wallachia (southern Romania) had become a tributary state in 1395.

The Ottomans combined the classic fluidity of Asian light cavalry tactics with an effective use of infantry. Their advance was delayed by the impact of Timur (whose victory was celebrated in Constantinople) and then by civil warfare, but in the 1430s the Ottomans resumed their pressure, driving the Venetians from Thessalonica in 1430 and overrunning much of Serbia in 1439. Another large Crusade was launched in 1443 in response and it was initially successful. The Hungarians captured Niš and

Sofia and supported rebellion in the Balkans, but, in 1444, the predominantly Hungarian army was heavily defeated by the Ottomans under Murad II at Varna on the Black Sea. King Wladislas I of Hungary (Wladyslaw III of Poland) was killed on the battlefield. Four years later, the Hungarians were defeated again at Kosovo. Like the earlier Mongol successes and the ultimate failure of the crusading attacks on the Middle East and Egypt, Ottoman triumphs underlined the weaknesses of European warmaking.

To speak of the Europeans might suggest a misleading coherence: in 1204, thanks to traditional enmity and particular Venetian interests, the Fourth Crusade led to the storming of Constantinople, and the creation of new Crusader states in Greece. This disruption of Byzantine rule, which was only reversed in 1261 when Michael Palaeologus recaptured Constantinople, greatly weakened the resistance to Muslim power. Nevertheless, it is still useful to consider relative European power. While the inroads of the eighth century had not been repeated and Western Europe was now largely free from the presence or threat of Islamic attack, the same was not true further east. Not only had the Crusades been defeated, but in 1453 Constantinople fell to the Ottomans.

In the meanwhile, military systems and methods within Christian Europe had been far from static. The long stretch of time generally called, in the West, the Middle Ages appears somewhat inconsequential in contrast to the modern age that is held to have succeeded it. Since modernity is presented as a reaction against medievalism, there is a tendency to downplay the latter and to treat it as conservative and reactionary. Furthermore, there is a tendency to reify the Middle Ages in order to present it as a single period with one set of characteristics. If there is a single idea that gives shape to the period it is that of feudalism – the ownership of land in return for military services. The related emphasis, in terms of force structure and tactics, is on heavy cavalry ('knights in armour') and castles. Furthermore, the standard chronology is a clear one: another bout of 'barbarian' invasions is thwarted, the feudal system develops and, in turn, is challenged from the fourteenth century by infantry weapons and related tactics, specifically longbows and pikes.

This account has a number of weaknesses. It certainly oversimplifies developments within Europe. With space at a premium, it is easy to present these in terms of the development of feudalism, but, aside from the problematic nature of that concept, which has been variously interpreted, it is worth noting a greater diversity of military forms. This can be seen by considering England, which was unified by the house of Wessex in the tenth century. The system of military recruitment and organisation devised by Alfred of Wessex in the late ninth century, including that of burhs (fortified towns) and the creation of a large navy, relied on public authority – although military systems in England, and on the Continent, were heavily based on lords and their retinues, and on landholding in various forms.

Alfred's opponents were the Danes, one of the most effective forces in the second wave of 'barbarian' attacks, that of the eighth, ninth and tenth centuries, which included Arabs, Magyars from the east, and Vikings (Danes, Norwegians and Swedes) from Scandinavia. In China, the Khitans from Mongolia took over the area around Beijing in the tenth century, while the Tanguts gained control of the north-west round Gansu: all benefited from their mobility. The pagan Magyars used horse archers, while the Arabs and Vikings attacked by sea and river. None, however, was adept at, or particularly interested in, siege warfare, and this lessened their strategic impact. Christian rulers responded with fortifications, such as the fortified bridges built in France under Charles the Bald (c. 843–77) in order to obstruct Viking passage up-river. No better armed than their opponents, the Vikings were not particularly effective in battle, in which their standard deployment was a siege wall.

Traders, colonisers and fighters, the Vikings spread east to Russia and west across the northern Atlantic. The main burden of their attack was on the British Isles, northern France and the Low Countries in the ninth century, with a fresh wave of attacks on Britain between 980 and 1075. Possibly with limited land available for colonisation in Scandinavia, they were motivated by opportunities for raiding and settlement in more prosperous and fertile lands that were vulnerable to the amphibious operations that the Scandinavians could mount so well. Viking longboats, with their sails, stepped masts, true keels, and steering rudders, although shallow and open, were effective oceangoing ships able to take to the Atlantic, but also able, thanks to their shallow draught, to be rowed in coastal waters and up rivers, even if there was only 3 feet of water. Thus in Ireland, where the wealthy monasteries attracted attack, the numerous rivers and lakes facilitated Viking movement. From the 840s, their military presence became stronger, with larger forces that overwintered and developed permanent coastal bases. In England, from the 850s, the Vikings came not to plunder, but to conquer and stay. They overran a large territory including East Anglia, Yorkshire, and the Midlands kingdom of Mercia, before being stopped by Alfred at the battle of Edington in 878. The Viking Great Army then turned to France where it did much damage but failed in the siege of Paris in 885–6.

In contrast, the entire English kingdom was to succumb to invasion in the eleventh century – but that did not prove the inherent superiority of the feudal model. Indeed, the first invasion was that by the Danes, which, thanks to the weakness of King Athelred, eventually led to Cnut ruling England from 1016 until his death in 1035. The house of Wessex was restored in 1042, but, in 1066, it faced its final crisis with separate invasions by Duke William of Normandy, who claimed the throne, and Harald Hardrada, King of Norway.

Chance played a major role in the outcome. King Harold of England concentrated his forces on the south coast, where effective logistics kept the army together, but William was delayed by contrary winds, so Harold marched north to confront the Norwegian invasion. The invaders had defeated the local forces and seized York, but they were surprised and crushed in their camp at Stamford Bridge.

Three days later, William successfully landed at Pevensey on the south coast: horse transports ensured that his army retained its cavalry. Harold rushed south to attack William before the Normans established themselves. The English army, however, was weakened by casualties at Stamford Bridge, the return home of levies whose sixty days'

Aerial view of Old Sarum, near Salisbury, clearly indicating the defensive character of this Norman site. Castles and other fortified sites fulfilled defensive and administrative functions. Towns were ringed by walls, providing both defence and an ability to control the entry of people and goods.

service was over, and fatigue; and was outnumbered by maybe 5,000 to 7,000 men – although the figures are tentative. Harold chose a strong defensive position on the slopes of a hill, thus offering protection against the Norman cavalry. Far from being a walkover victory by an advanced military system, the battle of Hastings was a hard-fought struggle between two effective systems, and its outcome far from certain. Eventually, the shieldwall of the English housecarls was disrupted by advances designed to exploit real or feigned retreats by the Normans and, at last, the English position was broken. The death of Harold was crucial. Without clear leadership, England fell, as William rapidly exploited his victory and seized the throne.

This led to a new political order; but the Norman 'system' of land tenure (what is usually called feudalism) only crystallised – as a legal system of landholding – in the twelfth century, in Normandy as well as in England. The Normans relied on knights (as likely to fight on foot as on horseback), who provided an effective striking force. The new order was entrenched by castles, of which there had been few under the Anglo-Saxons. They were very different to the characteristic feature of Anglo-Saxon fortification, the burh or fortified town. Early Norman castles in England and elsewhere were generally motte-and-bailey, earth and timber constructions thrown up in a hurry and able to give protection against local discontent. From the late eleventh century, many were replaced by stone works, becoming powerful means and symbols of control. Surviving examples provide ample illustration of how they literally towered

Beynac castle, France. A major fortification in the valley of the Dordogne, Beynac was built in the early twelfth century and subsequently played a major role in the struggles between the kings of England and France. On the opposite shore, there was a rival castle at Castelnaud.

over and commanded the surrounding countryside. This was true both of frontier areas and of more settled regions. Stone was not vulnerable to fire, but it was more expensive to build, as well as posing different problems for attack.

The Anglo-Saxons were not alone in creating an effective military system. The Carolingian rulers of France also did so in the eighth century, and this offered them an important range of capabilities, including good infantry, good cavalry and successful siegecraft. Sound logistics provided the basis for long-range campaigning, including into Italy in 754 and 755. It has been claimed that well-trained troops developed a degree of unit cohesion that made it possible to execute battle tactics successfully. Heirs to the later Roman military establishment, the early Carolingians were not primitives fighting in an inchoate Dark Ages; although, alongside the Roman legacy, it is necessary to stress the dependence of the Carolingians on the retinues and followers of the ruler's most prominent vassals (sworn followers). Compared to the Romans, military forces were small, less well trained, and frequently 'privatised' expressions of social power, rather than public expressions of state power. Furthermore, as troops were not paid cash, campaigning only really 'worked' if it produced land to distribute or plunder.

The Carolingian military system was developed under Charles Martel's grandson, Charlemagne (c. 742–814), who became sole King of the Franks in 771 and Holy Roman Emperor in 800. He conquered Saxony in northern Germany and Lombardy, the first leading to the imposition of control over a region that had successfully resisted Roman conquest, as well as defeating the Avars of Hungary (791) and advancing across the Pyrenees against the Muslims. Cavalry provided mobility, but Charlemagne also made extensive use of infantry. Against the Saxons, he advanced by building forts, linked by roads, whose garrisons were designed to consolidate control. Nevertheless, the conquest took over three decades and entailed 'anti-societal' methods including mass killings and large-scale deportations. Logistics, engineering and other organisational capabilities were important to Carolingian success. Charlemagne united most of Western Christendom, but it was divided among his grandsons by the Treaty of Verdun (843), and then further fragmented, while also coming under pressure from the Magyars, Vikings and Arabs.

From the late ninth century, the kingdoms of Western Europe found their authority challenged by local potentates who were to create feudal domains, producing a new political system with a clear military counterpart, including private, unlicensed castles. The integrated military system devised in Wessex by Alfred was not matched in West Frankia (later the kingdom of France) of the later Carolingians. Public order was weakened and noble families became more important. There was a parallel in China where, in the late ninth century, regional commanders wielded effective power, and strong bandit gangs, especially that of Huang Chao in the 870s and 880s, brought wide-ranging devastation. China finally splintered into regional states in the Five Dynasties period (907–60).

In Western Europe, rulers relied on their own military retinues, and supplemented their strength with those of their leading supporters. These retinues made up a warrior élite, but this was very different to the professional troops under central command of the leading European states of the period: the Varangians of Byzantium, or the slave-soldiers (also foreign) of the Islamic emirate of Cordoba in Spain. However, these forces were expensive. In China, Taizu (r. 960–76), a general who became first emperor of the Song dynasty, ended independent regional armies by bringing their best units into the palace army, which he kept under his own control, and by replacing military governors by civil officials.

The knight–castle system used by the rulers of Western Europe proved an effective one. Great numbers of fortifications restricted the mobility of the Magyars and, even more, restricted their ability to gain easy plunder. The terrain was increasingly unfavourable for them the farther they got from the Hungarian plain: unfavourable both tactically and logistically. Otto I (r. 936–73), ruler of the East Frankish kingdom (later Germany), used a heavy (in the sense of armour) cavalry based on his nobility to inflict a decisive defeat on the Magyars at the Lechfeld in 955. As was characteristic of Western European warfare, this cavalry relied not on archers but on weapons for close combat, principally swords.

The Frankish development of knights, castles and siege techniques enabled the rulers who were able to employ them in some quantity to extend their power, both against domestic opponents and on their frontiers, for example with the Baltic Crusades. The rulers of more peripheral regions, such as Scotland, Prussia and pagan Lithuania, felt obliged to adopt these devices. However, it is important to note the range of the military system. The development of the money fief in the late eleventh century helped weaken the link between knightly status and warrior activity. The Western European military included many soldiers who were not knights; and it was far more varied and flexible than discussion simply in terms of heavy cavalry and castles would suggest. Infantry played a major role in siegecraft and the defence of castles, and also an important role in battle. In addition, although trained to fight while mounted, knights frequently dismounted to fight, as also did their Japanese counterparts: in both cases, this underlined their flexibility.

Similarly, the Byzantine armies put a heavier stress on infantry from the tenth century, although that was as part of a diverse military system that had to cope with a variety of Muslim and Christian opponents. Alongside the long-established Byzantine emphasis on heavy cavalry and on the tactics of a shock-delivering wedge, came the need for light cavalry to compete with similar forces, and also for infantry both to hold positions and to take a role in the battle line. The increased use of mercenaries by the Byzantines helped in the spread of military techniques and also lessened the distinctiveness of Byzantine military traditions.

In Western Europe, the emphasis was on capturing castles and towns and on devastating territories. The frequency of battles varied and some monarchs with established military reputations fought no or few battles, for example Henry II and Richard I of England and Philip Augustus of France. There were, however, important battles too, while, in addition, armies had always to be ready for battle. Henry I of England established his control of

Krak (or Crac) des Chevaliers, one of the most impressive surviving medieval military sites, was originally built on by the Arabs to guard the route from Tripoli to Hamah. The Crusaders developed the fortifications under the Count of Tripoli, but the castle that survives was totally rebuilt by the Hospitaller military order after they obtained it from the Count in 1142. It successfully held out against Saladin in 1188, ensuring it was one of the few remaining Crusader castles in 1190. The defences were strengthened at the start of the thirteenth century, not least with the construction of an outer wall. Despite this, the fortress fell to the Mamluks after a siege of scarcely more than a month in 1271. It became the capital of a Mamluk province.

Normandy by defeating his brother Robert at Tinchebrai in 1106, thanks to the skilful use of a cavalry reserve, and he consolidated his position in northern France by defeating Louis VI of France at Brémule in 1119. King John of England's attempts to regain his French lands lost to Philip Augustus of France in a rapid conquest in 1203 and 1204 ended in failure when his allies were defeated at Bouvines in 1214, in large part due to the departure from the field of their most prominent leader, the Emperor Otto IV. Battles at Lincoln and at sea off Dover in 1217 were decisive in ending the attempt by Philip's son Louis to exploit John's unpopularity (and subsequently the minority of his son Henry III) by seizing the English throne.

Unlike in the Islamic world, light cavalry played very little role in Western Europe. This has been attributed to environmental factors, specifically the absence of extensive steppe grasslands. Light cavalry were, however, important in Spain.

Knights did not always prevail in Western Europe. They were of limited tactical value in capturing fortresses. Furthermore, the infantry of the Lombard League in northern Italy in the twelfth century, and of Flanders and the Swiss Cantons in the early fourteenth

Castle design in the Holy Land advanced more rapidly than in Western Europe. The outer walls of Krak were strengthened by semi-circular angle towers, while the nature of the site made mining difficult. The multiple character and interlocking strength of the defences ensured that, once the outer walls had been penetrated, it was still necessary to advance along overlooked corridors and ramps.

century, posed a formidable challenge to cavalry forces. At Legnano, in 1176, Frederick Barbarossa, the Holy Roman Emperor, was defeated by the League and its effective spearmen, while at Courtrai, in 1302, poorly deployed French knights were defeated by Flemish militia with heavy casualties. The Swiss were victorious at Morgarten in 1315 and Sempach in 1386: their pole arms – halberds and spears – proved very effective against Habsburg knights. At Sempach, the Habsburg emperor, Leopold III, was killed.

So also in the British Isles, where the Scots under William Wallace defeated the English at Stirling in 1297. When Edward I of England in turn triumphed at Falkirk in 1298, the Scottish pikemen, massed in tightly packed schiltroms, were able to defy the English cavalry, only to be broken by Edward's archers. At Bannockburn in 1314, however, Scottish pikemen on well-chosen ground routed the English cavalry. We have no definite numbers, but the English handled their archers very badly.

Nevertheless, archers also showed how infantry could defeat both cavalry and other infantry. The English were to develop this aspect of their force structure in the fourteenth century, deliberately seeking battle and defeating the Scots at Halidon Hill (1333) and the French at Crécy (1346), and Poitiers (1356), where John II of France was captured. These longbowmen lacked the operational and tactical flexibility of central Asian archers because, although they were sometimes mounted for movement on campaign, they could not fire from the saddle and tended to fight on the defensive, which ensured that they depended on being attacked; a general problem with infantry forces in the period. Edward III sought to overcome this by inflicting terrible devastation on rural France in order to provoke a French attack. However, this was not the major limitation of the English force structure. Instead, the problem was that triumph in battle could only achieve so much, and the English found it impossible to turn victory into a permanent settlement. This was seen in Scotland, Ireland and France.

To take the first, had the English been able to maintain and support a permanent military presence in lowland Scotland, then the Scottish kingdom might have been so weakened and divided as to cease to be a powerful challenge. Divisions among the Scottish nobility, which greatly helped the English, might have been exploited to spread the power of the King of England, who would have been able to mount a more effective claim to the Crown of Scotland, either for himself or for a protégé. However, the episodic military commitment dictated by Scotland's secondary role in English military policy from the late 1330s, as Edward III turned against France, exacerbated the natural logistical problems of campaigning there and ensured that fixed positions were given insufficient support. This left the Scots with the military initiative, which was fatal to the English cause in Scotland, although when the Scots invaded England in 1346 they were heavily defeated at Neville's Cross. When the English invaded Scotland, the defenders could avoid battle and concentrate on harrying the English force and denying them supplies, a policy that thwarted Edward III's invasion of Lothian in 1356. In addition, it would have been staggeringly expensive to maintain a large number of English garrisons, and, as Scotland itself would not have been rich enough to be made to fund its own occupation, the cost would have fallen on England.

The English also failed to conquer Ireland, which was invaded in 1169. Much was overrun over the following century, with progress marked by the construction of castles, such as Carrickfergus, Dundalk, Coleraine, Trim, Athlone and Kildare. A skilful combination of cavalry and archers provided a valuable military advantage. However, Ireland was too distant for a monarchy based in southern England adequately to deploy its resources. Furthermore, because it was politically decentralised, conquest was necessarily piecemeal and slow. By the 1320s, a Gaelic resurgence had compromised English chances of conquest and also ended the surplus that the Irish Exchequer had contributed to the English Exchequer.

Successful war in France, by contrast, was partially self-financing, although English forces were largely raised by contracts of indenture that specified payment in return for service. The financial viability of the English state was at issue, but the ability of European powers to develop quite complex systems of tax, created largely to finance war, was an important aspect of military capability. In Persia, the Il-Khans also developed some sophisticated financial techniques.

The Anglo-French conflict, subsequently known as the Hundred Years' War, arose from long-standing disputes over Gascony and, secondarily, in Anglo-French rivalry in the Low Countries. In 1340, in response to pressure from his allies, Edward III claimed the French throne. This claim was abandoned by the Peace of Brétigny of 1360, by which Edward was recognised as Duke of the whole of Aquitaine, as well as ruler of Calais. It was not a stable settlement, however. War was resumed in 1369 as a result of French encouragement of opposition in Aquitaine. Edward reasserted his claim to the French throne, but the war went badly both in Aquitaine and at sea and, by the time of the Truce of Bruges (1375), England held little more than Bayonne, Bordeaux and Calais.

Aside from pursuing external interests, troops were also used to suppress domestic opposition to rulers and nobles, including peasants' uprisings, as in England in 1381. Peasants who rose in Flanders in 1323 formed an army but it was destroyed by a French force at Cassel in 1328 after it unwisely attacked, a fate repeated at Westrozebeke in 1382. In France, the nobility suppressed the peasant jacquerie of 1358. Townsmen could also rebel. Those of Liège defeated Engelbert, Prince-bishop of Liège, at Voltern in 1346, only to be smashed at Othée in 1408.

Religious opposition also led to conflict: the ultimately successful Crusades against the Cathars in southern France in 1209–29, and those that failed against the Hussites in Bohemia in 1420–31. The Hussites held off the attacks by the Emperor Sigismund thanks to excellent leadership and innovative infantry tactics, including the use of fortified wagons to create effective defensive boundaries. The wagon fortresses – *wagenburgen* – were defended with crossbows and also handguns and cannon, the latter signs of a receptiveness to new armaments. The Hussite armies were able to inflict serious defeats, such as Domažlice (1431), on their attackers.

The problem of translating victory into permanent success recurred for the English in the early fifteenth century. In support of dismounted men at arms, Henry V's

The Hussite heretical movement in Bohemia was countered from 1420 when a crusade led by Sigismund, King of Hungary and Holy Roman Emperor-elect, led to an ultimately unsuccessful invasion. Further crusades in 1421, 1422, 1427 and 1431 also failed, and a compromise brought a settlement in 1436. The well-led Hussites used field fortifications, including wagon fortresses, to help protect their handgunners and crossbowmen from their frequently poorly-commanded attackers. Hussite raids into Germany underlined the failure of Sigismund and the German princes.

archers smashed the successive advances of the French at Agincourt (1415). Henry subsequently conquered Normandy, in part thanks to his use of siege artillery but more due to the weaknesses of the divided French, and, by the Treaty of Troyes (1420), he was recognised as the heir to Charles VI of France. Yet the struggle continued, especially when a charismatic peasant girl, Joan of Arc, inspired Charles VII and, in 1429, led an army that lifted the English siege of the strategic town of Orléans.

The political context, especially, in the 1420s and 1430s, the support of the Duke of Burgundy, first for Henry VI and then for Charles VI, was crucial to the course of the Hundred Years' War. However, the closing years of the conflict were also to see the effective deployment of another type of firepower. In 1449–51, English-held Normandy and Gascony fell rapidly to Charles VII's stronger army, not least his impressive train of artillery. The replacement of stone by iron cannon balls, the use of more effective gunpowder, improvements in the transport of cannon, and the development of the trunnion, which made it easier to change the angle of fire, all increased the effectiveness of artillery, although it helped drive up the cost of war. Charles VII's cannon helped bring the speedy fall of fortified positions, in marked contrast with the time taken in earlier sieges, as well as victory in battle over English archers at Formigny in 1450. An English counter-offensive was crushed at Castillon in 1453, the same year in which the fall of Constantinople, to an Ottoman army that had employed cannon to breach its walls, signalled the extent to which war could dramatically alter the political order. Over the following century, there were to be even more striking

An early firearm being fired, from a fifteenth-century manuscript. Although the ability to harness chemical energy was a valuable advance, and cannon have been referred to as the first workable internal combustion engines, gunpowder posed serious problems if its potential as a source of energy was to be utilised effectively. For a long period, cannon were not strong enough to make proper use of gunpowder. This did not change until the fifteenth century, with the development, around 1420, of 'corned' powder, which provided the necessary energy but without dangerously high peak pressures.

demonstrations. Hand-held gunpowder weapons also became increasingly important during the fifteenth century.

At the same time, the mid-fifteenth century serves as a reminder of the variety of military circumstances. It witnessed Aztec expansion and also a major Chinese defeat at the hands of the Mongols: in 1449 the Yingzong emperor was captured and his army destroyed at Tumu in a Mongol ambush, a defeat that greatly influenced Ming policy and brought to an end a period in which the Ming had launched numerous offensives beyond the Great Wall and taken the war to the Mongols. Thereafter, the Ming relied on a defensive strategy based on walls. The Great Wall of the first Qin emperor was reconstructed.

Seven years after Tumu, at Staraia Rusa, Vasilii II of Muscovy was able to defeat an army from Novgorod that was strong in lancers by making good use of horse archers, in part provided by Tatar auxiliaries. As a result, Novgorod was forced to accept Muscovite dominance, an important step in the consolidation of Christian Russia. Other Rus' principalities were subjugated and otherwise brought under control in the 1450s and 1460s. Staraia Rusa also marked a transition in force structures. Hitherto, Russian principalities had deployed armoured lancers, in part as a consequence of the impact of the Byzantine preference for heavy cavalry. In their place, came a shift in cavalry armament and tactics towards archers wearing padded hemp coats. This adaptation to the central Asian form of warfare also made it cheaper to deploy cavalry. As yet, there was nothing inevitable about the triumph of gunpowder weaponry. This can also be seen in the role of cavalry in the French and Burgundian armies in the late fifteenth century, and in the rise of the Swiss pikemen to prominence in the same period, not least as a result of their crucial role in defeating Charles the Bold, Duke of Burgundy in 1476–7.

Nor was there anything inevitable about the triumph of European maritime power. A Portuguese expedition had seized Ceuta in Morocco in 1415, Portuguese settlement of Madeira began in 1424 and of the Azores in the 1430s, and in the 1440s the Portuguese explored the African coast as far as modern Guinea. At the same time, however, the Chinese were far more wide-ranging. Under the Ming, whose fleet possibly carried cannon from the 1350s, a series of seven expeditions was sent into the Indian Ocean between 1405 and 1433 under Admiral Zheng He (1371–1433), and Chinese power was made manifest along much of its shores. The largest ships carried seven or eight masts, although claims that they were nearly 400 feet in length have been questioned, not least as the dimensions do not correspond to the figures for carrying capacity, tonnage and displacement. Nevertheless, these were probably the largest wooden ships built up to then and, thanks to watertight bulkheads and several layers of external planking, they were very seaworthy. At the same time that they were pressing Burma and attempting, albeit unsuccessfully, to annex Vietnam, the Chinese, in a major show of force designed to extend the Ming tributary system, reached Aden and Mogadishu and successfully invaded Sri Lanka in 1411 on the third expedition. South Asian trade patterns were greatly affected. It was by no means clear that the Europeans would dominate the oceans and eventually, therefore, the world.

3

THE RISE OF THE GUNPOWDER EMPIRES

Set against the previous chapter, it is easier to understand why a Eurocentric approach is adopted towards global military history in the period 1450–1600. This was the period in which European forces, employing firepower, were able to make a major impact across the world: on land in the 'New World', where Spanish *conquistadores* destroyed the Aztec and Inca empires, and by sea around the Indian Ocean, where Portuguese warships that had sailed round Africa created a far-flung maritime empire.

Yet, at the same time, other major changes were occurring, particularly in south Asia, and these reflected the fact that the gunpowder empires that arose in this period were not only European. Gunpowder weaponry had developed first in China, where the correct formula for manufacturing gunpowder was discovered in the ninth century, and effective metal-barrelled weapons were produced in the twelfth. Each of these processes in fact involved many stages. With gunpowder, it was necessary to find a rapidly burning mixture with a high propellant force – while with cannon, it was necessary to increase the calibre and to move from pieces made of rolled sheet iron reinforced with iron bands to proper castings.

Gunpowder was used at sea as well as on land. In 1161, gunpowder bombs fired by catapults helped the navy of the Song to defeat that of the Jurchen Jin. But even when gunpowder weapons had developed, their use was still restricted: by their limitations, by a preference for already established arms, and by the need to decide how best to employ them in battle and siegecraft. For example, in China there was no need for a revolution in fortification to counter the new weapon: Chinese city walls were already relatively low, extremely thick and made of packed earth, rather than the brittle stone which made European fortresses vulnerable. By the beginning of the sixteenth century, however, restrictions on the use of gunpowder weaponry had been overcome in a number of important areas, and it was to spread during the century. Nevertheless, alongside the widespread nature and increasing frequency of the use of gunpowder during the sixteenth century is the extent to which, among the number of dynamic

Ottoman military parade, *c.* 1579. Neither Suleiman the Magnificent (r. 1520–66) in his later years, nor his successors later in the century, were able to sustain the expansionism of the first fifty-five years of the century, but the Ottomans remained Europe's leading military power with an important mixed capability: in infantry, cavalry, artillery on land, as well as a formidable fleet.

powers in the period, not all of them made much, or, in some cases, any, use of gunpowder.

To start with the Europeans, and then note the existence of a few others might appear logical, given the global range of European power, but it risks minimising important developments involving the bulk of the world's population. It is also useful to contextualise European developments by considering those elsewhere.

The Ottoman empire was one of the most successful military powers of the period. The Ottomans initially relied on mounted archers, but, in the second half of the fourteenth century, they developed an infantry that became a centrally paid standing army, eventually armed with handguns and supported by field cannon. By the late fifteenth century, the Ottomans were using their firepower with great effect against Muslim rivals. In 1473, at Baskent, the impact of their handguns and cannon on Türkmen cavalry produced victory over Uzun Hasan, head of the Aqquyunlu confederacy that controlled Iraq and most of Persia. Hasan, in contrast, had a classic central Asian army centred on cavalry: the clans, armed with bows, swords and shields, and deployed in a two-wing cavalry formation, accounted for over 70 per cent of the army. Victory was not solely due to firepower. The Ottomans also benefited from having a fortified camp from which to resist cavalry attack, and from both numerical superiority and better discipline.

Under Selim I, 'the Grim' (r. 1512–20), the greatest challenges and opportunities for the Ottomans came not in Europe but in Asia. This reminds us of the danger of adopting a Eurocentric approach, whether to Ottoman history and geopolitics or to that of the Roman empire and, subsequently, Byzantium. At one level, there was an essential stability in south-western Asia. With the exception of Alexander the Great's short-lived empire, no state based in the Mediterranean was able to conquer Persia, just as Sudan eluded control. Similarly, after Alexander's destruction of the Persian empire, secure control over the lands to the Aegean was outside Persian capability. However, within these constraints, the Ottomans were able to create a far-flung empire.

In the early sixteenth century, the dynamism of Safavid Persia was as apparent as that of Ottoman Turkey, although, in Eurocentric accounts, an emphasis on the Ottoman threat to Christian Europe ensures that the role and importance of Persia are generally minimised; an instance of the more general neglect of non-European powers. The Safavids were a militant Muslim religious order that developed a powerful military dimension in order to wage what they saw as holy war. In 1501, the Safavid leader, Isma'il (r. 1501–24), and his nomadic Türkmen followers from Azerbaijan, defeated the Aqquyunlu at Sharur and captured Tabriz, where he had himself proclaimed Shah. The Aqquyunlu were totally defeated at Alme-Qulaq near Hamadan in 1503, one of the most decisive battles of the century. It led to the fall of most of the Iranian plateau, Baghdad following in 1508. By 1510, modern Iran and Iraq were under Safavid control. Isma'il had benefited greatly from Aqquyunlu disunity.

Like other major empires, the Safavids operated in, and were threatened from, a number of directions. They were under pressure from the north-east, from the

Uzbeks, as well as from the Ottomans to the west. Uzbek tribes from the central Asian steppes were highly mobile, and their successes reflected the continued potency of light cavalry. They repeatedly attacked Transoxania, seizing Bukhara in 1499, Samarkand in 1500, Tashkent in 1503, Kunduz in 1504, and Herat in 1507. In 1510, however, Isma'il defeated the Uzbeks in battle near Merv. The skull of their ruler, Muhammad Shaibani, was set in gold, made into a drinking cup, and sent to Isma'il's other major enemy, the Ottoman Sultan, Bayezid II (r. 1481–1512). Isma'il pressed on to capture Herat.

Support for the Safavids and their millenarianism among the peoples of eastern Anatolia threatened both Ottoman security and its sense of religious identity, especially when that support prompted rebellions in the area in 1511–12. Selim brutally repressed the rebels, and in 1514 invaded Persia. The initial Safavid scorched-earth strategy, a strategy that the economic system, the role of distance, and political culture all encouraged, created serious logistical problems for the Ottoman forces, but Isma'il chose to fight his far more numerous opponents at Chaldiran on 23 August.

The Safavid army was of the traditional central Asian nomadic type: archers on horseback who combined mobility and firepower, the ability to control vast spaces and to fight effectively on the battlefield. The Ottomans had made the transition to a more mixed force, combining their janissary infantry with the cavalry. Although the Safavids had used cannon in siege warfare, they had none at Chaldiran. Cultural factors were important: the Safavids thought firearms cowardly and, initially, adopted cannon with reluctance, preferring to use them for sieges not battles. Thanks to their numerical superiority and firepower, the respective importance of which is hard to disentangle, the Ottomans won a crushing victory over the Safavid cavalry. But the cannon were also important for another reason: chained together, they formed a barrier to cavalry charges. In response, the Safavids created a small unit of musketeers and gunners in 1516.

Unlike Baskent, which was not followed by any significant Ottoman territorial advance, Chaldiran was followed by the capture of the Persian capital, Tabriz, in 1514. However, an Ottoman-supported advance by the Aqquyunlu leader, Sultan Murad, was defeated near Ruha and Murad was killed. Furthermore, logistical problems, exacerbated by Persian scorched-earth tactics and the coming of winter, meant that Tabriz was not retained. Nevertheless, there was a major eastward shift in the Ottoman frontier. The Safavids were pushed on to the defensive for most of the century, although their use of scorched-earth tactics again limited Ottoman gains when the Ottomans invaded in 1534, 1548 and 1554. On the first occasion, Suleiman the Magnificent (r. 1520–66) overran northern and central Iraq. The Austrians also learned to avoid battle when Ottoman armies advanced.

The defeat of the Safavids in 1514 was a crucial precondition of the subsequent Ottoman advances against Mamluks and, later, Christians. The emirate of Dhu'l-Kadr, between Anatolia and Mesopotamia, was annexed in 1515, and Selim then achieved the rapid overthrow of the Mamluk empire. Firepower was decisive in the defeat of the

Mamluk heavy cavalry at Marj Dabiq (24 August 1516), which led to the capture of Syria, but other factors were also important. The Ottoman army was far larger, and the governor of the province of Aleppo made a secret agreement with Selim. This was important at Marj Dabia as the governor, who commanded the left flank, abandoned the battle at its height. The battle was swiftly over and the Mamluk sultan died, probably of a stroke. A counter-attack was defeated at Gaza (22 December 1516).

The Ottomans then advanced across Sinai and beat the Mamluks at Raydaniyya (23 January 1517) in less than twenty minutes. This led to the conquest of Egypt. Surviving resistance was rapidly overcome, and the new Mamluk sultan was captured and executed. A garrison of 5,000 cavalry and 500 arquebusiers was left by Selim. There were revolts – in Syria in 1520–1, and in Egypt in 1523 and 1524, the latter by the governor – but they were all put down. From Egypt, the Ottomans extended their power along the coast of North Africa (although Cyrenaica only acknowledged their authority in 1640) and down the Red Sea, where Aden was incorporated in the Ottoman system in 1538, thwarting Portuguese plans to seize the city.

Like the Safavids, the Mamluks put a premium on cavalry and did not associate the use of firearms with acceptable warrior conduct. Firearms were seen as socially subversive, as also in the case of samurai aversion to firearms in seventeenth- to nineteenth-century Japan. Hostility to the use of musketeers obliged successive Mamluk sultans in 1498 and 1514 to disband musketeer units they had raised. Like the Aztecs in Mexico, the Mamluks stressed individual prowess and hand-to-hand, one-to-one combat with a matched opponent, and this made them vulnerable to forces that put an emphasis on more concerted manoeuvres and on anonymous combat, particularly employing firepower.

The range of physical and military environments in which the Ottomans had to operate was striking. In the sixteenth century, aside from attacking the Safavids and Mamluks, with their large cavalry armies, the Ottomans fought the Europeans on land in Europe, North Africa and Abyssinia, and at sea in the Mediterranean, Red Sea, Persian Gulf and Indian Ocean, as well as fighting a series of less powerful polities, ranging from Bedouin Arabs to opponents in the Caucasus. This capability drew on a military system that required a considerable measure of organisation, especially in logistics. The Ottoman military combined the strengths of different systems: organisational/bureaucratic and fiscal strengths, alongside tribal forces, including allies and tributaries, especially the Crimean Tatars. The diversity of the Ottoman military system was an inherent source of strength, one that was linked to the breadth and depth of its recruitment pool. Ottoman success led other states to seek to imitate aspects of their military organisation and methods. The janissaries served as a model for infantry forces developed in Muscovy and Poland, the first of them the *strel'tsy* musketeer force created by Ivan IV in 1550.

Further east, the Mughals were another dynamic power, and they made far more of an impact on India than the Portuguese, whose arrival in Indian waters was of little consequence for military developments on land. Babur, the founder of the dynasty,

The siege of Belgrade (tower shown in flames on left), 1521. The garrison was only 700 strong and the absence of a relief effort helped Suleiman the Magnificent to a rapid success. This opened the route into Hungary that was to be taken in 1526. Earlier Ottoman sieges in 1440 and 1456 had failed.

Ottoman campaigning in Hungary, 1543–4. Suleiman the Magnificent intervened in Hungary again in the 1540s after the Emperor Charles V's brother, Ferdinand, the ruler of Austria, sought to enforce his claim there. The Ottomans conquered central Hungary, capturing Buda in 1541, Esztergom in 1543, Visegrād in 1544, Tenesvār in 1552, and Fülek in 1554.

descended from Chinggis and Timur, was another instance of the extraordinary military potency of central Asia. Yet again, cavalry forces from the region had a major impact elsewhere. This was partly a matter of numbers, with the Mughal cavalry more numerous than that of individual opponents, but also of the vigour with which they were employed. Mughal mounted archers fired volleys repeatedly in order to disorientate their opponent and make them vulnerable to a more direct attack.

Babur inherited the kingdom of Ferghana, one of the successor states to Timur's empire, in 1494, but was driven from it by the Uzbeks. He then captured Kabul and Ghazni in 1504, thus gaining control of eastern Afghanistan, took Kandahar in 1522, invaded the Punjab in 1525, and, on 20 April 1526, at the first battle of Panipat, decisively defeated the predominant power of northern India, the Lodi sultanate of Delhi.

Babur's opium-addicted successor, Humayun (r. 1530–56), was driven out of Hindustan, after defeats at Chausa and Bilgram, by the Afghan Sher Shāh Sūr in 1539 and 1540, but regained control of Delhi after defeating the Sur-Afghans near Sirhind in 1555. His son, Akbar (r. 1556–1605), rebuilt and extended his grandfather's empire, his conquests including Gujarat (1572–3), Bengal (1575–6), Kabul (1585), Kashmir (1585–9), Sind (1586–93) and Orissa (1592). Some of the Mughal gains cut short other expanding polities. Buhlol Lodi (r. 1451–89) and Secander Lodi (r. 1489–1517) had already extended the Lodi dominions east and south of Delhi, while the Arghuns of southern Afghanistan had conquered the Sammas of Sind in 1518–22 and the Langas of the middle Indus in 1526. This rush of names may appear confusing, but it serves to show the extent to which the military history of the period must not be thought of solely in terms of European power and personalities. Each of the campaigns just mentioned is worthy of detailed discussion, while, in combination, they greatly altered the geopolitics of south Asia. The Mughal state was transformed from being landlocked into an empire that stretched from the Bay of Bengal to the Indian Ocean.

Less striking, or well known, than that of the Mughals, Uzbek activity also testified to the vitality of central Asian military power. Aside from clashing with the Safavids, they pressed hard the Dörben Oirats of Mongolia, although the Uzbeks themselves were under pressure from another nomadic people, the Kazaks. The Uzbek nomadic system was politically fissiparous and much energy was spent on warfare between the tribes, lessening their wider impact. The Uzbeks' most dynamic leader, Abd Allah Sultan, sought to unite Transoxiana, seizing Balkh in 1573, Samarkand in 1578, Turkestan in 1584, and Herat in 1588, but he was unable to conquer Kabul, Khurasan and Kashgar, and in 1598 the Kazaks invaded the Uzbek lands. Abd Allah died that year, and the Uzbeks divided.

Elsewhere in Asia, once the Mongols had recovered from internal conflicts in the first half of the century, the Altan Khan revived their power and attacked Ming China every year from 1548 until 1566, riding beneath the walls of Beijing in 1550. With his army essentially of raiders, the Altan Khan was unable to breach the walls or maintain a long siege, and the garrison was unwilling to march out to fight him. It was easier to defeat the Oirat confederation of northern Mongolia, capturing Karakorum in 1552.

Helped by Portuguese auxiliaries using cannon and handguns, the Burmese kingdom of Toungoo under Tabinshwehti (r. 1531–50) and Bayinnaung (r. 1551–81) overran Pegu in 1535–41 and the rival kingdom of Ava in 1555. The resulting dynamic state expanded considerably in the 1550s and 1560s, defeating the Siamese state of Lan Na/Chiengmai in 1558 and capturing the Siamese capital of Ayuthia in 1564 and 1569. In 1564, the Burmese brought a number of large-calibre cannon with them, and this led to a rapid surrender. Vientiane fell in 1574, and Bayinnaung felt able to call himself the King of Kings. However, in the mid-1580s, Siam declared independence and in 1593 a Burmese attempt to reimpose control failed. It proved impossible to sustain the war effort. The demands of the Burmese army had placed too great a burden on economy and society, leading villagers to flee and hitting the ability to recruit. Further east, after the sengoku jidai, 'the age of warring states', a protracted period of civil war that had started in 1467, Toyotomi Hideyoshi reunified Japan by 1590.

In West Africa, Sonni Ali (r. 1464–92), ruler of the Songhay empire on the middle Niger, fought every year of his reign. Some of his campaigns, most obviously against the Tuaregs, can be characterised as defensive, but war was central to the Songhay state, as Sonni expanded his power at the expense of Jenne, the Fulani of Dendi, and the Mossi. These wars of expansion were continued by Askia Muhammad (r. 1493–1528), and the Songhay empire destroyed Mali in 1546, before itself collapsing after the victory of a Moroccan expeditionary force at Tondibi on the Niger in 1591: only about half of the 5,000 men sent across the Sahara survived the crossing, but they made a decisive difference to the politics of the middle-Niger valley. Sultan Mawláy Ahmad al-Mansur of Morocco wanted to secure gold as well as recognition for his claim to be caliph. Many of the troops sent were renegades: Christians who had become Muslim.

In many cases, decisive victory in this period reflected a technological gap in weaponry, specifically the role of cannon at sea and the advantage on land that firearms offered over cutting and thrusting weapons. At the first battle of Panipat, Babur employed both matchlockmen and field artillery successfully against the cavalry of the Lodis, whose armies did not use firearms. In 1527, Mughal firepower also played a role in the defeat of the cavalrymen and armoured war elephants of a confederacy of Rajput rulers at Kanua, although the flexible enveloping tactics of Babur's cavalry were also effective, and mounted archers were more important than infantry matchlockmen in the battle. The following year, Safavid artillery played a role in Tahmasp I of Persia's victory over the Uzbeks at Jam, which was followed by the conquest of Khurusan.

Tactics were similar at Baskent, Chaldiran, Panipat, Kanua, Jam, and the decisive Ottoman victory over the Hungarians at Mohacs (1526). The winning side employed a deployment known in Turkish as *tabúr cengí*: a row of carts linked by chains was arranged across the centre to block the advance of the opposing force, and, behind it, both artillery and infantry were deployed. Mounted archers were placed on the wings. The vital Ottoman addition to the notion of a wagon fort familiar to the Turco-

Ottoman campaigning in Hungary, 1543–4. The Ottomans had initially relied on mounted archers, but, in the second half of the fourteenth century, they developed an infantry that became a centrally paid standing army eventually armed with field cannon and handguns. The infantry played a major role in bringing victory over the Hungarian cavalry at Mohács in 1526.

Mongols of central Asia was firepower. Babur borrowed the tactic from the Ottomans, as did Ivan IV of Muscovy, helping the Russians to defeat the Crimean Tatars at Molodye in 1572.

Firepower also played a major role in other battles. In 1556, at the second battle of Panipat, Akbar's Mughal army, under the Regent, Bairam Khan, defeated a much larger insurrectionary force under Hemu, without the use of a tábúr cengí, or, apparently, artillery. Hemu relied on an elephant charge, but the Mughal centre redeployed behind a ravine and eventually prevailed thanks to their mounted archers. At Haldighati (1576), a Mughal force defeated a Rajput army, because only the Mughals had musketeers, and they and the Mughal archers killed the elephant drivers who were crucial in their opponent's army. Akbar took great interest in the improvement of muskets, maintaining a special collection that he tested himself. His artillery was superior to that of rivals and was instrumental in the capture of well-fortified positions, such as the Rajput fortress of Ranthambor in 1569. At Tondibi, Moroccan musketry defeated the cavalry of Songhay.

Firearms helped relatively small forces to defeat far more numerous opponents. This was true at Kanua, Jam and Tondibi, and also of the Spanish conquest of the Aztec and Inca empires. Firearms altered the balance of military advantage between states, peoples and areas. At the battle of Orsha in 1514, the Poles scored a decisive victory over a larger Muscovite army by using artillery and arquebusiers. This was the first significant Muscovite defeat attributable to superior enemy gunpowder firepower, and it pushed Vasilii III to begin developing an arquebusier infantry from volunteers at Novgorod and Pskov, although the Muscovites had deployed arquebusiers by 1480.

Nevertheless, in Muscovy and elsewhere, the social order was not dominated by those who used firepower. Promotion to *boyar* (noble) rank in sixteenth-century Muscovy depended in part upon service in the field army, and Ivan IV's Decree on Service (1556) held all nobles liable for lifelong service, including the most powerful boyars and princes with allodial estates. This was part of a social politics that bent the nobility to military service while compensating them with the enserfment of their peasant tenants.

Possession of, and expertise in, firearms became a priority in the struggle for predominance, or even survival. Without firearms, which he had unsuccessfully sought from the Venetians, Uzun Hasan was defeated at Baskent in 1473, but, five years later, the Aqquyunlu army had both field artillery and handguns. Although the first reference to gunpowder warfare in Muscovy relates to the use of a small cannon in the defence of Moscow in 1382, Ivan III felt it necessary to recruit Italian cannon-founders. By 1494, they had established a cannon-casting yard and powder yard in Moscow. It was not until the siege of Smolensk in 1514 that Muscovite artillery was sufficiently powerful to help determine the fate of a siege. In the early sixteenth century, the Portuguese, from their base at Ormuz in the Persian Gulf, were able to provide the Safavids with cannon to use against the Uzbeks, who understood the importance of artillery but, having no access to oceanic trade, found it difficult to

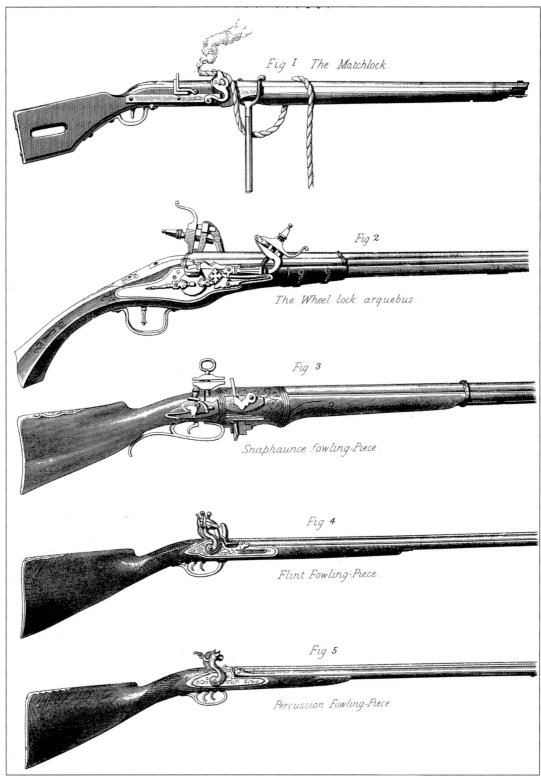

Examples of handgun firing mechanisms: matchlock; wheel-lock arquebus, snaphaunce fowling-piece, flint fowling-piece, percussion fowling-piece.

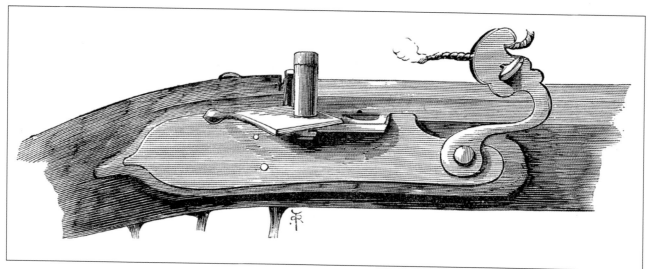

British matchlock, *c.* 1700.

Polish flintlock firing mechanism, *c.* 1650.

acquire. Persia also obtained cannon from Russia. By 1600, the Safavids had about 500 cannon. In turn, the Ottomans provided firearms or soldiers armed with firearms to the Uzbeks, the Khan of the Crimea, the sultanate of Aceh in Sumatra (an Islamic opponent of the Portuguese), and supporters in the Caucasus.

The new weaponry spread elsewhere in Asia and in Africa. In southern India, the Hindu state of Vijayanagara, under its dynamic ruler Rama Raja (r. 1542–65), maintained its position by deploying armies equipped with artillery manned by Portuguese or Muslim gunners. Ibrahim Qutb, Shah of Golconda (r. 1530–80), who played a major role in overthrowing Rama Raja, relied upon both heavy cavalry led by his nobility and a European artillery corps.

In the Horn of Africa, Iman Ahmad Gragn conquered Adal in the mid-1520s and launched a holy war against Christian Ethiopia, training his men in the new firearms and tactics introduced into the Red Sea region by the Ottomans after their conquest of Egypt in 1517. Better weapons were partly responsible for his victory over the Ethiopian Emperor Lebna-Dengel at Shimbra Kure in 1528, but he was unable to follow it up in 1529 because the tribal confederation he had built up collapsed. In 1530, however, Ahmad used loot from his 1528 campaign to buy seven cannon and recruited foreign experts to use them; although he also hired a force of Arabian archers. His cannon helped lead to victory at Antika in 1531. In 1541, the Portuguese, who had sent two cannon as a present in 1520, dispatched 400 musketeers to the aid of Ethiopia and helped defeat Ahmad. He turned to the Ottomans, who provided him with 900 musketeers and 10 cannon, with whose help he was victorious in 1542, only to be defeated and killed the following year at the battle of Woina-Dega on the shores of Lake Tana. Lebna-Dengel's son and successor, Galawdewos, then reconquered Ethiopia. The Ethiopians rewarded Portuguese musketeers with land in order to retain their services, and these musketeers and their descendants continued to play an important role into the following century.

The clash between Christianity and Islam in the Horn of Africa continued in mid-century to be intense. An Ottoman invasion in 1557 was driven back to the coast, but in 1559 Ahmad's nephew, Núr, led the forces of Adal on a fresh invasion in which the Ethiopians were beaten and Galawdewos killed. This provided an opportunity for the Galla peoples, nomadic pastoralists, who moved north into the Horn of Africa, helping undermine Adal, and thence into Ethiopia. The Galla's adoption of the use of horses increased their mobility. External pressure exacerbated divisions within the Ethiopian royal family and élite, and the latter further encouraged intervention. In 1562, Ottoman cannon fire helped decide the battle that temporarily determined the conflict over the Ethiopian crown.

However, Serse-Dingil, who became king at the end of 1562, changed the military system so that the traditional reliance on the private forces of provincial governors and other regional potentates was complemented by an expansion of the troops directly under royal control, both the bodyguard and the militia. Serse-Dingil's decision to lead the army in person also helped give new direction to Ethiopian

Fluted German armour being worn by John-Frederick, Elector of Saxony (r. 1532–47) by Cranach. Defeated and captured by Habsburg forces under Fernando, Duke of Alva at Mühlberg in 1547. The Electorate was transferred to the Habsburg ally Duke Maurice of Saxony.

energies. Adal was defeated in 1576, and an alliance of Ottoman forces with the governor of Tigre in 1578, ending Ottoman attempts to overrun Ethiopia. Serse-Dingil then expanded Ethiopia to the west. Susenyos (r. 1607–32) continued this, but also followed the traditional policy of those confronted by 'barbarians', by incorporating many of the Galla into his army and settling many into his domains. However, the king's conversion to Catholicism led to serious rebellions and he abdicated.

Alongside the customary stress on firepower, it is clear that other factors played a major role in conquest, including the ability to benefit from divisions among opponents, which greatly helped the Spaniards in the New World. Similarly, the Portuguese benefited in East Africa from the help of the rulers of Malindi in attacking those of Mombasa. In 1591, they cooperated in capturing Mombasa, the ruler of Malindi becoming Sheikh there while the Portuguese built a powerful fortress.

It is also clear that not all battles were decided by firepower. On the Ugra river in 1480, Khan Akhmet of the Golden Horde was defeated not so much by the arquebusiers of Ivan III of Muscovy as by his archers. At Alme-Qulaq (1503), the Safavids defeated the Aqquyunlu, in part because divisions among the latter undermined their attempt to unlimber cannon behind a wagon fort. Sieges were frequently determined not by wall-breaching artillery, but by the availability of sufficient light cavalry to blockade a fortress and ravage the surrounding country. This approach was best resisted by coastal positions when they could be resupplied by sea.

In India, Babur's victories owed more to his use of mounted archers than to firearms. The Mughal ability to control the supply of war horses ensured that they dominated mounted archery, and this played a major role in a relative decline in the importance of elephants, which had hitherto been much more valuable in north Indian warfare. The composite central Asian bows that the Mughals used were more effective in range and penetration than those of the Indians, most of which were made of bamboo. In 1581, Akbar's massive field army still only included 28 cannon in a force of 50,000 cavalry and 500 war elephants. In 1573, a rebellion in Gujarat was crushed by the Mughals in a cavalry engagement. Two years later, at Tukaroi, the Mughal army in east India under Todar Mal defeated the Afghan Sultan of Bengal, Daud Karani. After recovering from the initial shock of a successful elephant charge on the Mughal centre, they wore down their opponents in hard fighting in which archery played a major role.

The great extension of Mughal territory under Akbar reflected his energy and determination, the divisions among his opponents, the impressive demographic, economic and financial resources of Hindustan and the regions gained by conquest, and the strength of the Mughal military system. Aside from firearms, the Mughals also used heavy cavalry armed with swords and lances, horse archers and war elephants. The successful combination of a number of military traditions was important, while much of Akbar's success was due to his military skill and to the strong organisation of his state.

The limited role of firearms was not restricted to India, where, indeed, there was no major change until the spread of the flintlock musket in the eighteenth century. It could also be seen in Africa, China and Persia. When Shah Abbas I of Persia advanced on Herat in 1598, he defeated the Uzbeks at Rabát-i Pariyán, but the battle was decided by an old-fashioned charge by Abbas's mounted bodyguard, led by the Shah himself.

It is also appropriate to draw attention to the deficiencies of firearms in this period. The accuracy of smoothbore guns was limited. Spherical bullets were less aerodynamically effective than their nineteenth-century replacements. Recharging and reloading from the muzzle (rather than, as later, the breech) increased the time taken to fire, and the long reloading cycle led to acute vulnerability for the musketeers, especially from cavalry. Accuracy would have been increased by rifling the barrel, which helps give a controlled spin to the projectile fire, but this was not practical because of the difficulty of muzzle loading if the shot had to be pushed down rifled grooves.

The ability of spherical shot to inflict lethal wounds at other than short range was limited, and was further decreased by the impact on muzzle velocity of the large windage (gap between projectile and inside of barrel) made necessary by the difficulty of casting accurate shot. This limited ability helped account for the continued popularity of body armour, as it could provide protection against most gunshot wounds. This helped ensure a very different look among the troops to those on the twentieth-century battlefield.

In Africa, firearms had most impact along the savannah belt to the south of the Sahara, where Muslim influence from the Mediterranean littoral was strongest, although it is important not to exaggerate their impact. Idris Aloma, *mai* (ruler) of Borno (r. 1569–c. 1600), a Muslim state based in the region of Lake Chad, probably obtained his musketeers from Tripoli on the Mediterranean, which was captured by the Ottomans in 1551; but Ibn Fartuwa's contemporary account of his wars with Kanem makes no mention of guns playing a crucial role, and Fartuwa concentrated on other units of Aloma's army, which included archers, shield-bearers, cavalry and camel-borne troops. Camel columns were sent into the Sahara. There is no mention of cannon. In his campaigns, Aloma made careful use of economic measures, attacking crops or keeping nomads from their grazing areas in order to make them submit, both long-standing practices in such campaigns.

Although the Moroccans overran what became the Pashalik of Timbuktu in 1591, strong resistance in southern Songhay prevented further expansion. Campaigning there in 1593–4, the Moroccans suffered the effects of both guerrilla resistance and humidity. In 1594, the Moroccan Pasha was killed in battle by the animists of Hombori, who were effective despite the absence of firearms. In 1609, a Moroccan army was defeated by a Songhay force at Jenne. It is necessary to emphasise these obscure clashes because all too often warfare in the region is discussed solely in terms of Tondibi. This reflects not only limited knowledge but also a misleading preference for supposedly decisive battles that underrates the often lengthy and difficult process of conquest. Pressures of space also lead to a focus on particular battles, but these can provide a misleading impression of the weakness of societies that apparently succumbed so readily.

Maximilian (1459–1519), Holy Roman Emperor (1493–1519) and the creator of Habsburg power as a result of his marriage to Mary of Burgundy, as well as the marriage treaty with the Jagiellons that was, in 1526, to bring Bohemia and Hungary into the Habsburg fold. Maximilian was less successful as a war-leader, particularly in Italy, in part because he lacked the finances to sustain his ambitions. The French proved obstinate opponents, although Maximilian was able to win Artois and Franche-Comté from the Burgundian inheritance. A brave commander, Maximilian raised bands of Landsknechte in order to provide effective pikemen. *(From a woodcut by Hans Burgkmair)*

Sixteenth-century Spanish cannon. War on both land and sea was transformed by the spread and increased effectiveness of cannon and by the development of tactics to enhance their value. To a large extent, cannon for siege warfare, fortifications and naval warfare were interchangeable, although the mountings had to be changed. Field artillery was different as it had to be as light as possible.

Landscape with a cannon, Albrecht Dürer, 1518. The Nuremberg-born painter and engraver was greatly interested in the impact of cannon. In 1527, he published a treatise on fortification that proposed walls dominated by massive squat roundrels: towers that would also provide gun-platforms.

In inland West Africa, the spread from North Africa of larger breeds of horse, new equestrian techniques, and new tactics of cavalry warfare, which had begun in at least the fourteenth century, was more important than the use of firearms. Cavalry was particularly important in the savannah belt to the south of the Sahara, which was suitable cavalry terrain, but this ensured that operations were affected by the availability of water. In Ethiopia, as elsewhere, the use of firearms was restricted by the limited availability of shot and powder. In the early seventeenth century, no more than 500 musketeers took part in any one Ethiopian expedition. Throughout Africa, pillage and search for booty played a major role in conflict, and this contributed directly to the slave trade.

In east Asia, it is also appropriate to avoid a narrow focus on firepower. The use of cannon and other firearms spread from China to Burma, Cambodia, Siam, Vietnam and elsewhere in the fourteenth century; the Japanese received crude guns in the fifteenth. However, China lost the lead in handheld firearms. Matchlocks were introduced into China, probably from the Ottomans via the Muslims of Xinjiang, and from Portuguese merchant adventurers, either directly or via Japanese pirates. These European-style muskets and, later, European-style iron guns mounted on carriages, impressed the Chinese, who copied them.

Mongol and, later, Manchu success over Chinese forces reflected the effectiveness of their mounted archers. Horse archers also continued to play a major role in India. In addition, too close a focus on gunpowder weapons and, more generally, on firepower, makes it too easy to overlook the continued importance of cutting, stabbing and slashing weapons that could be wielded by both cavalry and infantry. In Europe, the pike proved devastating en masse in disciplined formations when used by the Swiss from the 1470s, until defensive Spanish firepower caused heavy casualties for the attacking Swiss at the battle of Bicocca in 1522. In sixteenth-century Russia, the cavalry increasingly did not employ the bow, but the switch was largely to swords, not pistols.

The first effective guns in Japan were brought by Portuguese traders in 1543. They were widely copied within a decade, as Japan's metallurgical industry could produce muskets in large numbers. However, the most important changes in Japan occurred earlier, from the late fifteenth century, as the pace of warfare within Japan accelerated. These changes included larger armies, greater preponderance of infantry, sophisticated tactics and command structures; and changes in weaponry, especially the spear, and armour. The sole major change introduced by the Portuguese was the gun. While this became an important weapon, and had far-reaching effects on armour design, its impact on Japanese warfare is a matter of controversy. Firearms certainly played an important role in war from the mid-1550s and, at the battle of Nagashino in 1575, 3,000 musketeers in the army of Nobunaga employed volley fire to smash the successive charges of Takeda cavalry. Firepower led to a stress on defensive tactics at the battle of Shizugatake in 1583, and in Kyúshú in 1587, where Hideyoshi's forces were deployed behind entrenchments. Cannon were known in Japan from at least 1551, although they did not become important until the last quarter of the century.

Toyotomi Hideyoshi, who united Japan by fighting his way into dominance over other *daimyōs* (important warriors), particularly by his skill in siege warfare, decided to conquer China after he had subdued the Shimazu of Kyúshú in 1587 and defeated the Hōjō in 1590, campaigns in which he had deployed at least 200,000 troops. The invasion would provide new lands for his warriors and enable Hideyoshi to keep his control over them. Continual success had led him to lose a sense of limits; the cult of the warrior, anyway, discouraged an interest in limits. Hideyoshi planned to advance via Korea, a Chinese client state, and to rule the world from the Chinese city of Ningpo. From there, he intended to conquer India. Hideyoshi also demanded that Taiwan and the Philippines submit to him.

Hideyoshi had exceeded his grasp. The invasion, with about 150,000 men, in 1592 was initially successful, winning victory at Ch'ungju, capturing Seoul, and advancing to the Yalu river, but Korean naval resistance eventually altered the situation. The Japanese fleet was defeated at the battle of the Yellow Sea by a fleet commanded by Yi Sun-Shin that included some of the more impressive warships of the age: Korean 'turtle ships', oar-driven boats, possibly covered by hexagonal metal plates in order to prevent grappling and boarding, that may also have been equipped with rams. In addition, Korean guerrilla tactics on land undermined Japanese control. In September 1592, the Chinese committed large forces that drove back the Japanese, recapturing P'yongyang in February 1593: the size of the army, not its technology, was important. The Japanese were pushed back to a bridgehead near Pusan, but the Chinese, who committed more than 200,000 troops to Korea, were unable to destroy the bridgehead.

The Japanese rapidly deployed cannon on their warships and used them with effect in 1593, and, again, in 1597 when a fresh invasion was mounted by 140,000 troops. However, the Chinese and Koreans were now prepared and the Japanese were unable to repeat their success of 1592, although the Chinese were affected by grave logistical problems. In 1598, the Koreans were supported by a Chinese fleet under an artillery expert, Ch'en Lin, and, that year, the Japanese fleet was defeated by Yi Sun-Shin at the battle of the Noryang Straits: the Koreans appear to have had a lead in cannon, although Yi was killed in the battle.

Hideyoshi died in 1598 and his plans against China were not pursued. His position was taken by Tokugawa Ieyasu, a daimyō that Hideyoshi had never trusted. His rise to power was resisted by a rival league of daimyōs, but Ieyasu had undermined his opponents by secretly winning several of them over, and this led to victory at the battle of Sekigahara in 1600. He then established the Tokugawa shōgunate, which lasted until 1868. Hideyoshi's son, Hideyori, and his supporters were defeated when Osaka castle was besieged in 1614–15.

During the seventeenth century, Japanese military capability did not develop either on land or at sea. There was considerable socio-cultural opposition to giving guns to ordinary people. No one outside the closed samurai élite was allowed to own any arms, including swords. The extent to which policies moulded opportunities was shown by the failure of Japan and Korea to develop a long-distance naval capability or to challenge the Iberian presence in Asian waters. The Japanese abandoned plans to develop ships protected with iron plates after Hideyoshi died, while the Korean turtle ships fought no further battles.

In China, the military strength of the Ming empire lay primarily in the size of its army and, to a lesser extent, in fortifications, rather than in firearms. In 1569, according to the Deputy Minister of War, the army had an authorised strength of 3,138,000 men, but the real strength was only 845,000. Of this the majority, about half a million, served along the northern frontier, where there was a series of major garrisons. This provision became more important as Mongol attacks became more serious in mid-century. To cope with the Mongols, there was a reliance on walls and on garrisons at strategic passes; just as Muscovy developed the Abatis Line of fortifications against the Crimean Tatars in the late sixteenth century. Steps were also taken to accommodate the Mongols. In 1571, the year in which Khan Devlet Girei of the Crimean Tatars was able to launch a devastating raid on Muscovy, the Chinese signed a treaty with the Altan Khan. Trade and gifts were used as effective means of defence.

Although better firearms and fortifications helped, in the 1550s the Ming used large numbers of men armed with traditional weapons – bows, lances and swords – to capture the Chinese bases of the *wako* (Japanese pirates) who attacked the coasts of the Yellow Sea and also mounted raids into the interior. Cannon were felt to be unreliable and/or inaccurate. The wako were defeated by 1567. Nevertheless, the spreading use of firearms pushed up Chinese military expenditure during the century. Much of the army was raised from a hereditary soldiery, although mercenaries became more important during the century, in part in response to the deterioration of the hereditary element.

Thanks to cultural assumptions, firearms also played a relatively minor role in south-east Asia and the East Indies, for example in warfare on Java. The emphasis was on the fighting qualities of individuals, and on warrior élites, some of whom duelled on war elephants, and not on large numbers. Firearms were expected to fit into existing tactics. Across the world, this frequently occurred when new weapons were introduced. Rather than a transformation of tactics or operational assumptions, there was often an attempt to use new weapons to give added power to existing practices. Although this could lessen the impact of the weapons, it was also a response not only to cultural conservatism but to the social norms influencing military service and warfare, as well as to the difficulty of training troops for new tactics.

In general, handgunners were treated badly in south-east Asia and the East Indies; they were not members of these élites. Effectiveness in the use of muskets, which were low-precision weapons, required their use in a regular manner in order to provide concentrated fire. The necessary discipline and drill did not match social assumptions about warfare in the region, because they subordinated individual skill and social rank to the collective, the disciplined unit. Furthermore, cannon were frequently used as symbolic supports of authority, rather than as killing machines. They were adjuncts of courts, and there was an emphasis on their size, not their manoeuvrability. European-type matchlocks were manufactured in Burma and Vietnam, but the provision of a large number of similar, let alone identical, weapons was beyond local metallurgical capability, and there were problems in making good gunpowder. The nature of the local environment ensured that in south-east Asia, and Kerala in southern India, war elephants remained important, while mounted archery did not play a role.

An emphasis on other expanding powers acts as a corrective to any tendency to see military history largely in terms of Europe, specifically of European initiatives with the addition of the Ottoman advance that took them to the gates of Vienna in 1529. Instead, the Europeans appear as distinctive because of their range. With the exception of Russian expansion – the conquest of Kazan and Astrakhan in the 1550s and expansion in Siberia from the 1580s – maritime power was crucial to this. It was through the projection of European power that the 'Old World' and the 'New' were connected. This power was not contested in American waters, for neither the Incas nor the Aztecs had naval capability (the Aztec canoes were used on lakes), while, in the Indian Ocean, the Portuguese defeated Egyptian and Indian rivals and were able to check Ottoman naval advances or to limit them by reliance on fortified ports.

Battle of Lepanto, 7 October 1571. The Holy League of Spain, Venice and the Papacy defeats the Ottoman fleet off the west coast of Greece. More than 100,000 men took part in the battle. Superior (at least more numerous) Christian gunnery, the fighting qualities and firepower of the Spanish infantry, who served on the Spanish and the Venetian ships, and the exhaustion of Ottoman gunpowder, all helped to bring a crushing victory in four hours fighting. The normal caution of the Christian galley commanders was overridden by the charismatic and determined leadership of Don John of Austria. The Ottomans lost perhaps 223 galleys sunk and captured; the victors about 12 galleys.

Initially, the most impressive naval power was Portugal. Her naval strength was based on full-rigged sailing ships, strong enough to carry cannon capable of sinking the more numerous but lightly built vessels of the Indian Ocean. Drawing on late fourteenth- and fifteenth-century developments in ship construction and navigation, specifically the fusion of Atlantic and Mediterranean techniques of hull construction and lateen- and square-rigging, and advances in location-finding at sea, the Portuguese enjoyed important advantages over other vessels. Developments in rigging permitted greater speed, improved manoeuvrability, and a better ability to sail close to the wind. Thanks to the use of the compass, and other developments in navigation, such as the solution in 1484 to the problem of measuring latitude south of the Equator, it was possible to chart the sea and to assemble knowledge about it, and therefore to have greater control than ever before over the relationship between the enormity of the ocean and the transience of man.

A key element in the Portuguese expansion along the coast of Africa and into the Indian Ocean was the creation of a series of fortified naval bases. The Portuguese chain of fortresses in the Indian Ocean included Socotra at the approach to the Red Sea, established in 1507 but rapidly abandoned because there was little water, Ormuz at the mouth of the Persian Gulf, established in 1507 and, after it had been lost, regained in 1515, Cochin (1503), Cannanore (1505), Goa (1510), Diu (1534) and Bassein (1534) on the west coast of India, and Malacca in the straits of that name (1511). In the decisive clash over the last, a well-coordinated and determined Portuguese force relying on pikes as much as firepower defeated the Sultan's war elephants.

In east Asia, the Portuguese accommodated themselves to the regional powers and traded with China and Japan. Whereas the Spaniards had exploited local divisions in Mesoamerica, and the Portuguese likewise in India, there was no comparable intervention in the divided politics of Japan. In 1521, the Chinese clashed with Portuguese ships off T'un-men when they tried to enforce an expulsion of all foreigners after the death of the emperor. The outnumbered Portuguese were put under heavy pressure and, in 1522, when three more Portuguese ships arrived, two were lost. Nevertheless, the quality of Portuguese cannon and ships was appreciated by the Chinese. Eventually, a process of mutual accommodation left the Portuguese able to trade at Macao. In what is now Indonesia, the Portuguese established fortified posts at Ternate (1522), Solor (1562) and Tidore (1578). However, as Islamic identity in the Moluccas increased, relations deteriorated and the Portuguese were driven from Ternate.

Portuguese capability on the high seas did not necessarily extend to inshore, estuarine and riverine waters where deep-draught sailing ships found it difficult to operate, and the Europeans achieved technological superiority and adequate force-projection capability only with the development of shallow-draught steamships from the 1820s. In addition, a number of south-east Asian powers, including Johor in Malaya and Aceh in Sumatra, developed naval forces that were able to challenge the Portuguese. The Chinese, however, had not persisted with their naval profile and expeditions of the early fifteenth century. More generally, naval strength did not play a major role in Chinese military history. China had established water forces from the northern Song dynasty, which gained power in the late tenth century, continuing into the southern Song, Mongol, Ming and Manchu periods. However, these forces were usually not organisationally differentiated from the ground forces; thus, the term navy is misleading and 'water forces' is a more appropriate designation. There was no imperial naval staff and no Admiral of China.

In the Mediterranean, the Ottomans, in contrast, developed a major naval capability. Their move, after the capture of Constantinople in 1453, to a port-capital whose support depended on maritime links, led to an increase in naval power. The Ottomans subsequently developed their fleet for more distant operations beyond the Aegean and to carry cannon, and used it with success against Venice in the war of 1499–1502. The most famous naval battle, that of Lepanto in 1571, was a crushing defeat for the Ottomans, but it did not indicate any marked deficiencies in their naval technology. Their opponents battered their way to victory thanks to superior gunnery, the fighting qualities and firepower of the Spanish infantry, who served on both the Spanish and the Venetian ships, and the exhaustion of Ottoman gunpowder. The Ottomans rapidly rebuilt their fleet and the Christian powers accepted the de facto establishment of Spanish and Ottoman spheres of influence in their respective halves of the Mediterranean.

The failure of the Ottoman invasion of Malta in 1565 was also important in this process. The ferocity of the fighting there indicates the intensity of religious conflict between Christians and Muslims. The few wounded captured Christian defendants of St Elmo fort, Malta, were nailed to crosses and floated back across the harbour with their bowels hanging out to discourage additional reinforcements. The two wounded commanders were torn limb from limb as both, too seriously wounded to remain on their feet, directed the final defence from chairs. Six years later, the Venetian commander of Famagusta was flayed alive after he surrendered.

Maritime range did not equate with dominance of the coastal littoral, let alone the interior. The European impact in Africa and south Asia was limited and major efforts in North Africa led to failure. The Spaniards were unable to retain most of their coastal positions, while, in 1578, at Alcazarquivir, Abd al-Malik of Morocco crushingly defeated the Portuguese, in part by making effective use of arquebusiers trained to fire from horseback. King Sebastian lost his life as Portuguese schemes for conquering Morocco were destroyed.

In contrast, the Spaniards made a major impact in the New World, conquering the Aztecs of Mexico in 1519–21 and the Incas of Peru in 1531. As they were most successful there in regions where there was much for them to gain, their failure to expand in some other parts of the Americas was not necessarily due to military factors. They never devoted military resources to the New World comparable to their efforts in Europe.

Spanish conquest was not solely a matter of initial military success. In overthrowing the Aztecs, the superiority in battle of the Spaniards, which owed much to steel

The Toxcatl massacre in Mexico: the slaughter of Aztec nobles by order of Pedro de Alvarado, 1520. The destruction of the Aztec leadership, by massacre, conflict and smallpox, was crucial to Spanish success, although it also owed much to the ability to win local allies among those hostile to the Aztecs, such as the Tlaxcaltecs. Second-in-command to Cortés, Alvarado was to conquer much of Guatemala and El Salvador in 1524.

helmets and swords, promised those who allied with them a good chance of victory, but the availability and willingness of Mesoamericans to cooperate against the Aztecs reflected the nature of Aztec rule, in particular the absence of a theory and practice of assimilation. Neither Incas nor Aztecs had firearms or horses. Their societies were reliant on wood and stone, not iron and steel. Slings, wooden clubs and obsidian knives were no match for the Spaniards' arms.

Intended to be more than raiding, Spanish conquest was followed by the arrival of colonists and their livestock, by Christian proselytisation and the destruction of rival religious rituals, by the introduction of administrative and tenurial structures, and by a degree of Spanish acceptance of local élites and local material cultures, as well as of local adaptation to the Spaniards. All of these helped as well in the expansion of Spanish power in the Philippines from 1565. Manila was swiftly conquered and burned down, and a walled settlement built in its place. This proved its value in 1574 when an attack by Lin Feng, a Chinese pirate with about 1,000 men, was driven off.

Philip II of Spain (r. 1556–98), after whom the Philippines were named, the ruler of the first empire on which the sun literally never set, had less success in executing his plans in Europe. Although, as a result of Malta and Lepanto, the Ottomans were held in the mid-Mediterranean, while Philip's forces successfully invaded Portugal in 1580, to enforce his claim on the throne, he was unable, despite major efforts, to suppress a

Glorification of Frederik Henry Nassau, Prince of Orange and Captain-General of the Dutch Republic from his brother Maurice's death in 1625 until his own in 1647 (Jan de Bray). A successful leader against the Spaniards, who took s'Hertogenbosch by siege in 1629, and Maastricht in 1632, but whose invasion of the Spanish Netherlands in 1635 failed to bring lasting gains.

rebellion in the Low Countries, to invade England successfully in 1588, or to ensure the outcome to the French Wars of Religion (1562–98) that he sought. As with the eventual failure of his father, the Holy Roman Emperor Charles V, in 1552, to suppress the German Protestants and defeat France, this reflected the extent to which hegemonic power was thwarted in Europe.

That was the end result of a century of conflict there that saw the greater use of firearms, both handheld and cannon, and resulting changes in tactics and fortification. The frequency of conflict in part reflected the extent to which the ability of European states to finance military activity increased in the late fifteenth and early sixteenth centuries, with their greater political consolidation, administrative development, and economic growth, as populations recovered from the fourteenth-century epidemic of bubonic plague known as the Black Death. Although this process of consolidation was to be challenged from the 1520s, as the impact of the Protestant Reformation increased domestic divisions, the demographic growth of the century helped ensure that more resources could be tapped, both manpower and finances.

Growing governmental strength and sophistication were most apparent at sea, where fleets far larger and more powerful than those of the fifteenth century were created and maintained. Maritime capability and warfare required detailed planning, logistical support, political commitment, administrative competence, leadership and training, as well as an ability to overcome the challenges posed by technological innovation. The maritime expeditions of the Mediterranean, Baltic and Atlantic were an important aspect of the warfare of the period.

The English developed a considerable expertise in maritime expeditionary warfare during Elizabeth I's reign (1558–1603). The capture of Cadiz in 1596 by an Anglo-Dutch force was one of the most impressive operations of its day and built on a military tradition that had developed steadily throughout the century. The amphibious taskforce fought its way into a defended anchorage under the guns of the city defences and carried out a successful opposed landing, followed by the storming of the city walls. Lengthy sea lines of communication, however, helped ensure that it was impossible to turn the victory to strategic advantage. English and Dutch success at sea enabled both powers to take a leading position in trade between northern and southern Europe.

The availability of resources that could be directed by governments was obvious in the ambitious fortification programmes of the period. Fortifications designed to cope with artillery were first constructed in large numbers in Italy, and were then spread across Europe by Italian architects. Cannon were most effective against the stationary target of high stone walls, so fortifications were redesigned to provide lower, denser and more complex targets. In the new system, known as the *trace italienne*, bastions, generally quadrilateral, angled, and at regular intervals along all walls, were introduced to provide gun platforms able to launch effective flanking fire, while defences were lowered and strengthened with earth. These improvements lessened the decisiveness of artillery in siegecraft. Furthermore, the new fortresses were defended by cannon, and states were willing and able to deploy large numbers of them. Newhaven, the English star-shaped fort built outside Le Havre in 1562, was equipped with 19 cannon, 15 brass culverins, 29 brass demi-culverins, and 2 cast-iron demi-cannon, plus another 70 smaller, wall-mounted pieces. The fortress fell in 1563 because of the severe impact of plague and because winds in the Channel delayed relief, not because its walls were breached or stormed.

Nevertheless, during the Thirteen Years' War (1593–1606), the Ottomans were able to capture many of the fortresses recently modified by the Austrians using the cutting-edge Italian expertise of the period, including Győr (Raab) in 1594, Eger in 1596, Kanizsa in 1600 and Esztergom (Gran) in 1605. Rather than providing a paradigm leap forward in the defensiveness of Christendom, it is necessary to consider the advances in fortification, like other developments, in terms of particular circumstances, and not least to remember that defences were only as good as their defenders and logistical support. The Ottomans had no equivalent to the trace italienne or to the extensive fortifications built in the Austrian-ruled section of Hungary and along the coasts of Naples and Sicily, but they did not require any such development as they were not under attack. However, Ottoman reports admiring Austrian cannon captured in the Thirteen Years' War suggest that a technological gap in cannon-casting had begun to open by then.

The term 'military revolution' has been applied to European military developments in this period, but combined arms tactics were, as ever, far easier to attempt than to execute successfully under the strain of battle. The contrasting fighting characteristics of the individual arms – muskets, pike, cavalry, cannon – operated very differently in particular circumstances, and this posed added problems for coordination. So also did the limited extent to which many generals and officers understood these characteristics and problems. 'Military adaptation' is a more appropriate term than revolution. The teleological language of governmental development and military revolution can be very misleading. Far from war being won by planned action, it was frequently the side that was less handicapped by deficiencies that was successful: coping with problems was the major skill of command. This was true both on campaign and on the battlefield. In the former, providing supplies was both difficult and vital, while, in the latter, the retention and use of reserves amid the uncertainty of battle was often crucial.

Alongside administrative development came a pressure on available resources that would have led most monarchs and ministers to smile at my remark that there were more resources to tap. This was particularly, although not only, the case with civil wars. In late sixteenth century France, lack of finance resulted in the steady decline in effectiveness of the royal army, and in a reduction in the size of forces deployed by the combatants. When the Huguenot (French Protestant) stronghold of La Rochelle was besieged by the royal army in 1572–3, it was impossible to constitute a naval force that could effectively blockade the port. The problems associated with raising sufficient funding to sustain high levels of operational warfare were faced by all the major

European combatants during this period, and was probably managed best by the Ottomans. In civil wars, desertion was also relatively easy, and was a regular occurrence as both leaders and men returned to their estates and their homes. For troops on campaign in foreign lands this option was not available, and this accounted for the prevalence of mutinies, when pay was not forthcoming and credit with the local communities was withdrawn.

Military adaptation in Europe took place in a variety of contexts. Warfare in Italy, France and the Low Countries, beginning with the Italian Wars of 1494–1559, has dominated discussion, leading to an underrating of the variety of types of force structure and conflict in Europe. Cavalry was more prominent in eastern Europe, but it developed in a different fashion. Whereas in France and the Low Countries, pistoleers played a major role, cavalry shock tactics continued to be central further east. In Ireland and Highland Scotland, infantry shock tactics were far more important than elsewhere in Europe.

This diversity developed within the context of the societies of the period. Within the gunpowder world, armies were mixed infantry/cavalry forces, and both infantry and cavalry involved troops that used firearms and those that did not. The varied response to firearms had to be understood not in terms of military progress, or administrative sophistication, or cultural superiority, but rather as a response to the different tasks and possibilities facing the armies of the period, within a context in which it was far from clear which weaponry, force structure, tactics, or operational method were better. More generally, models that assume some mechanistic search for efficiency and a maximisation of force do violence to the complex process by which interests in new methods interacted with powerful elements of continuity. A stress on the value of morale and the importance of honour came naturally to the aristocratic order that dominated war-making, and traditional assumptions about appropriate conduct were important in force structure and tactics. Across the world, the notion of effectiveness was framed and applied in terms of dominant cultural and social patterns.

As a reminder of the diversity of military arrangements around the globe, in New Zealand, where there were no firearms, fortified *pā* settlements (as opposed to *kāinga* or open settlements) spread, particularly on the North Island. Their number suggests serious competition for the resources of land and sea. Although they are difficult to date, and many would not have been occupied at the same time, over 6,000 pā sites have been found, and it has been suggested that there may have been about twice that number. Bellicosity was not restricted to the world of the gunpowder empires.

Maori clubs made from whalebone and jade timber. New Zealand was settled from Polynesia. Although it is unclear when, recent analysis suggests about 800 years ago. The settlers brought Polynesian practices of warfare and methods of fighting. Fortified pā were created more than 500 years ago.

Maori adze made from nephrite jade and with a kiwi feather, New Zealand.

Nephrite jade patu (club), New Zealand.

4

THE SEVENTEENTH CENTURY

China, the world's most populous state, found its fortunes transformed by war in this period and must take pride of place in any military history of the century. Nothing in the European world compared to the scale and drama of the overthrow of Ming China.

The Ming were to be replaced by the Manchu, descended from the Jurchen Jin who had controlled all of China north of the Huai river from 1126 to 1234. Originally based in the mountains of south-eastern Manchuria, the Jurchens expanded under Nurhaci (1559–1626) to dominate the lands to the north of the Great Wall in the early seventeenth century. He united the Jurchen tribes, by means of war, marriage alliances and exploiting the Chinese tributary system, and also developed a strong cavalry army based on horse archers. This was organised into 'banners': units that incorporated tribal groups. Nurhaci used this force to gain control of most of northern Manchuria by 1616. The efforts required to defeat the Japanese invasions of Korea in the 1590s had exhausted the Chinese treasury and led to a failure to maintain defences against invasion from the steppe.

Having renounced fealty to the Ming in 1616, Nurhaci consolidated the Manchu state before attacking the Chinese in 1618, capturing Fushun. Korean-supported Chinese counter-attacks failed disastrously in 1619, with defeats at Siyanggiayan and Niu-mao chai: Chinese and Korean firearms and numbers could not counteract the tactical mobility of the determined, well-led and numerous Manchu cavalry. Manchu adaptability led them to seek to benefit from the military technology of their rivals. A metallurgical industry developed in Manchuria by the end of the sixteenth century, and cannon production followed. In 1629, the Manchu captured Chinese artillerymen skilled in casting Portuguese cannon. The Manchu also emulated the political techniques and administrative structures of imperial China, creating a system that was recognisably different from that of tribalism. This left them better able to benefit from the flux of 1644.

Liaoyang had fallen in 1621, blocking the overland route between China and Korea. Nurhaci, instead of making over the conquered territory for looting and division among his banners, left it outside the tribal system to be administered by

Chinese bureaucrats. Thus a dual state, separately administering Chinese and Jurchens, was created. This helped increase the Manchu appeal to dissident and defeated Chinese.

After invasions in 1627 and 1636–7, Korea, China's most important ally, was reduced to vassal status: the Koreans surrendered within two months in the face of the Manchu winter invasion of 1636–7. Inner Mongolia became a Manchu dependency in 1633–4 as a result of disunity among the Mongols and a breakdown in relations between the Ming and the Čaqar Mongols, whose leader, Ligdan Khan, lost control of the steppe and was defeated by the Manchu. The Chinese had failed in their long-established policy of manipulating their steppe neighbours. The Manchu also benefited from marriage alliances with the Mongol élite, from matching Ming tribute and from purchasing Mongol horses. Mongol banners were organised by the Manchu. Mongol cooperation made it easier to attack China, not least by circumventing Chinese defences. The Chinese attempt to move troops on the northern frontier eastward, from facing the Mongols in order to confront the Manchu, was no longer appropriate. In addition, the Amur region was conquered, and the area further north to the Argun river brought under Manchu control from 1643.

Manchu attacks on China in 1626 and 1630 were unsuccessful. Nurhaci failed to storm the fortress of Ningyuan in 1626, but the fortress of Dalinghe fell in 1631 after Ming relief attempts were defeated. Cooperation with Chinese elements strengthened the Manchu militarily. In a battle near Dalinghe in 1631, the Chinese held off frontal assaults by Manchu cavalry, but were then disrupted by the artillery and fire arrows of the Manchu's Chinese allies. The Manchu cavalry therefore ultimately triumphed. Manchu plundering expeditions into northern China were followed by a major invasion in 1638–40 which captured many cities in Shandong and Zhili. Victory by Manchu cavalry at the battle of the Pass (Shanhaiguan) in 1644 led to the capture of Beijing. North and east China fell to the Manchu in 1644–5, Sichuan in 1646, Guangzhou (Canton) in 1650, much of the south by 1652, and Yunnan in the south-west in 1659.

This was a victory for cavalry over the static military system and warfare of China, but the lack of unity on the Chinese side was also important. This weakened resistance and, in some cases, directly abetted the Manchu advance. From 1582, there had been weak emperors, increasingly arbitrary central government, oppressive taxation, and growing financial problems. These encouraged both rebellions and a quest for power among ambitious leaders. Li Zicheng, a rebel who had become a powerful regional warlord, captured Beijing in 1644 and provoked the suicide of the last Ming emperor. He had established his base in Hunan in 1641 and benefited from the degree to which Ming forces and fortifications were concentrated further north and designed to resist attacks from the north. The garrison in Beijing marched out to confront Li's army, but proved unequal to the task. Allegedly, they fled when they heard cannon fire, leaving Beijing to rely on only 3,000 eunuch troops, who proved unable to hold off the attackers. Li proclaimed the Shun dynasty, but his army was poorly disciplined and he lacked the supports of legitimacy, powerful allies and administrative apparatus. It was the collapse of the Ming dynasty, and thus of the Chinese frontier defence system, thanks to Li, that gave the Manchu their opportunity.

Other powerful Chinese figures directly assisted the Manchu. Wu Sangui, who commanded the largest Chinese army on the northern frontier, refused to submit to Li and, instead, supported the Manchu. Wu and the Manchu together defeated Li at the battle of the Pass, forcing him to abandon Beijing in 1644. Wu pursued Li and was responsible for his death in 1645. Chinese units were reorganised by the Manchu and used to help conquer the rest of China. Hong Chengchou became a Manchu general, captured Hankou and Nanjing and pacified Fujian. Geng Jingzhong also became a Manchu general. The Manchu were earlier helped by fifth columnists when they gained Shenyang in 1619 and Liaoyang in 1621.

The overthrow of the Ming underlines the extent to which administrative continuity and sophistication did not suffice for victory. It is too easy to read back from later circumstances and to fail to note the extent to which, in the early–modern period, the degree of organisation required to create and support a large, permanent, long-range navy, or large, permanent, armies, was not required to maintain military forces fit for purpose across most of the world, nor to ensure success. Similarly, it is mistaken to read back from the modern perception of the effectiveness of infantry and artillery firepower, and of the attendant relationship between disciplined, well-drilled, and well-armed permanent firepower forces, and those that were not so armed. As with the 'decline and fall' of imperial Rome, and the role of 'barbarians', both in defeating Rome and in fighting for it, there were not clear-cut sides in seventeenth-century China, and the 'overthrow' that is to be explained is not as readily apparent as it might appear. Instead, the Manchu conquest involved redefinitions of cultural loyalty in which distinctions between Chinese and 'barbarian' became less apparent and definitions less rigid.

These problems of definition were even more apparent when the Manchu encountered strong resistance in southern China. They were challenged by Zheng Chenggong (known to Europeans as Coxinga) who, with the profits of piracy and trade, developed a large fleet based in Fujian and amassed a substantial army of over 50,000 men, some of whom were equipped with European-style weapons, although, like other Chinese armies, they did not use flintlocks. In 1656–8, he regained much of southern China for the Ming. The large force he led to the siege of Nanjing in 1659 was mostly armed with swords – two-handed long, heavy swords, or short swords carried with shields. The soldiers wore mail coats to protect themselves against bullets. Coxinga's army included cannon and musketeers, but also an archery corps that was more effective than his musketeers. This army was defeated outside Nanjing by Manchu cavalry and infantry attacks.

After the Manchu advanced into Fujian in 1659, Coxinga turned his attention to Taiwan, where he landed in 1661. The Dutch capitulated the following February. Dutch attempts to re-establish their position in 1662, 1663 and 1664 were all unsuccessful. In contrast, a Manchu expedition gained Taiwan in 1683. The Dutch failure to sustain a presence so close to China contrasted greatly with the situation two centuries later when, by the Treaty of Nanjing of 1842, the British were able to force the Chinese to accept their capture of Hong Kong. European powers never again established a presence on Taiwan, and, when it fell, it was to the Japanese as a result of the Sino-Japanese War of 1894–5.

The Manchu were challenged by the ultimately unsuccessful Sanfen rebellion of 1674–81. This War of the Three Feudatories was begun by powerful generals who were provincial governors, especially Wu Sangui, who controlled most of south-western China. The feudatories overran most of south China, but were driven back to the south-west by 1677 thanks to the use of Green Standard Troops: loyal Chinese forces. Earlier, Manchu units had failed to defeat the rebels, and this failure helped in the consolidation of a new political system in which Manchu tribesmen could no longer challenge the adoption of Chinese administrative techniques, personnel and priorities. Wu died in 1678, but the rebellion, which prevented Chinese opposition to Dzhungar expansion, did not end until 1681.

The west Mongolian tribes known collectively as the Oirats, had united in the dynamic new Dzhungar confederation from 1635. They conquered the domain of the last Altan Khan in north-western Mongolia and, in 1670, overcame his former vassals in the western part of Tuva. Under Taishi Galdan Boshughtu (r. 1671–97), the Dzhungars seized the Islamic oases near Mongolia from 1679; Hami and Turfan that year, Kashgar in 1680 and Yarkand soon after.

Before clashing with the Dzhungars, the Chinese had expelled the Russians from the Amur valley, which they had penetrated from the 1640s. In 1683–9, Chinese forces drove the Russians from both the Amur basin and from lands to the north. By the Treaty of Nerchinsk of 1689, the Russians acknowledged Chinese control of the region.

In 1687, the Dzhungars had intervened in a struggle between the two khans of the Khalkha regions of (eastern) Mongolia, and defeated the Tushetu khan. As the Khalkhas took refuge in China, many entering the Chinese army, this brought the Dzhungars into direct confrontation with China. In 1690, the two armies clashed at Ulan Butong, 300 kilometres north of Beijing. Galdan's defensive tactics, not least sheltering his men behind camels armoured with felt, limited the effectiveness of the Chinese artillery, but the Chinese drove their opponents from the field, although they were unable to mount an effective pursuit due to a shortage of food and because their horses were exhausted. The Chinese commander was happy to negotiate a truce.

In 1696, however, the Kangxi emperor (r. 1662–1723) advanced north across the Gobi desert, although this test of the logistical resources of the Chinese army led his advisers to urge him to turn back before it starved. Galdan's army was destroyed at Jao Modo, thanks in part to support from his rebellious nephew, Tsewang Rabdan. After another effective Chinese campaign, the following winter, Galdan died in suspicious circumstances. The Manchu system had delivered a decisive verdict, despite the difficulty of the terrain, the distance from Chinese sources of supply, and the long months of campaigning. The combination of effective forces and successful logistical and organisational systems made the Manchu army the best in the world. The banner system enabled Mongols, Chinese and Manchu to work together as part of a single military machine.

By the end of the 1690s, China had its strongest and most advanced northern frontier for centuries. The combination of Chinese and steppe forces and systems ensured that the problems that had beset Ming China had been overcome. The strength of Manchu China owed much to the extent to which the lands that had formed the initial Manchu homeland and the early acquisitions in eastern Mongolia had been the source of intractable problems for the Ming. The frontier had been overcome, or rather pushed back, a process underlined when settlement was supported in conquered areas in order to provide resources to support the army.

Mughal India, Safavid Persia and Ottoman Turkey did not face challenges comparable to those posed to Ming China by the Manchu invasion, but they all faced external pressures, as did lesser powers such as Ethiopia. In 1642, its army was destroyed by the Galla, after which much of Ethiopia was raided by them. This helped cause a protracted decline, with the weakness of the monarch ensuring that provincial independence grew. Iyasu I, who became king in 1682, made a major attempt to reverse the system. He built up the royal bodyguard as a separate army supported by a treasury to prevent it from following the militia in becoming overly connected to particular areas. Iyasu also built up a new militia among loyal Galla tribes who converted to Christianity. In the 1680s, 1690s, and 1700s, Iyasu took the war to the other Galla, but he found it very difficult to gain lasting success, and was assassinated by domestic opponents in 1706.

The Mughals, the leading land military power in the world other than China, encountered serious setbacks during the seventeenth century, both within India and in neighbouring regions. This was particularly the case where the terrain was not suited to their forces. For example, in the valley of the Brahmaputra, the Ahom, a Shan people originally from upper Burma, proved a serious challenge from 1612, not least because they mobilised all their resources for war. Although the Ahom were outnumbered, their fighting techniques were well adapted to the terrain. They relied on infantry armed with muskets or bows and arrows, used flexible tactics, including surprise night attacks, and rapidly created fortified positions based on bamboo stockades. The riverine and jungle terrain were very different from the plains and hills of Rajasthan where the Mughals had campaigned extensively and for which their weaponry and tactics were appropriate. The Mughals made little use of horses against the Ahom. Instead, both force structure and tactics were adapted. Elephants were used to provide shock power, both in battle and against stockades. The Mughals also made extensive use of boats equipped with cannon, including floating platforms carrying heavy cannon. A fierce war in 1636–8 led to a compromise peace, but in 1681 the Mughals were forced to retreat.

Afghanistan also proved difficult terrain for the Mughals. Some 50,000 cavalry and 10,000 infantry were sent to Kabul in early 1646. After the road had been improved, the army moved through the Hindu Kush, occupying Badakhshan, Kunduz, and Balkh. This was a formidable achievement which can be favourably judged after the difficulties faced by Britain, the Soviet Union and the USA when operating in Afghanistan from the 1830s. Little fighting was involved in the initial advance but again, like subsequent campaigns, it proved impossible to prevent the situation from deteriorating. Uzbek guerrilla raids inflicted a heavy burden on Mughal logistics, although Mughal firearms were effective against attacks by mounted archers. The range of Uzbek war-making included the fouling of the Balkh river which helped cause an epidemic.

In 1647, the Mughals sent reinforcements under Prince Aurangzeb. Unlike in 1646, they had to fight their way across the Hindu Kush, although they did so successfully, helped by the shock force of war elephants, as well as by firearms, including rockets. Once near Balkh, the Uzbeks employed the customary harrying tactics of horse archers in undermining the Mughal position. Mughal field artillery and musketeers were unable to defeat their more mobile opponents, even when the Mughals sought mobility by leaving their equipment behind, and they found it impossible to obtain adequate supplies from the harsh region where local knowledge, supplies and military adaptability were essential to success. In late 1647, Aurangzeb evacuated Balkh and retreated through the snowbound Hindu Kush mountains with heavy losses from local tribesmen.

This region remained a difficult one for Mughal forces. They were ambushed by the Afridi, a Pathan tribe near Kabul, in 1672–4. Aurangzeb came to rely on bribes to keep the Pathans quiet. The Mughals were no longer able to operate effectively in the lands of their forebears. Unlike Mongolia and Xinjiang for the Manchu in the 1690s–1750s, the operational range of the Mughals had been lessened, in part because of their Indianisation. In the 1640s, the Uzbeks had proved much better at living off the land.

Further south, in Afghanistan, the Mughals competed with the Safavids over Kandahar, the gateway for the Persians to southern Afghanistan and the Indus valley. Lost by the Mughals to Shah Abbas I of Persia in 1622, Kandahar had been regained in 1638, when the Persian commander surrendered, fearing execution by his sovereign. Helped by Mughal weakness in the aftermath of their campaign in Afghanistan, Shah Abbas II recaptured Kandahar in 1648 and Mughal attempts to regain it in 1649, 1652 and 1653 all failed. It was difficult to campaign effectively so far from the centre of Mughal power, and success had to be achieved before the harsh winter set in. Mughal siege artillery was also of poorer quality and less accurate than the Persian cannon which inflicted heavy casualties on the besiegers. In 1653, three specially cast heavy guns made breaches in the walls of Kandahar, but the onset of winter and logistical problems made it impossible to exploit them.

Despite their military strength and determination, the Mughals, therefore, were unable to prevail in adverse circumstances in frontier zones. They also suffered greatly from the 1660s at the hands of a new military force, the Marathas of the western Deccan. Maratha forces of mobile, lightly armoured horsemen avoided battle and, instead, concentrated on a strategy of *bargi-giri*: cutting supply links, launching devastating raids and using hit-and-run tactics. The Marathas did not defeat the Mughals in decisive battles, but rather denied the Mughals safe control of territory. However, the Maratha advantage of mobility was lost when they defended forts, which provided clear targets for the Mughals and their effective siege equipment: the Marathas lacked comparable artillery and their siegecraft was poorly developed. The Marathas were swayed by the view that forts were necessary for the symbol and reality of power, but Aurangzeb captured a whole series in 1689 and 1700–7. Nevertheless, he failed to conquer the Marathas, and they revealed an important weakness in Mughal warfare, its failure to sustain the mobility of its origins. By the seventeenth century, Mughal armies were large and slow-moving and their cavalry was preponderantly heavy. The Mughals sought battle, but were vulnerable to an opponent able to focus on mobility. The Mughals responded to the Marathas by fielding larger forces, which exacerbated the problem, and drove up the already high cost of campaigning.

The Mughals also had a number of important successes. To the south, they reduced the Deccan sultanates of Bijapur and Golconda to vassalage in 1636: Golconda swiftly complied, but Bijapur did so only after three Mughal armies invaded and ravaged the countryside. After they reasserted their independence, the sultanates were annexed in 1685–7 following successful sieges. These were massive enterprises in which strongly walled positions with large garrisons fell to large armies, the supply of which was a formidable undertaking. Golconda fort eventually fell when its defences were betrayed and a gateway left open.

To the north, the Mughals pushed into Baltistan and Ladakh in the Himalayas in 1637–9. They were also able to maintain dominance of northern India, even when Aurangzeb and most of his army were engaged in protracted conflict with the Marathas. Although the Mughals paid insufficient attention to the quality of their firearms, they maintained a formidable mixed-arms army. In 1647, Abdul Hamid Lahori listed Mughal military strength as 200,000 stipendiary cavalry, 185,000 other cavalry, and a central force of 40,000 garrisoned musketeers and gunners. Aurangzeb's successors were unable to sustain his gains, or indeed to prevent the empire from rapid collapse following his death, but he had succeeded in gaining a degree of hegemony within India that neither the Habsburg rulers of Spain and Austria nor Louis XIV of France could match in Europe.

Compared to the developments already discussed, the European military impact on India was of minor importance. Poorly fortified Portuguese positions in the Bay of Bengal fell to Indian powers, although in 1683, when Portuguese positions at Goa and Chaul were attacked by the Marathas, they were saved by their fortifications and because the Mughals attacked the Marathas the same year. In 1686, Aurangzeb vigorously pursued a dispute with the English East India Company, which was forced

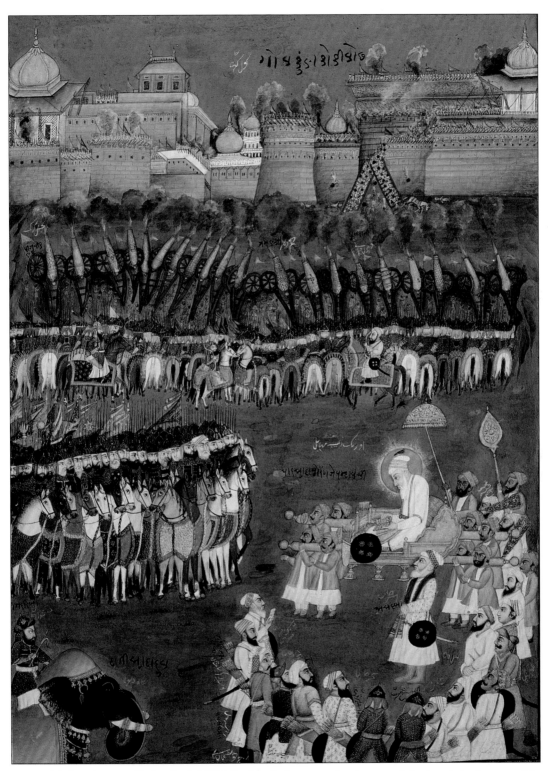

Siege of Golconda, near Hyderabad, 1687. The Mughal army under Aurangzeb besieged the fortress with its four-mile-long outer wall. Two mines were driven under the walls, but they exploded prematurely. The fortress finally fell by betrayal: Mughal forces entered through an opened gateway.

to abandon its base at Hooghly and to surrender its position at Bombay. Defeated, the company was able to continue trading only after they apologised for their conduct and paid an indemnity. There was scant evidence of European strength on land.

Abbas I of Persia (r. 1587–1629) also sought to develop a strong, centrally controlled force. Based on Caucasian military slaves (*ghulams*), this included a 12,000-strong corps of artillerymen with about 500 cannon, although most of the ghulams fought with traditional weapons. By increasing the land under his control, Abbas was able to fund this system which contributed to a string of successes, including the capture of Herat from the Uzbeks in 1598 and Kandahar from the Mughals in 1622. Continuing the Safavids' struggle with the Ottomans, Abbas also captured Tabriz in 1603 and Erivan in 1604, defeated the Ottomans at Súufiyán in 1605, and took Baghdad from them in 1623.

European impact on Persia was restricted to the Persian Gulf, where, in 1684, a blockade by a Dutch East India Company squadron was part of a process by which European commercial interests were defended, rather than an attempt to create a network of bases. The Dutch were able to capture the island position of Qishm, but restored it to Persian control in 1685 in order to forward negotiations. The Portuguese had similarly used a naval force in 1674 to secure their share in toll revenue.

Another instance of centrally controlled force was the corps of black slaves, personally attached to the sultan by religious ties, created in Morocco by Mawlay Isma'il (r. 1672–1727), who wanted to be free of local political pressure. Slave children were trained in horsemanship and the use of spears and firearms, and then married to slave girls to produce more slaves, while slave raids were also mounted south into the Sahara. However, under his successor, the slave corps became a force for chaos, trying, like the Praetorian Guard of imperial Rome, to sell their political support.

The Ottoman empire is generally noted in histories of seventeenth-century warfare for its failure to take Vienna in 1683 and for the subsequent loss of Hungary, culminating in the overwhelming victory of the Austrians under Prince Eugene of Savoy at Zenta in 1697. These were important episodes, but they need to be set aside against examples of Ottoman resilience, including the recapture of Baghdad in 1638 (after unsuccessful sieges in 1625–6 and 1630), the conquest of Crete from the Venetians in 1645–69, the successful invasion of southern Poland in 1672, and the ability of the Ottomans to regain the initiative in the Balkans, at least temporarily, in 1690 and 1695–6. There was no significant disparity between Ottoman and European abilities to mobilise and finance major campaigns until the mid-seventeenth century, and maybe even later. The Ottomans were effective in feeding and supplying their troops and their logistics were important to their operational capability.

The defeat of the Ottoman besieging army outside Vienna in 1683 can be seen as a sign of a more general failure in Asian military systems, but it is necessary to be careful before pushing this argument too far. There was clearly no equivalence with the Dutch failure in Taiwan or the Russian loss of the Amur valley, because the

Vienna campaign involved the main Ottoman army. In addition, the warfare between the Christians and the Ottomans indicated the strength of Christian infantry firepower and the value of its ability to operate in a disciplined fashion on the battlefield. Ottoman war-making no longer had an edge in battle. However, it is less clear that the Christian powers had developed a superior logistical system to the Ottomans, and there is no reason to suggest that European war-making was superior to that of the Manchu, Mughals or Safavids.

Nevertheless, there was also an important shift in Russia. Earlier in the century, the Crimean Tatars had been a considerable problem. Their invasions of central Muscovy helped force Tsar Mikhail's government to negotiate peace with the Poles in 1634 and to turn attention to the securing of Muscovy's southern steppe frontier. This was done by developing the earlier programme of constructing new fortress towns and defensive lines. In the last two decades of the century, the Russians made major efforts to project their strength south across the steppe in order to crush the Tatars and establish bases on and near the Black Sea. Expeditions in 1687 and 1689 fell victim to logistical difficulties, exacerbated by Tatar scorched-earth opposition, but, in 1696, Peter the Great captured Azov on his second attempt. However, he had to return it in 1711 when his invasion of the Balkans disastrously failed when he was outmanoeuvred and surrounded by the Ottoman army at the Pruth river.

Where Europe did have a clear edge was at sea, where only the major Western European powers controlled fleets of deep-draught vessels able to operate at great distances. Only Western European warships and merchantmen sailed across the Atlantic or Pacific or between the Atlantic and the Indian Ocean. The power that made the greatest impact for much of the seventeenth century was the United Provinces (modern Netherlands). The profits made from shipping spices back to Europe led to the foundation of the United East India Company, which was granted a charter giving it political and military powers, including the right to make war, peace and treaties, and to construct fortresses. Jayakěrta, where the Dutch had a trading base from 1603, became the centre of Dutch power in the East Indies from 1619 after the town was stormed and the forces of Bantam defeated. It was renamed Batavia.

The Dutch actively sought to displace competitors and drove the Spaniards from Taiwan, the English from Ambon in the Moluccas, and the Portuguese from Sri Lanka, Ambon, the Malabar coast of India and Malacca; although, in the 1640s and 1650s, they failed to drive the Portuguese from Angola, Macao, and, despite major efforts, Brazil. In turn, the Dutch were challenged by the French and by the English. French pressure was most serious in the Low Countries; that from England at sea and in the colonies. The three Anglo-Dutch Wars (1652–4, 1665–6 and 1672–4) led to the loss of New Netherland, New Amsterdam being renamed New York.

The forces involved in colonial conflict between Europeans were far smaller than those committed for conflict within Europe. Thus, in 1642 a Dutch force of 591 men took Keelung, the Spanish base on Taiwan, which had a garrison of only 115 Spaniards and 155 Filipinos. In 1751, Charles de Bussy led a surprise attack by 411 Frenchmen,

Eugene of Savoy (1663–1736), one of the foremost European generals of the age, served the Austrians against the Ottomans and the French. Although he deployed his troops in the conventional manner, he placed a greater premium on manoeuvre on campaign and attack in battle than did his French rivals. In Italy, he did not allow the French emphasis on the defence of river lines and fortified positions to thwart his drive for battle and victory. In part, this was a consequence of his personality: the preference for excitement and acceptance of risk that took him into the thick of the battle.

Battle of Belgrade, 16 August 1717. Austrians under Prince Eugene defeated the Ottoman army seeking to relieve besieged Belgrade. In a difficult position, Eugene resolved on a surprise attack and won. It was a confused engagement that was not a matter of clear-cut formations exchanging fire and was followed by the surrender of Belgrade.

as well as Hyderabadi troops, that routed a Maratha force, although the French lost the campaign as the Marathas used their mobility to cut off grain supplies. When such small forces were involved, there was a premium on experience, morale and command that was at once bold and skilful.

Non-European powers could also take a role at sea. The Mataram, Aceh, Mughal and Magh fleets all played a local role in south Asian waters, although Sultan Iskander Muda of Aceh was defeated when he attacked Malacca, then Portuguese-controlled, in 1629. Large squadrons of Mughal riverboats, carrying cannon, played a major role in defeating the fleet of Arakan in 1666, although the expansion of Mughal power against Arakan also owed much to operations on land, particularly road-building.

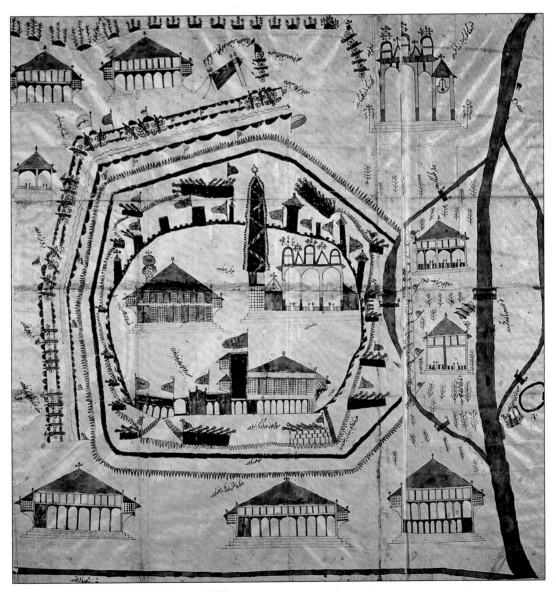

Ottoman plan of the siege of Vienna, 1683.

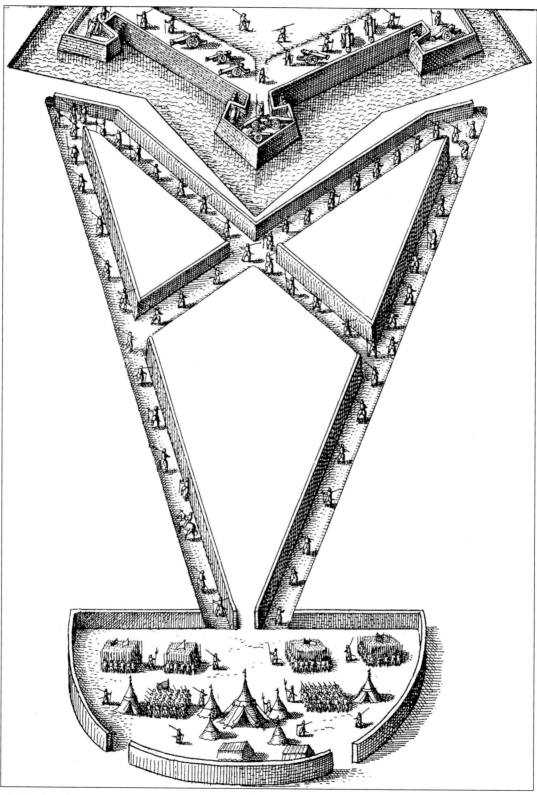

Idealised design for encampment outside a besieged fortress, engraving from Robert Fludd's *Utriusque Cosmi . . .* (1617–24). Siegecraft led to extensive interest in the mathematisation of aspects of war.

In east Asia, a Chinese fleet intimidated a Dutch squadron into abandoning the Penghu Islands (Pescadores) in 1604. In 1622, another Dutch fleet occupied the islands and began to construct a fort. They also threatened to attack the Chinese coast unless the Chinese accepted Dutch commercial demands. Refusal to comply led to Dutch attacks on towns and shipping later that year. In 1623, a compromise reached by local representatives was rejected by their superiors on both sides, and the Dutch tried to capture Chinese ships bound for Spanish-ruled Manila: after a twelve-year truce expired, the Dutch were at war with Spain from 1621 until 1648. Early in 1624, the Dutch raided the Chinese coast, but the Chinese sent a large force that occupied most of the main island, and cut the fort off from its water supplies. This led the Dutch to agree to evacuate the position, and they did not subsequently attempt to reverse their loss.

The Omani Arabs were successful in becoming a regional power. They captured the Portuguese base of Muscat in 1650 and, on the basis of the ships they seized and the hybrid culture they took over, created a formidable navy with well-gunned warships. It was the largest fleet in the western part of the Indian Ocean. Benefiting from the use of European mariners and from the assistance of Dutch and English navigators, gunners, and arms suppliers, the Omanis were also helped by the degree to which the extensive Portuguese overseas empire had already been weakened by persistent Dutch attacks. The Portuguese had only a small military presence on the East African coast: they were short of men, ships and money. In 1661, the Omanis sacked Mombasa, although they avoided Fort Jesus, the powerful Portuguese fortress there. In 1670, the Omanis pillaged Mozambique, but were repulsed by the fortress garrison. The Omanis also pressed the Portuguese in India.

Yet the Omanis did not match the naval range of the Europeans, any more than did the Barbary states of North Africa. The Omani impact on India was limited, and their campaigns on the East African coast scarcely revealed a major power. Fort Jesus fell in 1698, but the siege had lasted since 1696 and the Omanis had no siege artillery. The Portuguese, instead, were weakened by beri-beri and other diseases that killed nine-tenths of the garrison.

The value of garrison positions and European weaponry was revealed in Manila in 1603 when a rebellion by the large Chinese population, who lived outside the city, led to an assault on its walls. Reliant on the traditional methods of siege towers and ladders, the untrained Chinese were beaten off by musket and cannon fire, and their towers were destroyed. Subsequently, in the face of sorties, the Chinese fled, only to be hunted down and about 15,000–25,000 killed. Another Chinese rising in 1639 was brutally suppressed, while, in 1662, the danger of Chinese invasion led to a fresh massacre. Similarly, in 1652, the firepower of 150 Dutch musketeers cut short a Chinese rebellion in Taiwan.

However, the Portuguese experience in Africa revealed the limitations of European land warfare outside its home continent. Their attempts to operate up the Zambezi were thwarted, while in Angola they were effective only in combination with African soldiers, as in the victory over Antonio I of Kongo at Ambuila in 1665. In Angola, the Portuguese were subsequently defeated at Kitombo in 1670, while their wars against the kingdom of Ndongo, begun in 1579, ended in stalemate in the early 1680s.

There was no resumption of the conquest of North Africa on which Portugal and Spain had devoted much effort in the fifteenth and sixteenth centuries. Instead, Moroccan pressure drove the Spaniards from La Mamora (1681), Larache (1689) and Arzila (1691), and the English from Tangier, although the Spaniards held on to Ceuta despite the lengthy siege of 1694–1720. Major European powers, however, maintained their ability to project naval power successfully, and in 1682, 1683 and 1688 Algiers was heavily bombarded by the French, as was Tripoli in 1685, while, under the threat of bombardment, Tunis in 1685 agreed to return all French captives. This was still a long way from the ability to project power successfully on land, and also very different to the situation in the nineteenth century, when the French occupied Algiers and Tunis in 1830 and 1881 respectively.

In the seventeenth century, the European powers were most successful in expanding their power in north Asia and North America. In the former, the Russians were attracted into Siberia by its fur, a vital form of wealth and prestige. A vast area, inhabited by small numbers of nomadic and semi-nomadic peoples, Siberia was subjugated by the Russian construction of forts, while resistance was weakened by local divisions as well as the level of military technology. With their gunpowder weaponry, the Russians had a clear technological edge, and they used firearms effectively against Siberian aborigines and against the remnants of the Tatar Golden Horde. The inroads of smallpox also greatly weakened resistance. Yakutsk was established as a Russian base in 1632, the Pacific was first reached in 1639, and Okhotsk was founded as a base in 1647.

In North America, the European impact was less sweeping, in large part due to stronger local resistance, but also because the Europeans devoted much of their effort to fighting one another. Local resistance was helped by the acquisition of firearms and horses by the Natives, to which (as in West Africa) rivalry among the European powers directly contributed. As experts with bows and arrows, the Native Americans were adept at missile warfare, and thus more readily able to make the transition to muskets, which were easier to aim, and the bullets of which, unlike arrows, were less likely to be deflected by brush, and also could not be dodged. The Natives' general lack of fixed battle positions made it difficult for the Europeans to devise clear military goals, and ensured that there was scant role for volley fire. The ability of the Europeans to travel by sea became less valuable once they moved away from coastal regions. As with the Portuguese in Angola, European success in frontier warfare depended on Native assistance or adaptation to the Native way of war. Thus, in King Philip's war in New England in 1675–6, the English colonists moved in loose order, adapted to the available cover, fired at specific targets, and benefited from Native support.

The power balance in North America was shifted less by weaponry than by demography. The Europeans came to colonise rather than to trade, and they, especially the English, came in increasing numbers. In contrast, hit by smallpox, Native numbers did not grow. It was the rising number of Europeans and their ability, thanks to advantages of mobility, logistical support and reinforcement, to concentrate forces at points of conflict, which proved crucial along the St Lawrence valley, which was under French control, and on the east coast of North America, which was increasingly under English control, north of Florida, where there was a Spanish presence.

Further south, both Spain and, in Brazil, Portugal expanded their power. In central America, Nojpeten, capital of the Maya people known as Itzas, the last unconquered powerful native New World kingdom, fell to Spanish attack in 1697, with very heavy losses among the defenders. This was no easy conquest, for the Spaniards found it difficult to support their new position. They were helped, however, by the rapid

Fort Jesus, Mombasa. The major Portuguese position on the Swahili coast of Africa, the fort fell to the Omanis in 1698. This was part of a more widespread crisis of Portuguese power round the Indian Ocean from the 1620s, which included losses not only to the Dutch but also to non-Europeans, in the Persian Gulf, India and East Africa.

decline of the Itzas under the pressures of Spanish seizures of food, terrible epidemics, probably influenza and later smallpox, the capture of much of their leadership by the Spaniards, and subsequent disputes among the Itzas. An Itzas rebellion in 1704 was ultimately unsuccessful, and the Spaniards were able to impose a measure of control, thanks to moving the population into towns and Christian missions; those who evaded the control lived in isolated forest areas, but were no longer able to challenge Spanish dominance. The Spanish conquest of the region indicated that the techniques that were to be employed by European imperial powers in Africa in the late nineteenth century were already well developed.

Within Europe, there was no hegemonic power to match that of Manchu China or Mughal India. The branches of the Habsburg dynasty that ruled Austria and Spain had appeared close to this state in the late 1620s and again in 1634, after their victory over the Swedes at Nördlingen, during the Thirty Years' War (1618–48), and Louis XIV of France (r. 1643–1715) seemed also to wield hegemonic power in the late 1670s and early 1680s.

In each case, however, their position was precarious and they were swiftly challenged: the Habsburgs by Gustavus Adolphus of Sweden from 1630 and France from 1635; and Louis XIV by the growing power of Austria, once it had defeated the Turks in 1683, and the British Isles, after it was taken over by Dutch forces under William III of Orange following his successful invasion of England in 1688 and his defeat of his pro-Stuart opponents in Scotland and Ireland in 1689–91. The latter was an instance of the potentially decisive nature of warfare in Europe. So also was the conquest of the British Isles by Parliamentary forces in 1642–52 during the civil wars of that period, and the capacity of the Swedes to crush the Danes in 1643–5 and 1657–8 in rapid and overwhelming campaigns. In the Nine Years' War with England, Austria, the Dutch and their allies (1688–97), France won a number of battles, including Fleurus (1690), Steenkerk (1692) and Neerwinden (1693), but had to accept peace terms that led to the cession of territory.

In Europe, as elsewhere, battles were usually won by experienced and motivated troops whose dispositions had been well arranged, as with the Swedish victory over Catholic German forces at Breitenfeld in 1631. If armies were evenly matched, battles were either inconclusive encounters or were determined by other factors, such as terrain, the availability and employment of reserves, and the results of cavalry clashes on the flanks, which were frequently decided by which side attacked first. These clashes could lead to the victorious cavalry attacking the enemy infantry in flank or rear where it was very vulnerable, as in the French victory over the Spaniards at Rocroi in 1643 and the Parliamentary triumph over the Royalists under Charles I at Naseby in 1645, the latter the decisive battle of the English Civil War of 1642–6. Experienced and well-deployed infantry were usually safe against frontal attack. This threatened a tactical impasse in infantry warfare that led to a particular need for skills in generalship and for flexible and effective cavalry. Innovative ideas about deployment and tactics were not necessarily superior, as was shown in the Thirty Years' War, while numbers alone were only of value if they were handled ably.

In eastern Europe, Polish victories over the Swedes at Kircholm (1605) and over a far larger Swedish and Muscovite army at Klushino (1610) suggests the limits of effectiveness of musket and pike against cavalry, in this case hussar lancers. Generalship was also important. At Konotop in 1659, a Muscovite army was defeated by the Cossacks largely because of poor reconnaissance and generalship: they let their main corps get lured into a swamp. Better-disciplined and effective cavalry also played a major role in the battles that determined the Mughal civil war, the war of succession of 1657–60, especially Dharmat (1658) and Samugarh (1658).

Alongside an emphasis on battles and sieges in 'functional' terms, as stages in the defeat of opposing forces, it is necessary in Europe, as elsewhere in the world, to adopt a broader approach to victory and to underline the extent to which success had a symbolic value. From this perspective, decisiveness has to be reconceptualised, away from an emphasis on total victory, understood in modern terms as the destruction of opposing armies and the capture of their territory, and towards a notion that may have had more meaning in terms of the values of the period. This would present war as a struggle of will and for prestige, the ends sought being, first, a retention of domestic and international backing that rested on the gaining of *gloire*, and, second, persuading other rulers to accept a new configuration of relative gloire. This led, for example, to a concentration of forces on campaigns and sieges made important largely by the presence of the king as commander. Like other rulers, Louis XIV enjoyed both commanding and reviewing troops. His triumphs, such as the crossing of the Rhine in 1672 and the successful sieges of Maastricht (1673), Ghent (1678), Mons (1691), and Namur (1692), were celebrated with religious services and commemorative displays. In the Salon de la Guerre at the royal palace of Versailles, finished and opened to the public in 1686, Antoine Coysevox presented Louis as a stuccoed Mars, the God of War. By the 1690s, over 20,000 French nobles were serving in the army and navy, a bond that testified to aristocratic confidence in Louis.

Force was also used to contain domestic disaffection. An emphasis on fortified positions away from external frontiers was one result. For example, Louis XIV built a citadel at Marseille, while, after the rebellion of Messina in Sicily was suppressed in 1678, Carlos II of Spain imposed a substantial garrison in a new citadel. The absence of police forces meant that troops were frequently used for policing purposes; but the limited nature of royal control in many, especially frontier, regions was such that the army was the appropriate solution anyway. Major risings were suppressed across Europe, including in Brittany (1675), Bohemia (1680) and south-west England (1685).

The size of several European armies grew in the second half of the century, especially those of France and Prussia, but such a rise exacerbated supply problems. Failures to provide sufficient food both sapped the strength of soldiers and affected their morale. Logistical demands pressed on societies that could not readily increase their production of food or munitions. The low level of agrarian productivity ensured

King Ferdinand of Hungary and Cardinal Infant Ferdinand, by Peter Paul Rubens. The victorious generals at the Habsburg victory over the outnumbered Swedes at Nördlingen, 6 September 1634. This was followed by the Swedish loss of southern Germany and by France's entry into the Thirty Years' War in order to resist Habsburg hegemony. *(Kunsthistorisches Museum, Vienna)*

that the accumulation of reserves of food was difficult. In addition, the ability of states during sustained conflict to retain their military effectiveness was affected by factors over which there was limited control, principally the weather, which could greatly affect the harvest. Logistical difficulties encouraged an emphasis on the strategic offensive, because it then became possible to tap the economies of occupied areas, either by pillage or by 'contributions': taxes enforced under the threat of devastation. This system of transferred costs both enhanced the destructiveness of war and made it more important not to lose control of territory. The armies Tsar Aleksei sent into Polish-ruled Belarus and Ukraine in 1654 were enormous, of unprecedented size in

Gustavus Adolphus, King of Sweden (r. 1611–32). One of the most prominent European military figures of the century, Gustavus fought Denmark and Russia in the 1610s, before attacking Poland in 1617–18, 1621–2 and 1625–9, and intervening in Germany in the Thirty Years' War from 1630, winning a major victory over the Imperial army at Breitenfeld in 1631.

Battle of Lützen, 17 November 1632, a fog-shrouded and bitterly fought clash between the equally matched Swedes under Gustavus Adolphus and the Imperial army under Albrecht Wallenstein. Austrian cavalry helped deny the Swedes a victory to match Breitenfeld. Leading his infantry, Gustavus died, shot three times. At close of battle, advantage lay with the Swedes. Both sides lost about one-third of their strength, and Wallenstein retreated after nightfall.

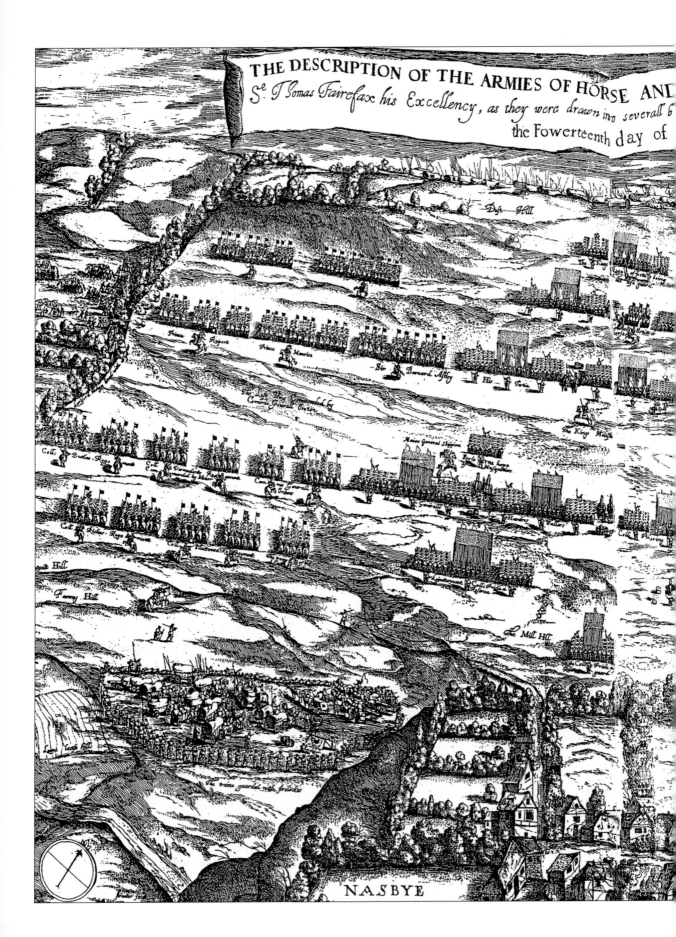

THE DESCRIPTION OF THE ARMIES OF HORSE AND
Sᵉ Tʰomas Fairefax his Excellency, as they were drawn into severall b
the Fowerteenth day of

Dʳt Hill

Prince Rupert   Prince Maurice   Sᵉ Bernard Astly   Hir Torie

The Kings Maj

The Le Mⁱ
Comis Generall Ireton

Mꜩⁱꝝ Generall Skippon

Colt Butler Rege   Colt Vʳⁿⁿⁱ...   Coⁿⁱꜱ Gᵉ   Colt Pickering

Coⁿⁱꜱ Commⁱꜱⁱꝝ   Come   Gᵉⁿⁱⁱꝝ Ireton

Colt Richer Regt

...quit Hill

Fanny Hill

Gⁱⁱꝝ...

the Mill Hill

Ye Coll Prids guard

The traine guardes with ...ides

...i Coll hill

NASBYE

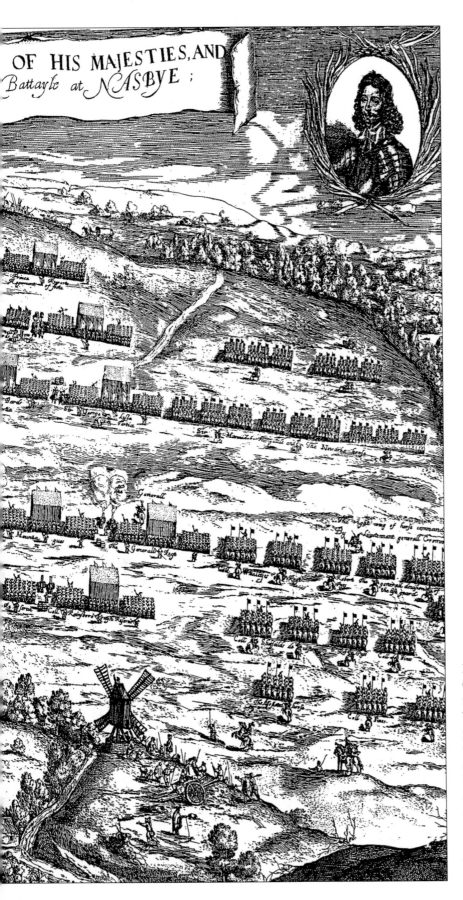

Battle of Naseby, 14 June 1645.
Crucial Parliamentary victory over
the Royalists in the English Civil
War. Infantry in the centre, with
pikemen flanked by musketeers.
Cavalry on the flanks. Well-
disciplined cavalry on the
Parliamentary right under Oliver
Cromwell defeated the Royalist
cavalry opposite and then turned
on the veteran but heavily
outnumbered Royalist infantry
who succumbed to an
overwhelming attack.

Muscovite history, and responsible for a terrible amount of devastation. The burden of war for individual powers rose if armies were forced to fight on the defensive on their own territory. This happened to the French after they were defeated by Anglo-German forces under the Duke of Marlborough and Prince Eugene at Blenheim in 1704 and then withdrew across the Rhine.

Towards the close of the seventeenth century, the development of the bayonet altered warfare in Europe. The early plug bayonet, which was inserted in the musket barrel and therefore prevented firing, was replaced by ring and socket bayonets, which allowed firing with the blade in place. This led to the phasing out of the pike, which was now redundant. Bayonets were a better complement to firearms in fulfilling the pike's defensive role, and also had an offensive capability against infantry and, on occasion, cavalry. This rapid change was largely carried out in the 1690s and early 1700s. It had been very complicated to coordinate pikemen and musketeers in order to ensure the necessary balance of defensive protection and firepower. The new system led to the longer and thinner linear formations, and the shoulder-to-shoulder drill in order to maximise firepower, that were to characterise European infantry in the eighteenth century both within Europe and overseas.

Similarly, changes in seventeenth-century European naval warfare were responsible for the distinctive character of warfare at sea during the following century. Naval combat with artillery came clearly to replace the earlier preference for boarding. The development of line-ahead deployment and tactics for warships encouraged the maximisation of broadside power. This stress on cohesion reflected a move away from battle as a series of struggles between individual ships. Instead, fighting instructions and line tactics instilled discipline and encouraged a new stage in organisational cohesion that permitted more effective firepower, one that was further enhanced when merchantmen ceased to appear in the line of battle of European fleets. A breakthrough in European iron gunfounding, that was not matched elsewhere, aided production of large quantities of comparatively cheap and reliable iron guns, and this helped ensure the increase in total firepower in the leading European navies.

Navies were expensive, and an important aspect of the degree to which war and military capability increasingly became a matter of the intersection of capitalism and the state. This was central to the ability to marshal resources, and was focused, and symbolised, in institutions such as the Bank of England, founded in 1694. This military-financial combination preceded, and helped finance, the military-industrial complexes of the nineteenth and twentieth centuries. An economic system stressing values of labour, thrift, efficiency and accumulation contributed to military capability.

The ability to organise and direct resources could also be seen in non-Western states, most obviously China and the Ottoman empire. However, the liberal political systems of, in particular, Britain and the United Provinces (Netherlands) were notably successful at eliciting the cooperation of their own and indeed other

John Churchill, 1st Duke of Marlborough at the battle of Blenheim, 13 August 1704. The Anglo-Dutch-Austrian victory over the Franco-Bavarian army was largely due to Marlborough's tactical flexibility, in particular to his ability to retain control and manoeuvrability, an ability that contrasted with the failure of his opponents. The decisive factors were mastery of the terrain, the retention and management of reserves, and the timing of the heavy strike in the centre where the opposing line was broken. Victory was followed by the conquest of Bavaria. (*Blenheim Palace, Woodstock, Oxfordshire*)

capitalists, producing a symbiosis of government and the private sector that proved both effective and especially valuable for developing naval strength. Government policy was also important. The Western industrial system was well adapted to producing and supporting a large number of warships, but Manchu China, Japan and the Mughal empire did not seek to do so. Their conception of power was based on, and defined by, territorial control of land. This choice not to develop large navies was very important to the military history of the world, both in the seventeenth century and subsequently.

5

THE EIGHTEENTH CENTURY

China remained the leading land power during the eighteenth century, although the naval strength and transoceanic advances of the British, at the expense of the French in North America in 1758–60 and at the expense of the French and native powers in India from the 1750s, ensured that Britain was the strongest global power. Just as the British faced the French in a long-standing series of conflicts, so the same was true of China and the Dzhungars until the latter were overcome in the 1750s. This was a war waged entirely on land and only in east Asia. It lacked the range and variety of the Anglo-French struggle, but it was just as dramatic.

In the early eighteenth century, the Chinese and the Dzhungars vied for control of Tibet. The Manchu used Lamaist Buddhism to control the Mongols and therefore needed to dominate the Tibetan centres of Buddhism, which had been under the partial control of the Mongols since 1642 when the last king was deposed. In 1706, a Chinese protégé deposed the Dalai Lama, but in 1717, in a campaign in which cavalry played a major role, the Dzhungars invaded Tibet and defeated his army, eventually storming the capital, Lhasa. The Chinese launched a counter-attack in 1718 and, although one army was wiped out that year, concerted operations by two armies under Nian Gengyao led to the fall of Lhasa in 1720. A permanent Manchu garrison was established, an important extension of Chinese power, as when Tibet had earlier accepted tributary status there had been no Chinese garrisons.

The chief characteristic of the Chinese military was a remorseless persistence. The army, the largest in the world, was impressive in its operational range, acting in very different terrains including the Tibetan plateau and the Gobi desert. Long-range operations were the principal military challenge for China in the eighteenth century: there was no comparable power on China's borders deploying similar forces, and the Chinese made no attempt to conquer Japan. The ability to deliver power at a great distance was crucial in Tibet, Xinjiang, Burma and Nepal. In the 1690s and 1750s against the Dzhungars and in 1720 in Tibet, the Chinese successfully employed co-ordinated advances. Overwhelming force was combined with thorough planning.

With the addition of divisions and smallpox among the Dzhungars, this combination led to Chinese success in the 1750s. The Dzhungar ruler, Dawaci, was defeated and captured at the Ili river in 1755, but his rival, Amursana, who had helped the Chinese, then sought to gain independence, leading to another successful Chinese campaign in 1755–7. The personal determination of the Kangxi (r. 1662–1723) and Qianlong (r. 1736–98) emperors was crucial. Both made victory over the Dzhungars a personal crusade and pushed hard those generals who were more hesitant about campaigning on the steppes. Kangxi wanted victory. He understood the transient nature of the possession of territory: for him, victory in battle was crucial. The Qianlong emperor wanted to surpass the achievement of his grandfather by putting an end to the frontier problem. The importance of personality is illustrated by the role of the intervening Yongzheng emperor (r. 1723–36), who launched only one expedition against the Dzhungars, and did not persist after the defeat at Hoton Nor in 1731, when the Chinese force had been lured into a trap. Had he ruled as long as his predecessor or successor, the Dzhungars might have expanded once again and become a more powerful central Asian empire.

China under the Manchu successfully solved the logistical problems central in managing steppe warfare, which was considered the supreme strategic threat by all Chinese dynasties. In the 1750s, the Chinese established two chains of magazine posts along the main roads on which they advanced. Supplies were transported for thousands of miles, and the Mongolian homelands controlled by their eastern Mongol allies provided the horses and fodder. These improvements in logistics – partly due to a desire to keep the troops from alienating the populace – ensured that the Chinese armies did not disintegrate as Napoleon's did in Russia in 1812. In order to wage war with the Dzhungars, there was a massive transfer of resources from eastern to western China: the application to military purposes of the great demographic and agricultural expansion of China during the century. Organisational factors were therefore a crucial precondition for campaign success, as also with the contemporary effectiveness of the British navy, and the eventual victories of the British in India over Mysore and the Marathas in 1792–1803.

Chinese weaponry was less impressive in relative terms than Chinese logistics. Eighteenth-century Chinese soldiers were frequently armed with muskets, but they were far worse than their European counterparts. The Chinese had poor matchlocks: they had not made the transition to flintlocks. Chinese gunpowder was low-grade. Partly as a result, the Chinese continued to use bows and arrows, as well as swords, spears, pikes, halberds and shields. They had cannon, but not field artillery.

The Chinese were less successful against Burma than against the Dzhungars. War began in 1765 over what had hitherto been the buffer zone of the Shan states. In 1766, the scope of operations widened to include a Chinese invasion of Burma proper. This, and the two subsequent expeditions, were outmanoeuvred by skilful Burmese generals and in 1769 the invading Chinese army was trapped at Kaung-ton and forced to accept peace. The Chinese also failed when they intervened in Vietnam in 1788–9: their attempt to capture Hanoi was defeated by Nguyen Hue and, the following year, the Chinese were reported as routed. The Vietnamese were well familiar with the use of firearms.

The Chinese were less successful along their southern frontiers than they were in central Asia; partly because the area was of less strategic interest and because the heavily forested environment was very difficult for large-scale operations. Furthermore, Burmese military strength had been improved from mid-century by Alaung-hpaya. The Manchu were much more comfortable with the people and cultures of central Asia than with the south. The banner armies garrisoned north China and were also in garrisons along the Yangzi, but had little presence in the south. There, the Manchu relied on the Green Standard (Han Chinese) troops, but preferred not to allow large concentrations of them, because they were far more numerous than the banner armies: by about 630,000 to about 250,000 men in 1764.

Alongside these failures, the Chinese had other operations to record. The army acted against risings, both by Chinese, for example the huge and very costly millenarian White Lotus rebellion of 1796–1805 in Shaanxi, and by non-Chinese subjects, such as the Jinchuan tribal rising in Sichuan in 1746–9, and the Miao revolts in Hunan and Guizhou in 1735–6 and 1795–1805. The 1795 revolt was in response to the spread of Han settlement and the attempt to increase government power. The army responded by creating more garrisons, building a wall, introducing military-agricultural colonists, and using brutal repression. Similar brutality was also employed against the White Lotus rebels who made extensive use of guerrilla tactics and benefited from the hilly character of their core area. The rising was only put down after a formidable military effort, including the use of banner troops from Manchuria as well as raising local mercenaries and militia. The Green Standard troops especially were used for these 'pacification' duties.

On their frontiers, the Chinese benefited from their successes in Xinjiang and Tibet to project their power even further. To the west, they annexed eastern Turkestan from the Afaqi Makhdumzadas: Kashgar fell in 1759. In 1792, the Chinese advanced to Katmandu, where the Gurkhas of Nepal, whose expansion had begun to challenge their position in Tibet, were forced to recognise Chinese authority. By the end of the century, China was at peace with all its neighbours, and on its own terms. Russia respected China's treaty boundaries, but not those of the Ottoman empire or Persia. China's other neighbours, including the Kazakhs, were tributary powers. Had the other major non-European empires matched, at least part of, the success of China then the military history of the period would have been similar to that of the seventeenth century, and the impression of a relative rise in European power on land would have lacked substance.

However, both Mughal India and Safavid Persia collapsed in the eighteenth century. In the last years of Aurangzeb's reign, and even more after his death in 1707, as the Mughal empire rapidly weakened, Indian provincial potentates were provided with the opportunity, and also the need, to grasp power. Thus, Asaf Jah, the Nizam of Hyderabad, defeated the governor of Khandesh at Shakarkhera in 1724 and became, in effect, independent, sundering one of the major achievements of the Mughals, the control of Hindustan over the Deccan. The Nawab of Bengal also became independent in 1733.

The decline of Mughal strength provided an opportunity for other Indian powers, including the Marathas, the Gurkhas and, in the south, the dynasty founded by Haidar Ali when he seized power in Mysore in 1761. The Marathas made important gains from the 1730s onward. The Mughals fielded large forces against them, especially in 1735 and (with the Nizam) 1738, when the Mughals were routed at Talkatora; but the more mobile Marathas generally refused to engage in a major battle. Instead, they concentrated on cutting off their opponent's grain supplies and reinforcements, forcing the Mughal general to buy them off with a cash tribute in 1735, and ensuring that they made major gains from the Nizam in the Treaty of Bhopal (1739). The same year, another cavalry force, that of the Persian ruler, Nadir Shah, routed the Mughals at Karnal, north of Delhi. He then sacked the city, which had fallen without resistance. As a result, the Mughals ceded Sind and all territories west of the Indus. This campaign was a crippling blow for Mughal power. In 1741, the Marathas raided as far as Bengal. From 1745 to 1751, Orissa was raided every year, and the Carnatic between 1753 and 1757. Maratha armies grew larger and more professional, which, however, increased the cost of their operations.

To a certain extent, from mid-century the French and the British East India Companies were part of the same process of state-building in the shadow of Mughal decline, although they were also linked to international power systems, in the shape of French and British interests. The European impact in India could, moreover, be seen in the spread of flintlock rifles, bayonets, prepared cartridges, and cast-iron cannon. It was in the eighteenth century, and not earlier, that the advantage swung in India from cavalry to infantry armed with firearms, while artillery also became more effective. Superior firearms – flintlocks mounting bayonets – and effective tactics were important in this shift.

The specific context of military operations, however, was also relevant to the effectiveness of particular weapons and tactics. British infantry was more effective in operations on the Carnatic coast, near their base at Madras, and in the marshy Lower Ganges valley, near their base at Calcutta, than in conflict against the Marathas and Mysore in regions that favoured their light cavalry. The Indians fought in different ways. The Gurkhas, for example, relied on infantry, but both the Marathas and Haidar Ali focused on light cavalry. British East India Company forces could triumph over Surajah Dowla, the Nawab of Bengal, at Plassey in 1757, and over a coalition of Indian powers at Buxar in the Ganges valley in 1764, but were outfought by Haidar Ali of Mysore in 1769 and defeated by him at Perumbakam in 1780. The Company's conquest of Bengal in 1757–65 was attributed by contemporary Persian-language histories not to their military superiority, but to the factionalism and moral decline of the ruling Indian families of the region. The British had certainly benefited from their ability to win local allies. Nevertheless, weaponry and tactics were important. The impact of European infantry and artillery was noted by the Marathas, some of whom tried to adapt their forces and tactics. So also did Mysore: in 1792, a British officer noted: 'the enemy fire heavily at the rate of about 800 shot a day'.[1]

Like other powers deploying regular forces, the British used them not only against their counterparts but also to impose control, or at least constraints, on people and territories that were outside the matrix of governmental authority, or only precariously within it. Dean Mahomet, a quartermaster with the Bengal army of the British East India Company, recorded the advance of a brigade from Bihar to Calcutta in 1772–3 and the response to resistance by the hill people of the passes through which Bengal was entered. He clearly thought weaponry and discipline were important, and also commented on the savagery of the conflict. After the 'licentious savages' had attacked those cutting grass and gathering fuel for the camp, two companies of sepoys advanced:

> our men, arranged in military order, fired . . . the greater part of them [savages], after a feeble resistance with their bows, arrows, and swords, giving way to our superior courage and discipline, fled . . . two hundred . . . prisoners . . . severely punished for their crimes; some having their ears and noses cut off, and others hung in gibbets.[2]

Nadir Shah's victory at Karnal, a triumph for the determined leadership of mobile forces, was repeated on 14 January 1761 when Afghan invaders under Ahmad Shah Abdali, the founder of the Durrani empire based in Afghanistan (r. 1747–73), defeated the Marathas at the third battle of Panipat, probably the largest land battle of the century. This battle helps explain why it is anachronistic to criticise Indian rulers for failing to match the force structure of the British. Instead, as in 1739, the principal threat to northern India came from cavalry invaders from across the Indus. More generally, this acts as a reminder of the folly of judging war largely in terms of Western models of military progress.

At Panipat, both sides were about equal in manpower, but the Maratha army suffered from problems of control and coordination caused by its composite nature and the lack of a satisfactory command structure. The slow-firing Maratha artillery made little contribution to the course of battle. The Afghan cavalry reserve helped determine the battle. It broke through the Maratha centre, leading to a rout in which thousands were slaughtered.

Earlier, Afghan cavalry had overthrown Safavid Persia in 1721–2, a triumph, both strategic and tactical, over the poor leadership and divided counsels of Shah Husain (r. 1694–1722). The Safavid attempt to impose Shi'ite orthodoxy on Sunni Muslims led to opposition in the Afghan regions of the empire, particularly among the Ghalzai tribe, who rebelled in 1704 and, more successfully, in response to a harsh governor of Kandahar, in 1709. The Safavid army sent to suppress the rebellion mounted an unsuccessful siege of Kandahar in 1711, and was heavily defeated as it retreated. This defeat was followed by a rebellion of the Abdalis of Herat, another Afghan tribe, and the Safavid failure to suppress them also testified to the respective fighting quality of the two sides. Herat fell to the Abdalis in 1716. The recent lack of Safavid war-making ensured an absence of experience. The Safavids were also weak in the vital political

Maharajah Jagat Singh II of Mewar riding in procession, *c.* 1745. Mughal decline had led to the leading Rajput houses gaining effective independence, but from the 1740s they were increasingly subject to Maratha attacks.

dimension, which was particularly crucial in the handling of 'barbarian' opponents by settled empires. They failed to exploit divisions among the Afghans.

In late 1721, the Ghalzai force advanced into the centre of Persia. On 8 March 1722, at Gulnabad, east of Isfahan, it fought a far larger Persian army (much of which was tribal cavalry), but the Persians were poorly commanded and the Persian artillery made no contribution to the battle. Superior Afghan fighting quality and command skills led to Persian collapse. Afghan weaponry included *zanbürak*, camel-mounted swivel guns. The Ghalzais then blockaded Isfahan, defeating attempts at relief. Famine in the city led to its surrender on 23 October, the Shah abdicating in favour of Mahmud, the Ghalzai leader.

The Ottomans intervened, overrunning western Persia, while the Russians, under Peter the Great (r. 1689–1725), advanced south along the western shores of the Caspian Sea. More seriously, Mahmud was unable to bring stability to Persia. His successor, his cousin Ashraf (r. 1725–9) had Shah Husain beheaded in 1726, but the latter's third son, Tahmasp, opposed him, and Tahmasp's supporter Nadir Kuli (1688–1747), a Turcoman tribesman, defeated Ashraf at Mihmandust and Murchakhur in 1729, leading to the capture of Isfahan. Tahmasp himself was a poor commander, and was heavily defeated by the Ottomans at Kurijan in 1731. This paved the way for Nadir's successful pressure on Tahmasp in 1732 to abdicate in favour of his infant son, Abbas III. Four years later, Nadir himself took total power when he made himself Shah.

Their garrisons badly affected by disease, the Russians returned their gains to Persia in 1732 and 1735, while Nadir defeated the Ottomans in a long war, especially at Nahavand (1730), near Kirkuk (1733), at Baghavand (1735), and near Erivan (1745). He and his generals campaigned widely from Khiva to Muscat, and Daghestan to Delhi, creating a short-lived empire reminiscent of those of the Middle Ages. Nadir also faced Safavid pretenders and rebellious governors and tribes. Nadir's operations were in part designed to gain spoils in order to reward his army, and also to transfer the burden of its support from Persia. They included the capture of Kandahar in 1738, after a year-long siege, Kabul (1738), and Delhi (1739), and the conquest of Sind (1740), the central Asian khanates of Burkhara and Khiva (1740), Kirkuk (1743), and Armenia (1745), although he was unsuccessful in Daghestan (1741–3), and failed to capture Baghdad and Mosul from the Ottomans. Siegecraft was a field in which Nadir's army was deficient.

Nadir's model was not the Safavid one but a more far-flung imperial ambition similar to that of Timur. Like Napoleon, Nadir Shah was a bold practitioner of warfare; he put the emphasis on mobility, and made the areas he campaigned in support his forces and provide recruits. Nadir also had bold religious and political ambitions. He sought to resolve the schism within Islam, and to integrate Shi'ism into Sunn'ism. Like Napoleon, Nadir's continual wars and heavy taxation, enforced with torture and slaughter, placed a terrible burden on his subjects and, again like Napoleon, his empire proved ephemeral. Nevertheless, it still had a major impact, for example in seriously weakening the Mughals.

The empire split apart after Nadir was assassinated in 1747 by Persian officers concerned about his favour to Afghans and Uzbeks. The resulting divisions led to sustained conflict with battles, such as Chamchamal in 1754 and Urmiya in 1757, in which betrayal was as important as military tactics. The eastern part of the empire was taken over by Ahmad Shah Abdali, with a client buffer state in Khurasan until the Persians conquered it in 1796. From 1763, the Zands dominated the south-western part of the empire, although only after much conflict. The Qajars, who were to destroy the Zands in 1794, were dominant in northern Persia.

Other instances of the pressure on settled societies from pastoralists, although less serious than that from the Afghans, were Berber incursions on the plains of Morocco, and Tuareg raids out of the Sahara against Timbuktu. The city was raided in 1729, its trade routes were attacked in 1736 and 1737, and in 1737 the Tuareg were victorious in battle. The city was besieged by the Tuareg again in the early 1770s.

Aside from Nadir, other dynamic Asian rulers included Alaung-hpaya in Burma and Tashin in Siam. The former, and his successors, expanded Burmese territory to west, east and south. In 1757–8, Manipur to the north-west was successfully invaded and, in 1759, Tenasserim to the south. Ayuthia, the Siamese capital, which had successfully resisted a siege in 1760, was stormed in 1767. The campaign had persisted through two rainy seasons, the soldiers growing their own rice so that the army did not fade away. Chinese attacks on Burma were checked. In 1784, Arakan to the west was overrun. The Burmese were able to deploy large armies: about 200,000 men were conscripted for the 1785 and 1786 expeditions against Siam.

Burmese success was challenged by a Siamese revival under Tashin, who reunited the country and drove the Burmese out. Burmese invasions of Siam in 1775–6, 1785 and 1786 all failed. Tashin had gained control over Cambodia and the Lao principalities in the 1770s, but his subsequent invasion of Vietnam encountered difficulties and was unpopular. Tashin's growing insanity led Chakri, a general, to overthrow him in 1782: he became ruler as Rama I.

Further east, from his base of Hué, Nguyen Hue reunited Vietnam after nearly two centuries of division and proclaimed himself Emperor as Quang-trung (r. 1788–92). After he died, his opponent, Nguyen Anh, conquered all of Vietnam, becoming Emperor Gia-long (r. 1802–20). Although interested in Western military technology, the Vietnamese did not really Westernise: as with other cases of adopting Western methods, it proved difficult to extend this to cultural attitudes.

The Ottomans did not face any crisis comparable to the Mughals or Safavids, but they were hit hard in wars with Austria and, more especially, Russia. The Russians were particularly successful in the wars of 1736–9, 1768–74 and 1787–92, and, in the latter two conflicts, advanced south of the Danube. In 1770, a Russian fleet that had sailed from the Baltic defeated the Ottoman fleet at Cesmé in the Aegean, and more naval victories in the Black Sea followed in 1788 and 1790. The Russians were also able to annex the khanate of the Crimea in 1783, and to defeat an Ottoman attempt to regain the Crimea in 1787. They were increasingly effective in battle and on campaign, with column formations employing both firepower and bayonet charges, and more flexible supply systems, which permitted better strategic planning.

The Ottomans had also found Nadir Shah a formidable foe; while, in a fresh war with Persia in 1774–9, Basra was blockaded into surrendering to the Persians in 1776. The Ottomans were also faced by serious rebellions, for example in Egypt in the 1780s and by Kara Mahmoud, the governor of Scutari, in the 1780s and 1790s. In addition, it proved difficult to maintain authority over the nomadic tribesmen of the Arab borderlands.

Yet, it proved possible to counter some of these challenges. The Venetians seized the Morea from the Ottomans in the 1680s, but were driven out in 1715. The Austrians were beaten by the Ottomans in 1737–9, having to return Belgrade, which they had captured in 1717, and the Russian attempt to exploit Cesmé in order to overthrow the Turks in Greece was unsuccessful. In 1786, an Ottoman expeditionary force landed in Egypt and defeated the rebels, capturing Cairo. However, the rebel leaders retreated to Upper Egypt and, unable to impose a settlement, the Ottomans had to negotiate terms in 1787. The episode serves as a reminder of the difficulties that all empires faced in maintaining their power and enforcing their authority. This was true not only of the Safavids and the Ottomans, but also of the European empires: they lost most of their positions in the 'New' World in 1775–1830.

There were impulses of military reform in the Ottoman empire, generally linked to a desire to emulate the West, and often organised by renegade Westerners. In the 1730s, a French nobleman, Comte Claude-Alexandre de Bonneval, sought to develop a modern artillery service and a modern corps of bombardiers, but he was thwarted by janissary and political opposition. A French-trained Hungarian nobleman, Baron François de Tott, again concentrated on the Ottoman artillery in the 1770s. In the 1790s, recent defeats led Selim III, the new sultan, to reform both the *sipahis* (feudal cavalry), which increasingly acted as a repository of conservative military practice, and the janissary infantry, by now a hereditary caste. Selim developed the Nizam-i Cedid, a new army trained and commanded by Western officers. However, janissary hostility helped to thwart Selim's plans.

The Ottomans were not alone in responding to Western power, although it did not pose much of a problem in east Asia. Indeed, the negative British response to requests for assistance against the Chinese invasion of Nepal in 1792 and the relative lack of interest by the Chinese in a British diplomatic advance in 1793 were noteworthy.

By contrast, in North America, the expanding 'Western' powers – Britain from the eastern seaboard, France from Québec and Louisiana, Spain from the frontier of settlement north of Mexico and in Florida, and Russia in the Aleutian Islands and Alaska, and, subsequently, the newly independent United States – created serious problems for Native Americans. For example, the Fox tribe of Mississippi–Illinois was nearly wiped out by French-allied Native attacks in 1712–34, while, in 1766, the Russians overcame resistance on the Fox Islands, part of the Aleutian chain. As earlier in Siberia, massacre and disease secured the Russian 'achievement'.

Nevertheless, Native military potential was considerable given their hunter-warrior training, and their not inconsiderable numbers, particularly in the South, especially in comparison to the backcountry whites. The heavy losses inflicted on the Tuscarora in North Carolina in 1713 owed something to European artillery, but the army consisted of fewer than 100 Europeans. The support of over 700 Catawba, Cherokee and Yamasee was crucial. In the Yamasee War of 1715–17, South Carolina was devastated. Further north, there was effective resistance to British and colonial forces in Pontiac's War (1763–4) and to American revolutionaries in the American War of Independence (1775–83). The Cherokee resisted British and colonist forces successfully in 1759–60, but a shortage of ammunition and British scorched-earth tactics led them to opt for peace.

The pattern of Cherokee activity in 1776 was fairly typical of conflict with European regulars and colonists, including when the latter won independence. Having attacked the Virginia and Carolina frontier, the Cherokee lands were invaded by columns of American militia. Instead of resisting, the Cherokee largely abandoned their towns to be burned by the militia, disappeared into the mountains, and repeatedly returned, once the militia had departed, to cause sufficient trouble to provoke repeated militia incursions. This style of war had become a standard pattern, as Natives had come to appreciate that defending any given point against a large force was dangerous and, instead, had developed alternative strategies reliant on the likelihood that the militia would not remain for long. The Natives had abandoned their traditional fortification systems in the face of European siegecraft capabilities. They lacked the numbers to man any fortification system, and individual positions could, justifiably, be seen as traps, presenting targets for their opponents' cannon. In turn, 'Western' forces focused on destroying crops and shelter, which made life difficult for the Natives in the long run, and made them more likely to negotiate.

There was also pressure on Native peoples in South America, which is generally, misleadingly, denied any military history between Pizarro's overthrow of the Incas in the 1530s and the successful Wars of Liberation against Spanish rule in the early nineteenth century. In fact, the *conquistadores* had taken only a fraction of South America and, over the following three centuries, conflict between Spanish and Portuguese colonies and Natives continued. The Portuguese made considerable advances in Brazil, where the discovery of goldfields in the interior led to an intensification of activity and a Native response. For example, resistance by the Paiaguá began in the 1720s, but they were affected by Portuguese expeditions, disease and attacks of the Guaicurú Natives, and by the 1780s the Paiaguá had been largely wiped out. The use of local allies was important: Portuguese troops were unable to defeat the Caiapó, who ambushed Portuguese settlements and convoys, but the Bororo, under the leadership of a Portuguese woodsman, pressed them hard in a bitter war between 1745 and 1751. The ability to win and exploit local allies reflected the lack of Native unity. This, and disease, all helped the Portuguese far more than any particular success in contact warfare. Portuguese firepower was important, but natives, such as the Mura in central Amazonia, learned to avoid it. They made very effective use of bows and arrows in attacks on canoes and isolated settlements, but they could only check the Portuguese, not defeat them. The same was true of the Caribs on St Vincent in 1772–3: guerrilla tactics and the impact of disease hindered their British assailants and the Caribs retained most of their land.

The acquisition of Western weaponry, seen in North America, provided firearms not only for use against Westerners but also against other Natives, and indeed against animals. The arrival of the horse gave Native Americans a far greater mobility, allowing them to follow bison or deer for hundreds of miles. The resulting improvement in diet led to a larger and healthier population. Tribal warfare was affected by competition for hunting grounds, and by trade and animal movements. Firearms also came to play an important role in conflict between the Natives.

Firearms were also used in the central Pacific. The 'Napoleon of Hawaii', Kamehameha I, fought his way to supremacy in the Hawaiian archipelago in the 1790s, in part thanks to his use of muskets and cannon, rather than spears, clubs, daggers and slingshots. His power was based on the west coast of the island of Hawaii, a coast frequented by European ships, and he employed Europeans as gunners. By 1789, he was using a swivel gun secured to a platform on the hulls of a big double canoe. Soon after, he had a large double canoe mounting two cannon and rigged like a European schooner. Kamehameha won dominance of the island in 1791, and of the islands of Maui and Oahu in 1795. In 1796 and 1809, the difficult waters between Oahu and Kauai, and outbreaks of disease, ended his plans to invade Kauai, but, in 1810, Kaumualii, the ruler of the islands of Kauai and Niihau, agreed to serve as a client king.

This was very different to the level of military attainment across much of the Pacific or in Australia, where the absence of horse and gun limited the capacity of humans to kill either animals – or one another. Without the horse, distance was a far greater obstacle to human activity.

Within Africa, the availability of horses was an important aspect of the variety of warfare, as they were not present across much of the continent. Furthermore, areas of low population density and limited governmental development, such as the deserts of south-west Africa, had a different level of military preparedness and warfare from that of polities able to deploy armies of more considerable size. In the Horn of Africa, in the 1760s, Mika'el Suhul, the Ethiopian imperial Ras, built up an army 30,000 strong, and equipped 8,000 of them with muskets. He defeated his master, Emperor Iyoas, in 1769 at Azezo, his musketeers wrecking the opposing cavalry. Iyoas was killed after the battle. Later in the year, Mika'el's musketeers overcame resistance at the battle of Fagitta. However, in 1771, at Sabarkusa, in a battle that lasted several days, Mika'el was defeated by rival provincial warlords, especially Wand Bewasen of Begemder, whose army made successful use of shock tactics. This underlines the extent to which firearms alone could not determine conflict, as was also shown at Amed Ber in 1787, where an Ethiopian army equipped with cannon and thousands of muskets was defeated by the cavalry of the Yejju.

In Madagascar, firearms played a major role in the powerful kingdoms of Menabe and Boina. In 1719, the crew of a Dutch ship recorded their surprise at the skilful use of muskets by the 4,000–5,000-strong army of the King of Menabe, and three years later another Dutch commentator was impressed by that of Boina. Indeed, by mid-century, the King of Boina had at least thirty large cannon, while his army was estimated as 15,000 strong in 1741. Plentiful firearms were obtained from European traders in return for slaves. The availability of these arms probably played a role in the consolidation of powerful kingdoms in Madagascar and elsewhere, but there were also political and economic dimensions to this process.

In the forest zone of West Africa, muskets replaced the bow and javelin in the armies of states such as Dahomey, Asante, and Kongo, and they were able to obtain arms from European traders, often in return for slaves. Dahomey owed its rise under Agaja (r. 1716–40) to an effective use of European firearms combined with standards of training and discipline that impressed European observers.

In the savannah zone further north, Babba Zaki was the first ruler of Kano to have a guard of musketeers, probably in the third quarter of the century, although he also had a large force of cavalry. Where it occurred, the adoption of firearms by cavalry made relatively little difference to tactics in the savannah. Clashes between cavalry-centred and infantry-dominated armies occurred where the savannah met the forests. Dahomey was subjected to invasions by the cavalry of Oyo in a series of conflicts between 1726 and 1748; although the cavalry could be held off by musketeers sheltering behind field fortifications, their mobility enabled them to pillage Dahomey and force it to surrender and pay tribute. Asante, which sought to expand further west, could not defeat the cavalry of the savannah and became reliant on winning allies who had their own cavalry. Away from the forest belt, Tuareg cavalry conquered Timbuktu.

Within forest Africa inland from the Atlantic coast, and its European influences, there was greater reliance on the traditional use of shield-carrying, heavily armed infantry, fighting hand to hand, especially with swords. In so far as there were missile weapons in support, they were generally bows and javelins. This was true of such armies as those of Matamba, Kasanje, Muzumbo a Kalunga, and Lunda (in modern eastern Angola).

In Africa, as in most of the non-European world, military capability was largely a matter of land power; but there were also a series of coastal polities that controlled flotillas operating in inshore, estuarine, deltaic and riverine waters. These boats were shallow in draught and therefore enjoyed a range denied to European warships. Their crews usually fought with missile weapons, increasingly muskets, and some canoes also carried cannon. By the end of the century, the fleets of outrigger canoes of the Betsimisaraka and Sakalava of Madagascar raided as far as the mainland of northern Mozambique.

Substantial navies were deployed by only a handful of non-European powers, principally the Ottoman empire, the Barbary states of North Africa, the Omani Arabs, and the Maratha Angria family on the Konkon coast of India. The ships of these powers had a greater range than war canoes and approximated more closely to

European warships, but they lacked the destructive power of the latter. When, in 1735, the Pasha of Basra defeated a Persian naval attempt to seize the port, he did so by commandeering British ships. The British were far less successful in 1765 when they attacked the piratical Banu Ka'b of Khuziztan at the head of the Persian Gulf. The Barbary, Omani and Angria ships were commerce raiders that emphasised speed and manoeuvrability, whereas the heavier, slower ships of the line of European navies were designed for battle and emphasised battering power.

Under the strain of conflict, however, to qualify what has just been said, European navies found it hard to fulfil their potential. At the outset of wars, even Britain, the leading naval power, found it difficult to ensure victory, as was shown in indecisive clashes with the French off Malaga (1704), Toulon (1744), Minorca (1756), and Ushant (1778). Particularly in the last two cases, the individual ships' companies were newly recruited or pressed, their captains were still working up the sailing capabilities of their ships and crew, and the admiral was still working up and determining the capacities of his captains, who were equally unsure of their commander. More generally, thanks in large part to the combination of the wind and the poor manoeuvrability of warships, naval battles frequently did not develop as suggested by fighting instructions, and admirals had only limited control once battles had begun.

The range of European fleets owed something to overseas bases, such as Batavia, Cape Town, Halifax, Havana, and Port Royal, Jamaica, but more to the systems of supply that supported their warships. Thanks to these systems, European forces in the eighteenth century were able to sustain transoceanic struggles with other European forces at a hitherto unprecedented rate. Conflict between them was concentrated in North America, the West Indies and southern India, in each of which the British clashed with the French. In hindsight, the course of this conflict appears all too clear: France would be on the defensive, increasingly pressed by a power that was stronger at sea and thus able to take the initiative; while, with the support of their North American colonies, which were far more heavily populated than their French counterparts, the British were bound to win there.

In fact, triumph in the Seven Years' War (1756–63), known in America as the French and Indian War (1754–63), was far from easy. Already, in 1690 and 1711, the British had launched unsuccessful attacks on Québec, while in 1746 the French took the initiative in India, capturing Madras. In 1754–60 there were a number of serious British failures, including, in North America, the successful French–Native ambush of General Braddock's larger army at the battle of the Monongahela in 1755. These failures serve as a reminder that the French were helped by the difficulties of the British task, not least among them the complications of amphibious operations, the problems of operating in the interior of North America, the need to allocate limited resources across a number of operations, logistical problems, and the resourcefulness of the leading French commanders: Lally in India and Montcalm in Canada. Major British successes were frequently obtained only with considerable difficulty. Thus, the capture of Québec in 1759 followed a frustrating two months in which the natural

Battle of Zenta, 11 September 1697. Victory of the Austrian army under Prince Eugene over Ottomans. Eugene employed effective offensive tactics, immediately attacking the Ottomans, who were vulnerable as they crossed the river Tisza. The Grand Vizier was among the heavy Ottoman casualties. Zenta ensured Habsburg dominance of Hungary.

strength of the position, French fortifications, and the skilful character of Montcalm's dispositions, had thwarted the attacking British forces under James Wolfe. The British completed their conquest of New France the following year with concerted advances on Montréal that led to French surrender.

The relatively small forces involved in transoceanic operations, and the close similarity of their weapons and methods of fighting, put a great premium on leadership – an ability to understand and exploit terrain, and maintain morale and unit cohesion – as well as on firepower. The British were generally adept at both of these, but so also were the French, and sometimes more so. Montcalm made effective use of French troops and Native allies and understood how best to operate in the interior of North America. He was particularly successful in 1756–7.

However, British naval predominance and success in European waters meant an ability to apply resources and grasp the initiative outside Europe. This was the crucial interconnectedness of British power. The blockade of Brest, the leading French naval base, hit French imperial links hard. This blockade led ultimately to British naval victory in Quiberon Bay in 1759, when a fleet preparing to invade Britain initially evaded the blockade, but was then caught and defeated by its pursuers. Without a large hinterland to provide support or shelter, French colonies were vulnerable to amphibious attack.

By the war's close, the French imperial system had collapsed, with only Louisiana and St Domingue not conquered by Britain; while that of France's ally, Spain, had been badly damaged by the British capture of Havana and Manila in 1762. The capture of Havana wrecked Spanish naval power in the Caribbean, and the Spaniards had to cede Florida at the subsequent peace to regain Cuba. However, heavy British losses to malaria and yellow fever during the siege destroyed much of the army that had been brought to a high pitch of combat readiness during the conquest of Canada, weakening the subsequent military response to the American Revolution in 1775.

French intervention in the American War of Independence (1775–83) turned that conflict into a worldwide struggle that seriously tested the British empire. Having earlier supplied weapons, France entered the war on the American side in 1778, Spain following a year later. Thanks to much shipbuilding by these powers in the late 1760s and 1770s, the British were now outnumbered at sea, and were able to gain control of neither European nor American waters. French naval success in blockading a British army at Yorktown in 1781 was crucial to the triumph of the American and French besiegers on land. In the event, the British empire held during the war, particularly in India, but the American success in winning independence was of great long-term importance. This success was a matter not merely of avoiding being crushed, but even of forcing British armies to surrender, at Saratoga (1777) and Yorktown.

The American War of Independence was a political as much as a military struggle, one in which it was necessary for the revolutionaries to convince themselves and the British that there was no alternative to independence. The resulting politicisation of much of the American public and the motivation of many of their troops were important aspects of modernity. However, there was little of the emphasis on large armed forces and the mass production of munitions that were to be such obvious aspects of the industrial warfare of the late nineteenth and early twentieth centuries. In addition, a popular fight for independence was scarcely unprecedented. Within the European world, it was possible, for example, to point to the Swiss and the Dutch, both of whom had overthrown Habsburg forces and created republics. In the eighteenth century, the American war was not a new departure, but rather a uniquely successful war in a series of unsuccessful popular risings within the British empire. This focuses attention not on the political causes of the rebellion, nor on the military consequences of popular warfare, but, instead, on the political and military factors that led to a successful outcome. Among them, it is important to stress America's geopolitical exceptionalism, as the first of the European overseas colonies to rebel, as well as issues that bridged politics and war. For example, the federal nature of the revolution ensured that there was no one single centre or region of power, control over which would lead to the suppression of the revolution.

There was little novelty in battlefield operations during the war. The American response to battle was to adopt the line formations of musketeers seen in European warfare, a course advocated by George Washington, the commander of the Continental army. However, compared to war in Europe, both sides were lightly gunned. The Americans did not inherit a significant artillery park; while, for both sides, the distances of America and the nature of communications discouraged a reliance on cannon, which were relatively slow to move. As a result, although cannon played a role in battles such as Monmouth Court House (1778), these clashes were not characterised by the efficient exchanges of concentrated and sustained artillery fire seen in Europe.

The British faced serious problems in North America, particularly with logistics and with defining an appropriate strategy, and their military command structures had major deficiencies. However, the greatly outnumbered American naval forces were unable to cut British supply routes or threaten British positions, while the American cause was greatly handicapped by the problems of creating an effective war machine, largely because the anti-authoritarian character of the Revolution and the absence of national institutions made it difficult to create a viable national military system. By creating the Continental army, military decisions were taken out of the ambit of state government. In theory, this made the planning of strategy easier; in practice, the creation of the army, although essential to the dissemination of a new notion of nationhood, did not free military operations from political intervention and disputes. Nor did the army enjoy the support of a developed system for providing reinforcements and supplies, let alone the relatively sophisticated one that enabled the British armed forces to operate so far from their bases. The provision of men and supplies created major problems, preventing or hindering American operations, and producing serious strains in the relationship between the new national government and the states. This was exacerbated by British control of the sea, which threw an excessive burden on the land transport available to the Revolutionaries.

Compared to the American War of Independence, conflict within Europe was of limited long-term consequence. Again, it served to prevent the emergence of a hegemonic power. The bayonet–flintlock musket combination altered battlefield tactics, helping to lessen the role of cavalry, and ensured that casualty rates could be extremely high, particularly as a result of the exchange of fire at close quarters between lines of closely packed troops, the formation chosen to maximise firepower. Soldiers fired by volley, rather than employing individually aimed shot. Despite the bayonets, hand-to-hand fighting on the battlefield was relatively uncommon and most casualties were caused by shot. The accuracy of muskets was limited, and training, therefore, stressed rapidity of fire, and thus drill and discipline.

There was a tension between firepower and shock tactics, for infantry, cavalry and siegecraft. The different choices made reflected both the views of particular generals, and also wider assumptions in military society; they were not dictated by technology. An emphasis on the attack can be frequently seen in the case of Gaelic, Polish, Russian and Swedish forces. Marshal Saxe, the leading French general of the 1740s, and Frederick II, the Great, of Prussia (r. 1740–86) were also skilled in attack. The strategic, operational and tactical offensive in Western Europe had not been banished by the enhancement of firepower from the 1690s with the widespread addition then of socket bayonets to flintlock muskets. Shock won over firepower in the case of cavalry tactics. Furthermore, shock played a major role in victories over non-Europeans, particularly in the defeat of the Ottomans by the Austrians at Vienna (1683), Zenta (1697) and Belgrade (1717), and by the Russians in 1770 and 1774.

An emphasis on shock does not necessarily lessen the value of firepower, especially because the latter could be used to prepare for the assault. However, it suggests that any account that approaches tactical success in terms of the technological (weaponry) and organisational (tactics, drill, discipline) factors that maximised firepower is a limited one. The real point of drill and discipline was defensive: to prepare a unit to remain intact in the face of death, regardless of casualties. The issue of shock versus firepower – of offensive efficacy or effectiveness in causing casualties – was not as important as a unit remaining able to act, and tractable to its commander, while receiving casualties.

Firepower played a major role in sieges, but many fortresses, often major ones, such as Prague in 1741 and Bergen-op-Zoom in 1747, fell to assault. Furthermore, many positions were not strengthened in accordance with the latest fortification techniques as they were too expensive to be comprehensively adopted.

The European armies of the period were 'standing' permanent forces under the direct control of the rulers. The spread of conscription greatly altered the social politics of military service and war, although systems of conscription were less effective than in the twentieth century, not least because of the limited amount of information at the disposal of the state and the weakness of its policing power. In 1693, each Prussian province was ordered to provide a certain number of recruits. This was achieved by conscription, largely of peasants. The same year, French militia were sent

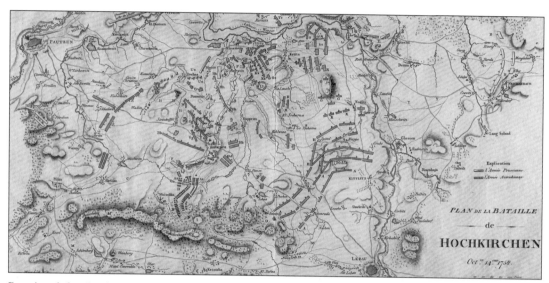

Prussian defeat by the Austrians at Hochkirch on 14 October 1758 underlined the degree to which the armies of the period were not rendered inflexible by the notion of linear tactics. Field-Marshal Daun used columns to great effect against the over-confident Frederick.

Victory of outnumbered Prussians under Frederick the Great over Austrians at Leuthen, 5 December 1757. A hard-fought victory by a well-honed army reflecting Frederick's skilled exploitation of the terrain, Prussian firepower, and the fighting quality of the Prussian cavalry. Victory was followed by Austrian abandonment of most of their gains in Silesia.

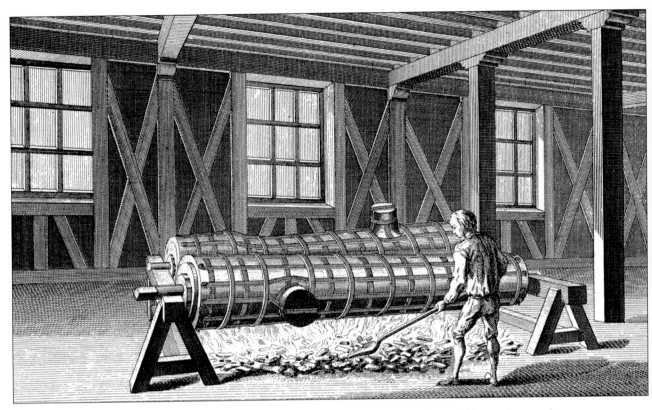

Eighteenth-century method of casting cannon. Drying clay patterns which would be used to produce a mould into which molten metal would be run. (From Diderot's *Encyclopédie*)

to fight in war zones; from 1688, they had been raised by conscription among unmarried peasants. Conscription was imposed in Denmark in 1701, Spain in 1704, Russia the following year, and Austria and Bohemia in 1771. In Prussia, a cantonal system was established between 1727 and 1735. Every regiment was assigned a permanent catchment area around its peacetime garrison town, from where it drew its draftees for lifelong service. Such systems increased control over the peasantry, who were less able than mercenaries to adopt a contractual approach towards military service.

These recruitment practices were as important an aspect of rising state military power as the number of troops in armies, which is sometimes employed in a somewhat crude fashion as the sole indicator of such power. New recruitment systems were mediated by aristocratic officers, but they reflected an enhanced control on the part of government, and there was no longer a figure equivalent to Wallenstein – the independent entrepreneur who raised and commanded armies for the Emperor Ferdinand II in the 1620s and 1630s, and was finally assassinated when his loyalty became suspect – and no system of military entrepreneurship to sap governmental control, both politically and operationally. This was crucial to the ability to think and act in strategic terms effectively.

This ability was scarcely novel, but the increase in discipline, planning, and organisational regularity and predictability that characterised European armies and

Eighteenth-century method of casting cannon, by tapping a furnace to allow molten metal to run into the moulds. On the right, a puddler is skimming off impurities. (From Diderot's *Encyclopédie*)

navies, enabling them to match the Chinese in this period, made it less difficult to implement strategic conceptions. The greater effectiveness of military forces was demonstrated by Russia under Peter the Great (r. 1689–1725) and by Prussia from 1740, but there were other examples. The Spanish army had been very weak in the 1670s, but in 1717 the island of Sardinia was successfully invaded by Spain, and in 1734 Naples and Sicily. The Spanish army was given a new structure in 1702–4, while the navy was revitalised in the 1710s.

Enhanced European organisational capability was not simply a matter of financing, supplying or moving armies, but also improved the organisational and operational effectiveness of individual units. The Europeans moved most towards a large-scale rationalisation of such units: they were to have uniform sizes, armaments, clothing, command strategies, etc. Such developments made it easier to implement drill techniques that maximised firepower. Allied and subsidised units could be expected to fight in an identical fashion with 'national' units, a marked contrast to the situation in the Asiatic empires where there were major differences between core and ancillary troops. The Europeans extended this model to India, training local units to fight as they did.

European conflict could deliver decisive results in both battle and war. In the 1700s, the military reputations of Sweden and France were dealt heavy blows by Russia and Britain respectively, with defeats at Poltava (1709) and Blenheim (1704) having major long-term effects on European power politics. The rise of Prussian power under Frederick II, the Great (r. 1740–86), owed everything to success in battle, particularly against Austria in the 1740s and Austria and France in the late 1750s.

In 1745, Frederick developed the attack in oblique order, so as to be able to concentrate overwhelming strength against a portion of the linear formation of the opposing army. Frederick devised a series of methods for strengthening one end of his line and attacking with it, while minimising the exposure of the weaker end. This depended on the speedy execution of complex manoeuvres for which well-drilled and well-disciplined troops were essential. The oblique attack was used to great effect in defeating the Austrians at Leuthen in 1757. However, the Austrians soon developed effective counter-tactics, retaining reserves that could be moved to meet the Prussian attack.

The Prussian army enjoyed the highest reputation in Europe until the triumphs of the forces of Revolutionary France from 1792. This reputation led to an under-valuation of the achievement of the Russians, who had demonstrated fighting quality, unit cohesion, discipline and persistence on the battlefield against the Prussians in the late 1750s. In their wars with the Turks in 1768–74 and 1787–92, the Russians went on to display flexibility and success.

Over a longer timescale, the potential of European warfare changed. The century witnessed the linkage of Newtonian science to military engineering, artillery and military thought. Ballistics was revolutionised between 1742 and 1753 by Benjamin Robins and Leonhard Euler. Robins invented new instruments enabling him to discover and quantify the air resistance to high-speed projectiles. He also furthered understanding of the impact of rifling. The author of *Neue Gründsatze der Artillerie* (1745), Euler also solved the equations of subsonic ballistic motion in 1753 and summarised some of the results in published tables.

Theoretical and empirical advances greatly increased the predictive power of ballistics, and helped turn gunnery from a craft into a science that could and should be taught. These developments affected the use of artillery and influenced military education. The latter was encouraged by both major and minor powers. For example, an artillery school was opened in Naples in 1744, and an engineering academy ten years later, and in 1769 they were amalgamated into the Reale Academia Militare. It taught ballistics, tactics, experimental physics and chemistry to officer cadets, all of whom were supposed to attend classes.

European warfare in the century before the outbreak of the French Revolutionary Wars in 1792 can be dismissed as rigid and anachronistic only if a very narrow and misleading view of it is taken. Its dynamism and flexibility should not, however, detract attention from the variety of military systems and conflict elsewhere in the world.

6

FROM THE FRENCH REVOLUTIONARY WARS TO 1914

Whatever the situation previously, it would be perverse to begin any discussion of the warfare of this period without reference to Europe. Although the Spaniards lost control of much of Latin America with the wars of independence there in the 1810s and 1820s, and Brazil won independence from Portugal, the Western empires, including, at a later stage, the United States of America, came to dominate much of the world, militarily, politically and economically.

Most English-language accounts of warfare in this period are preoccupied with conflict between European states (with the inclusion of the American Civil War 1861–5, a conflict fought in a similar fashion), but, on the global scale, the most important product of war was the spread of the West's military capacity to dominate the world. There was, of course, a common basis to both types of conflict: the availability and improved application of resources. These included population growth and industrialisation in the Western world, plus the utilisation of these through effective systems of conscription, taxation and borrowing, which provided yet more resources.

There were also important technical developments in battlefield capability and operations. Land warfare was transformed by the continual incremental developments in firearms, such as the introduction of the percussion rifle and the Minié bullet, both in the 1840s, and, subsequently, of breech-loading cartridge rifles. The net effect, for both handheld firearms and artillery, was very substantial changes in precision, mobility and speed of use. In the century after Napoleon's final defeat at Waterloo in 1815, greater and more predictable production of munitions flowed from a more streamlined and systematised manufacturing process. The overall result was a degree of change far greater in pace and scope than that over the previous century.

This is even more the case if logistics, command and control, and naval warfare are considered. Steam power, the railway and the telegraph made a major difference for the Western powers, both to nearby operations, for example the mid-nineteenth-century conflicts in Europe, such as the Franco-Prussian War, and the American Civil War,

Revolutionary élan: the battle of Lodi, 10 May 1796. The storming of the bridge over the River Adda was important to the French victory, as was Napoleon's able siting of the cannon.

and to wars waged at a greater distance, such as the Crimean and Spanish-American Wars. The combination of the three made it possible to apply and direct greater resources, and in a more sustained fashion, than hitherto. This did not necessarily determine the course of conflict with those who lacked such technology, but it did make it far easier to organise war. A comparison, for example, of the British capture of Manila in 1762 and the American conquest of the Philippines from 1898 reveals very different military systems; the Americans were able to deploy and sustain far larger forces by land and sea. A comparison of the very limited French presence in Madagascar in the seventeenth and eighteenth centuries, and their conquest of the island in 1894–5, illustrates the same point. Technological advances made European operations in Africa and elsewhere easier in the 1880s and 1890s than they had been earlier.

Yet the mechanisation of European warfare should not be exaggerated. When the First World War broke out in 1914, there was an average of only one machine-gun per thousand troops. The French Revolutionary and Napoleonic Wars (1792–1815) had seen experiments with submarine warfare, as well as the first use of the air for conflict (reconnaissance balloons for artillery spotting in 1794), and the first use in the West of rockets, but none of these made any real impact in the period, and investment in all of them combined was very small. It was not until the twentieth century that the actual dimensions of conflict expanded with effective air, submarine and rocket warfare. Furthermore, it was only then that the chemistry of war acquired the tool of gas, and thus introduced an entirely new type of conflict on land.

The French Revolutionary and Napoleonic period left examples of conflict along the continuum from rapid and victorious offensives to slogging matches. Particularly spectacular instances of the first were provided by Napoleon's operations, in command of the French army of Italy, against the Sardinians and, especially, the Austrians, in northern Italy in 1796–7, and by his successful command of the Grand Armée against Austro-Russian forces in 1805 and against the Prussians in 1806. In 1805, the Austrians were outmanoeuvred and forced to surrender at Ulm, before Napoleon successfully pressed on to occupy Vienna and then to defeat an Austro-Russian army at Austerlitz. In 1806, thanks to defeat at Jena, the Prussians were also rapidly overthrown. These were impressive eastward projections of French strength, far surpassing anything achieved under the *ancien régime* prior to the French Revolution. It was necessary to go back to Charlemagne to see such range on the part of a French ruler, although the context was very different. Napoleon exceeded Charlemagne's range with his operations against the Russians in Poland in 1807.

Napoleon, however, found it impossible to secure decisive victory over the Austrians in 1809 and over the Russians in 1807 and, far more obviously and seriously, 1812. The slogging match of the battle of Borodino (1812), seen in France as a victory, was followed by similar battles at Leipzig (1813) and Waterloo (1815) that were clearly French defeats. As a military commander, Napoleon had benefited from the operational and organisational advantages that the French enjoyed over their opponents from the outbreak of war in 1792, and from the commitment of the Revolutionary political system to war. The *levée en masse*, a general conscription ordered in 1793, raised large forces, such that French armies were able to operate effectively on several fronts at once, to sustain heavy casualties, and to match the opposing forces of much of Europe. Although there were major difficulties in the 1790s, especially in logistics, the French army was successfully moulded and sustained as a war-winning force.

In the British Parliament in April 1797, the playwright and opposition spokesman Richard Brinsley Sheridan mocked governmental assurances about the ease with which the French would be destroyed: 'I will not remind those gentlemen of their declaration so often made, that the French must fly before troops well disciplined and regularly paid. We have fatal experience of the folly of those declarations; we have seen soldiers frequently without pay, and without sufficient provisions, put to rout the best-paid armies in Europe.'[1]

The aggressive style of French war-making, in strategy, operations and tactics, was matched by a battlefield deployment in independent attack columns. Preceded by skirmishers that disrupted the close-packed lines of opponents, and supported by massed cannon, these columns proved effective, as at Jemappes in 1792, after which Belgium was conquered – but they did not guarantee success. Alongside victories for the Revolutionaries, there were defeats, as at Neerwinden in 1793 and Amberg in 1796.

Although revolutionary radicalism was not sustained in the 1790s, the French regime remained bellicose, and France was still at war when Napoleon seized power in 1799. He had made his name with a campaigning characterised by swift decision-making and rapid mobility. France's relative advantages, however, were eroded in the 1800s. The French lacked a lead comparable to that enjoyed (although not without anxiety) at sea by the British after Horatio Nelson's shattering victory over a Franco-Spanish fleet at Trafalgar in 1805.

As so frequently in European military history, a capability gap on land had been swiftly closed. Combined with the widespread reluctance within Europe to accept Napoleonic views, this ensured the end of his drive for hegemonic power. Opposition to French hegemony required a skilful response, both military and political. Napoleon could not provide this. His retreat from Moscow at the end of the 1812 campaign, with his army ebbing away into the snows, was a fitting symbol of the folly of his attempt to dominate all of Europe.

In 1813, Napoleon wrote 'War is waged only with vigour, decision and unshaken will. One must neither grope nor hesitate.' However, that year, at Leipzig (16–19 October), the 'Battle of the Nations', the French were outgeneralled and outfought; the most serious defeat in battle Napoleon had hitherto faced. At the outset of the battle, he exploited the advantage of the interior lines on which he was operating, while his mutually suspicious opponents faced the difficult task of cooperation on exterior lines. On the 16th, the Allies took heavy casualties, but made important gains. In particular, the Prussians under Blücher were successful at Möckern, a clash that demonstrated the continued role of cavalry. Under pressure from greater numbers, the French were finally defeated, leading to the collapse of Napoleon's position in Germany. The 1813 campaign clearly indicated that symmetry had revived in Western warfare. It was possible to defeat the main French field army, and without the benefit of the distances and climate of Russia. The aura of Napoleonic invincibility had been wrecked by the Russia campaign, the Austrians had now learned to counter the French corps system by using one of their own, and the Prussians had improved their army, not least by developing a more coherent and comprehensive staff system.

In 1814, France itself was invaded. Outmanoeuvred, despite initial successes, and abandoned by many of his generals, Napoleon was obliged to abdicate. Returning from exile in 1815, he regained power and invaded Belgium, only to be defeated at Waterloo, as defensive firepower beat off successive, poorly coordinated French frontal attacks. The French army was not at its peak; but nor was it well commanded. The individual arms were not combined ably, and there was a failure to grasp tactical control. After the battle, France was easily invaded and Napoleon surrendered to a blockading British warship.

After the Napoleonic Wars, there was a preference for long-service regulars, rather than large numbers of conscripts. Experienced troops were seen as more valuable both in battle and for irregular operations, as well as being more politically reliable. Combat certainly required a disciplined willingness to accept hazardous exposure. When British

Napoleon's victory over the Mamluks at the battle of the Pyramids, 21 July 1798. This was a victory for defensive firepower over shock rifles. French rifles were described as 'like a boiling pot on a fierce fire'.

troops approached the Egyptian coast in a landing contested by the French in 1801, 'the enemy commenced their attack upon us with round shot and shell which as we approached nearer was changed into the hottest discharges imaginable of grape, cannister and musquetry without our being able to make any return. In spite of this destructive opposition the boats still advanced', and, indeed, the landing was successful.[2]

The continuum in European warfare from rapid offensives to slogging matches seen in the French Revolutionary and Napoleonic Wars remained the case throughout the period. The Austrians rapidly crushed liberal uprisings in Naples and Piedmont in 1821, and in central Italy in 1830; the French did likewise in Spain in 1823, and the Russians in Poland in 1831, although the Dutch failed to do the same in Belgium in 1830 and 1831. In mid-century, there was the swift and successful Austro-Russian defeat of a Hungarian rising in 1849, a conflict that receives insufficient attention, but also the long siege of the Black Sea naval base of Sevastopol (1854–5) during the Crimean War (1853–6) between Russia and a coalition, eventually, of Britain, France, Sardinia and the Ottomans.

The Anglo-French effort in the Crimean War has been frequently criticised and, indeed, there was a lack of purposeful planning. Yet, the Allies successfully deployed forces into Russia and kept them there until they had achieved their task, a goal that had eluded Napoleon. An indication of the growing scale of combat made possible by industrialisation was provided by the siege of Sevastopol in which the Russians were supported by over 1,000 cannon, while the Allies fired 1,350,000 rounds of artillery ammunition. Such figures suggest that the Crimean conflict can be seen as the first industrial war. One British officer wrote to his beloved 'now I am so accustomed to the noise that I believe I could go to sleep in a battery when the enemy were firing at it'.[3]

The Allies benefited from steamships in transporting and supporting their forces, an aspect of the use of new means of transport. In 1859, during the Franco-Austrian war in Italy, both sides employed railways in the mobilisation and deployment of their forces. However, in contrast to the Prussian leadership in the 1860s, there was a lack of planning and of command coherence in the Crimean War.

The Anglo-French forces were fortunate that the Russians lacked modern rifles and artillery: they were still reliant on smooth-bore muskets. In contrast, the British had adopted the Enfield rifle in 1853. This percussion-lock rifle was more accurate and effective than the musket. The rifled barrel gave bullets a spin, which led to a more stable and thus reliable trajectory. The percussion cap, coated with fulminate of mercury, produced a reliable, all-weather ignition system. Positioned over the fire hole, it ignited the main charge, replacing the flintlock mechanism. There had also been a development in the shot. In place of the musket ball came the Minié bullet. Developed

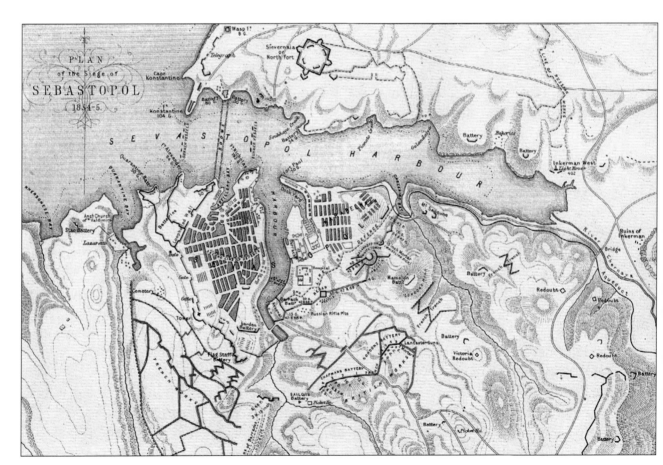

In the Crimean War, the Allies surrendered mobility by besieging Sevastopol in 1854–5, and the siege was not fully effective as road links to the north stayed open. The Allies also had to face both particularly bad weather, which hit supply links across the Black Sea, and attempts by the Russian army in the Crimea to disrupt the siege. The city was well defended, and an Anglo-French naval attack in 1854 failed, as did initial land assaults in 1855. The attackers lacked adequate experience in siegecraft, and had to face a type of trench warfare that was different to earlier sieges.

by Captain Claude-Etienne Minié in 1848, this easily loaded cylindro-conoidal lead bullet expanded when fired to create a tight seal within the rifle, obtaining a high muzzle velocity. These innovations increased the effective range of infantry firepower. The casualty rates inflicted on close-packed infantry rose dramatically. At Inkerman (1854), attacking Russian columns, seeking to close to bayonet point, took heavy casualties from the Enfield rifles of the British and were defeated.

The war between the USA and Mexico in 1846–8 was more decisive in its consequences: it left the USA with what was to become California, Nevada and Utah, as well as most of Arizona and parts of Colorado, New Mexico and Wyoming. In 1846, an American army advancing from Texas under Zachary Taylor drove the Mexicans back over the Rio Grande, invaded northern Mexico, and captured Monterrey after difficult street fighting. The following year, an amphibious expedition under Winfield Scott captured Vera Cruz and then successfully advanced on Mexico City. Other American forces captured California and New Mexico in 1846 and held them against rebellion in the winter of 1846/7.

American campaigning was high-tempo, its aggressive and fast-moving character necessary for political as well as military reasons. The Americans were helped by naval superiority, as well as better artillery, which made a major difference in battle. Horse artillery provided firepower as well as mobility, while Scott's effective generalship displayed strategic insight, a skilful transfer of this insight into effective operational direction, and an ability to gain and retain the initiative. Always favouring the attack, Scott repeatedly tried to turn the Mexican flank. The American conviction of superiority encouraged both operational and tactical boldness; this boldness was reinforced by the very nature of the enemy whose own mobility made it difficult to force him to an engagement. The Mexicans benefited from numbers and from the fighting quality of their troops, but they were poorly armed and supplied and both outgeneralled and outfought. American battlefield quality owed much to the calibre of the junior officers who helped turn recruits and volunteers into effective soldiers.

The American reliance on infantry accorded with a more general long-term trend in which the battlefield value of cavalry decreased. Cavalry remained most important in reconnaissance and in action against other cavalry. Horses also provided crucial mobility for long-range movements away from rail links. While important in all these spheres, cavalry had been marginalised from battle. There were also specific problems with horses, not least their requirements in fodder and water, and the difficulty of transporting them safely by sea.

One of the direct consequences of the increased power of government, as well as, but less directly, of industrialisation, was the creation of large armies in the second half of the century in Europe; and also during the American Civil War. They were raised in Europe through conscription. These large armies led to serious problems in training, equipment and command. Such problems were not readily apparent in peacetime, but conflict exposed the military's inability to operate as envisaged. In practice, bulk did not equal mass, nor movement manoeuvre. Logistical support was frequently inadequate. In Europe, as in North America, these problems encouraged an emphasis on attack, in order to obtain a quick decision, contributing to the high-tempo warfare of the period.

The problems of effectively directing and maintaining large armies were not fully appreciated until the First World War (1914–18). Instead, there was an element of delusion arising from Prussian successes against Denmark (1864), Austria (1866) and France (1870–1), the second of which was particularly swift. These led to the conclusion that offensive operations, carefully planned by an effective and professional general staff, that drew on the logistical possibilities provided by railways, would rapidly lead to decisive victories, such as at Sadowa in 1866. In 1870, the Prussians outmanoeuvred the more concentrated and slower-moving French armies. This reflected Prussian superiority in command and control, a clearly planned strategy, and tactical differences, not least the French preference for tight defensive formations and the Prussian stress on open-order deployment and small-unit fire tactics.

Yet Field Marshal Moltke, the architect of these campaigns, himself warned of the hazards of extrapolating a general principle of war from them, and was increasingly sceptical about the potential of the offensive. Prussian skill, at the operational and tactical levels, had not prevented many difficulties from arising, not least at the hands of Austrian artillery and French rifles. Furthermore, deficiencies in leadership and strategy on the part of Austria and France had played into Prussian hands, enabling them to outmanoeuvre their opponents. Napoleon III proved a particularly maladroit leader for the French, but the calibre of his generals was also poor. In these cases, as more generally, for example with German successes in 1939 and 1940, it is necessary to focus on relative capability, and on the extent to which offensives were (or were not) countered by defensive skill, not least by the availability and use of reserves.

European commentators also did not draw appropriate lessons from the American Civil War (1861–5). Contemptuous of the Americans, they underrated the role of resources in the conflict, its length and, in part, attritional quality, the signs of what were to be seen as total war, and the development of trench tactics; the first recorded battlefield appearance of barbed wire (originally devised to pen cattle) occurred at Drewry's Bluff in May 1864. Over one million died or were wounded in the conflict, in part because of the use of new firearms, especially the percussion-lock rifle. The Springfield rifle, which had become the army issue in 1855, had a greater effective range than its predecessors, with rifling offering greater effectiveness than smoothbore. A further innovation in artillery was that some cannon now used timed fuses. However, in neither case did these weapons match in effectiveness the breech-loaders that were soon to dominate battle. Use of the machine-gun was also limited: the Gatling gun, patented in 1862, could continue firing as long as the hand-operated crank was turned, but, aside from mechanical problems, high rate of ammunition usage and expense, it suffered from being considered eccentric to battlefield dispositions and tactics. The same problem affected use of the French mitrailleuse machine-gun in the Franco-Prussian War.

In the American Civil War, the strength of entrenched troops was accentuated because the opposing artillery did not find an effectual way of suppressing them. The devastating consequences were captured in Colonel William Aylett's account of Pickett's Charge, an unsuccessful Confederate attack during the battle of Gettysburg (1–3 July 1863):

> The brigade moved on across the open field for more than half a mile, receiving, as it came in range, fire of shell, grape, canister and musketry, which rapidly thinned its ranks; still pushed on until the first line of the enemy, strongly posted behind a stone wall, was broken and driven from its position, leaving in our hands a number of pieces of artillery, how many is not known.
>
> By this time the troops on our right and left were broken and driven back, and the brigade exposed to a severe musketry fire from the front and both flanks and an enfilading artillery fire from the rocky hill some distance to the right. No supports coming up, the position was untenable, and we were compelled to retire, leaving more than two-thirds of our bravest and best killed or wounded on the field.[4]

Attacking in columns, not lines, which Union forces increasingly did in 1864 and 1865, was designed to reduce the target for defensive firepower and to increase the speed and mass of attack. The effectiveness of the defence was increased by the manoeuvrability of riflemen within the relatively compact battlefields. This permitted the ready presentation of new defensive fronts, although that required adequate intelligence and skilled generalship. At the same time, it has been argued that a reliance on holding fire or the effects of advances through wooded terrain meant that the increased range of rifled muskets was not fully exploited. It has also been suggested that a failure to advance to a bayonet assault and, instead, the halting of advances in order to engage in close-range firefights, led to a failure to press home attacks that caused indecisive combat. In practice, it was difficult to assimilate new military techniques. This interval between military innovation and battlefield effectiveness was to be a recurring feature of industrialised warfare.

Ulysses Grant, appointed General-in-Chief of the Union army in 1864, eventually added a strategic purposefulness and impetus to Union military policy, and subordinated the individual battle to the repeated pressure of campaigning against the Confederates and inflicting cumulative damage. For example, after the battle of the Wilderness (5–6 May 1864), the Union forces pressed on towards Spotsylvania Court House, where the two sides fought it out around the Confederate entrenchments from 8 to 21 May. On 3 June, Grant attacked again, against Cold Harbor.

At any time in history, protracted conflict placed a premium on the organisation of resources. The Franco-Prussian War was total in that Moltke's systematised warfare offered a hitherto unprecedented degree of methodical effectiveness, although there were serious logistical problems for the Prussians in 1870, with confusion on the railways and, ironically, a return to dependence on horses. However, the scale, duration and mobilisation of resources of the American Civil War provided a different type of totality: the Union raised a total of 2.1 million troops, as well as creating a National Bank and introducing income tax and paper currency. War bonds provided about two-thirds of the Union's expenditure. The North also had a formidable advantage in bullion, manufacturing plant, and railway track. The railways helped the Union mobilise and direct its resources, although they took troops to the battlefield, rather than giving them mobility on it.

The willingness of the more industrialised North to seize and, even more, destroy civilian property was also very marked. Grant pressed for attacks on private property from the spring of 1862, in order to hit Confederate supply capacity and thus war-making. This was declaring war on an entire people. Europeans and European-Americans had used these techniques in imperial conquest but not against each other. Sherman destroyed $100 million worth of property as he set out to wreck the will of Confederate civilians in 1864 by making 'Georgia howl'. Sherman's ability to spread devastation unhindered by Confederate forces across the Southern hinterland helped to lead to Confederate surrender, and thus to ensure a decisive end to the war.

Yet it is important not to overestimate the sophistication of the organisation on either side in the Civil War. They cannot be described as war machines, if that is intended to suggest predictable and regular operating systems that could be readily controlled and adapted. Organisation was not only a matter of raising resources, but also of their effective use on the battlefield. In this, both sides experienced major limitations, with the Union lacking the advantage it had in overall resources. Training was inadequate on both sides: this was seen in particular with infantry–artillery coordination. Rapidly raising large forces created serious problems of supply, training and command. Numbers alone could not suffice: it was the way in which men were integrated into existing military structures that was crucial, as the Prussians showed.

More generally, the American Civil War revealed serious deficiencies in the operational dimension of war. Resource strength was applied through inadequate logistical systems. It also proved difficult to secure adequate tactical concentration and cooperation on the battlefield; the situation was to be very different in 1918 in the closing stages of the First World War. During the Civil War, too many assaults were uncoordinated between units and also between arms (infantry, cavalry and artillery). A preference for linear formations made it harder to retain unit coherence on the advance, to resist flanking attacks, and to switch from firepower to shock attack. Partly for these reasons, it was difficult to achieve a decisive tactical triumph. In the end, Grant defeated Robert E. Lee, the commander of the leading Confederate army, with an attritional pounding, whereas in 1866 and 1870 Moltke won victories of manoeuvre (although attritional pounding also played a role), in which he was fortunate in the folly of his opponents.

As an instance of the variety of campaigning, and the limited role of actual battle in some wars, the French intervened in Mexico in the same years. French forces landed in Vera Cruz in 1861, and in 1863 advanced to capture Mexico City. Napoleon III encouraged opponents of the republican government of Benito Juárez to offer the throne to Archduke Ferdinand Maximilian, the brother of the Austrian Emperor. However, Maximilian's attempt to take over the country was mishandled and met a strong nationalist response. There was a long guerrilla war, led by Juárez, with few conventional battles, and French backing for Maximilian, although 40,000 troops at the peak, was both insufficient and unsustained. The French benefited from naval support on both coastlines, and on land were able to seize positions, but they could not stabilise the situation. Maximilian also had a 7,100-strong Austrian volunteer corps, but they were hit by yellow fever and only infrequently encountered the enemy. Following the conclusion of the American Civil War, American pressure led the French to withdraw. Refusing to go, Maximilian was defeated by the Mexicans at Queretaro in 1867 and executed.

Aside from conflicts arising from foreign interventions, there were also wars in Latin America between states, as well as rebellions, for example that of 1835–45 arising from the opposition of the Farrapos of the Brazilian province of Rio Grande do Sul to the national government, and the successful rebellion in Texas against Mexico in 1835–6. These types of conflict overlapped as a result of the instability of a number of countries and of the clashes between them. In 1851–2, for example, Brazilian troops intervened in divided Argentina, and played a major role in overthrowing its dictator, Juan Manuel de Rosas. In 1854, they intervened in Uruguay at the request of the government, and, in 1864–5, intervened again, this time overthrowing the government. President Francisco López of Paraguay determined to strike back and invaded Brazil, following up with an invasion of Argentina. This led to a bitter war characterised by logistical problems. The outnumbered Paraguayans were defeated in the field in 1868–9, but the war then became a guerrilla struggle as the Brazilians tried to hunt down López in the barren vastness of northern Paraguay. In the end, as with other counter-guerrilla struggles, this required the adoption of more flexible operational units, specifically flying columns, and the development of a successful intelligence system. The combination of the two led to López being surprised in his encampment in March 1870, defeated, and killed.

The wars waged by the major powers between 1871 and 1914 did not challenge contemporary military assumptions about the effectiveness of the offensive. For example, by putting the stress on success rather than casualties, observers saw the Balkan Wars of 1912–13 as confirming their faith in the offensive, more specifically in massed infantry assaults. This lesson was taken in particular from the Bulgarian victories over the Turks in 1912, such as Kirkkilese and Lyule Burgas, which appeared to show the effectiveness of high morale and of infantry charging in to the attack. There was a general failure to note the degree to which the effectiveness of rapid-firing artillery and machine-guns might blunt infantry attacks. The power of entrenched positions supported by artillery when neither had been suppressed by superior offensive gunfire was shown in the failure of the Bulgarian attack on the Turks at Chataldzha in 1912. Although the defensive advantages resulting from the new breech-loading, smokeless, quick-firing firearms were understood, and the benefits of field fortifications had been shown in the Russo-Japanese War of 1904–5, there was a firm conviction within the General Staffs that sooner or later the supply of artillery firing high-explosive shells combined with the élan of infantry advances would overcome trenches, barbed wire and automatic weaponry. In the Balkan and Russo-Japanese Wars, as in the Spanish-American War of 1898, the attacking power had won.

There was no major conflict at sea between European powers in this period, although war between the USA and Spain in 1898 and between Japan and Russia in 1904–5 made it possible to test theories of naval capability. The radical technological developments in warships and gunnery after 1815, in particular the switch to steam and iron, had become a continuous process, as ship designers sought to juggle the desirable qualities of speed, armament and armour, while responding to new hull materials, such as nickel-steel, and to changes in gunnery, particularly the introduction of high-explosive armour-piercing shells fired by guns mounted in centreline turrets. The first clash between ironclads in history, the inconclusive duel between the *Monitor* and the *Merrimack*, occurred during the American Civil War in 1862; although that was because the three European navies that already had commissioned ironclads (Britain, France and Italy) had not fought one another. In this duel, cannon shot could make little impact on the armoured sides of the two ships, even though they fired from within 100 yards.

While advanced warships were designed and built to cope with the fleets of other leading powers, navies were also used to project strength at the expense of lesser states. In the 1850s alone, the USA, not then a leading naval power, made a demonstration along the coast of Palestine after foreigners, including Americans, were killed at Jaffa in 1851, while the protection of American interests led to the deployment of forces in Buenos Aires in 1852–3, Nicaragua in 1853, Shanghai in 1854, 1855 and 1859, Fiji in 1855 and 1858, Uruguay in 1855 and 1858, Panama in 1856, and Canton in 1856. In 1853, four American warships entered Tokyo Bay, wintering on the Chinese coast, itself an important display of capability, and returned to Japan in 1854, securing an opening of Japan to American diplomatic and maritime interests. This expedition also made naval demonstrations in the Ryukyu and Bonin Islands, which secured a coaling concession from the ruler of Naha on Okinawa. In 1854–5, another American naval expedition, the North Pacific Surveying Expedition, greatly expanded hydrographic knowledge of Japanese waters.

A major American deployment to South America occurred in 1858. As a result of disagreements with Britain and France over the treatment of their citizens in Paraguay, its dictator, López, closed the Paraguay and Paraná rivers to all foreign warships. In enforcing this policy, his forces in 1855 fired on the *Water Witch*, a lightly armed American naval steamer which had ascended the Paraná on a mapping expedition. The Americans responded in 1858, sending a squadron up the Paraná.

López apologised, paid an indemnity, and let the mapping proceed. By early 1859, the American navy had eight ships deployed on the rivers of Paraguay.

During the American Civil War, the capability of ironclads increased. Whereas the *Monitor*, a ship that symbolised the power of the machine, had two guns in one steam-powered revolving turret, the Union laid down its first monitor with two turrets in 1863. Less powerful than the British navy, the Union navy still became the second largest in the world, with over 650 warships, including 49 ironclads; although after the war most of it was rapidly decommissioned as the Americans returned to imperial expansion against Native Americans, rather than overseas power-projection.

The development, from the 1860s, of a submerged torpedo driven by compressed air and, eventually, equipped with gyroscopes to provide an automatic means of steering; and, from the 1880s, of electric-powered submarines, made the situation at sea more volatile, and encouraged debate about naval tactics, strategy and force-structure. Rather than focusing on conflict between battle fleets, the French Jeune École, particularly in the 1880s, argued that France should respond to British naval power by emphasising commerce raiding, a strategy that required fast cruisers, while the torpedo was seen as a way to undermine British battleships.

Towards the close of the nineteenth century, however, command of the sea through battle was emphasised by theorists, particularly the influential American, Alfred Thayer Mahan. This approach led to a stress on battleships. From the 1890s, the leading powers all developed battleship navies. States that hitherto had no major fleet of this type, such as the USA and Japan, began work on them. The potency of naval gunnery increased as breech-loaders replaced muzzle-loaders and as quicker-firing guns were introduced. In response, the strength per ton of armour also increased, which led to pressure for still more powerful gunnery.

In 1906, the British launched HMS *Dreadnought*, the first of a new class of all big-gun (12-in) battleships, and the first capital ship in the world to be powered by the marine turbine engine. Completed in one year, her construction reflected the industrial and organisational efficiency of British shipbuilding. Other powers, particularly Germany, rushed to match Britain's new class of warship. By the outbreak of the First World War in 1914, Britain had 21 dreadnoughts in service, the Germans 14; and 12 and 5 respectively were under construction. The Americans laid down their first dread-nought in 1906, the Japanese theirs in 1909.

The potency of battleships was tested in the Russo-Japanese War of 1904–5, a conflict in which naval power played a major role. Tsushima (1905) was the most important naval battle in the war, and a crippling defeat for the Russian navy, with 31 out of 39 warships destroyed or captured that day or in the immediate aftermath. The battle was the only example of a clash between modern battleships in the century that led to the destruction of one of the fleets. Tsushima saw hits scored from unprecedented distances, which led to pressure for the development of big-gun battleships. Rapidly followed by the end of the war, Tsushima appeared to vindicate Mahanian ideas: a high seas encounter would occur, it could be a decisive battle, and it would then affect the fate of nations. The war also saw the use of mines, torpedoes and destroyers, although not submarines, the potential of which was greatly underestimated by most naval commanders.

Thanks to the development of radio, there were also important advances in naval communications by 1914. Germany developed a highly sophisticated radio network which enabled communications with her vessels over the entire globe, with the exception of a dark spot on the western side of the Americas.

Developments, and the pace of development, in the military capability of Western states, with their industrial economies, were not matched elsewhere; although, from the start of the period, efforts were made to increase effectiveness by emulating European armies and navies. At the close of the eighteenth century, Selim III attempted to introduce changes in the Ottoman army. He created a new force, the *Nizam-i Cedid* (new order army), organised and armed on European lines. However, the overthrow of Selim in 1807, when he tried to reform the janissary auxiliaries, the dissolution of the Nizam-i Cedid, and the failure of Mahmud II to re-establish control over the janissaries in the 1810s, indicated the deeply rooted ideological, political and social obstacles to Ottoman military reform. The war with Persia in 1820–3 revealed serious deficiencies, and the Ottomans avoided serious defeat largely as a result of the inroads of cholera in the Persian army.

Although military improvements were to play a role, the Ottoman empire owed much of its survival in the nineteenth century to the concern of European powers about the geopolitical consequences of its collapse. In 1807, French advisers helped Ottoman forces to deploy cannon to prevent a British fleet seeking to force acceptance of British mediation of their war with Russia. In those pre-steamship days, the British navy was also held back by contrary winds. Anglo-French intervention in the Crimean War was designed to protect the Ottoman empire against the Turks, and in the late 1870s the British threatened war against Russia to the same end.

There were also attempts elsewhere to adopt European weaponry and other related aspects of modernisation, such as institutionalised military education. Thus, Mehmet Ali, Viceroy of Egypt from 1805 until 1848, organised an impressive military system. This included a staff college, established in 1825, and the introduction of conscription in the 1820s, which enabled him to create an army 130,000 men strong. A ministry of war was the first permanent department of state to be instituted. In 1813, Mecca and Medina were retaken from the Wahhabis, an orthodox Muslim sect that energised much of Arabia, after an Egyptian expedition launched in 1811 had been ambushed. However, a fresh rebellion led to initial disaster for the Egyptians until, in 1814, the Wahhabi forces were defeated. In 1816, the Egyptians resumed the offensive into the deserts of Arabia, seizing the Wahhabi strongholds, culminating with the capture of their capital, Dar'iyya, in 1818 after a six-month siege. The resilience of the Wahhabis was shown by their continued opposition, and in 1824 the second Sa'udi-Wahhabi state was founded in the interior. This demonstrated that the regular forces of settled societies could achieve only so much.

To the south of Egypt, Massawa and Suakin on the Red Sea were occupied by the Egyptians in 1818, and Nubia (northern Sudan) in 1820. Relatively well-equipped Egyptian forces operated from 1824 against Greeks revolting against Ottoman rule, while in Yemen the Egyptians made major gains over the Asir tribes in 1833–8. When Mehmet Ali turned on his Ottoman overlord, he won major victories at Koniya in 1832 and Nezib in 1839. In both Greece and Asia Minor, the Egyptians were only stopped by Western powers, the Ottoman-Egyptian fleet being sunk in Navarino Bay in 1827 by British, French and Russian warships; this was the decisive battle in the struggle for Greek independence. In the 1830s, Mehmet Ali built a large battle fleet with French technical support, launching ships of the line (ten of them very large) within a decade. However, he was unable to sustain his position in Syria. In 1840, a British squadron blockaded the Egyptian fleet in Alexandria, while British and Austrian warships and marines helped overthrow the Egyptian position in Lebanon and Syria. Sidon was stormed, the marines joined the Ottomans in defeating the Egyptian army at Boharsef, and Acre was heavily bombarded, leading to its evacuation by the Egyptians and to occupation by the Allies. Mehmet agreed to evacuate Syria. Further south, the British occupied Aden in 1839, and in 1840 their diplomatic pressure led to the Egyptian evacuation of Yemen.

A similar process of reform also occurred in the Sikh and Persian forces. In 1803, the Sikh leader Ranjit Singh, who had established Sikh dominance in the Punjab in 1799, began to create a corps of regular infantry and artillery on the Western model to complement the Sikh cavalry and, in 1807, he set up factories in Lahore for the manufacture of guns. These reforms were sufficiently successful that, two years later, Richard Purvis, an officer in the Bengal army of the British East India Company, worried about the prospect of forcing a crossing of the Sutlej river in the face of Ranjit's army: 'his artillery must occasion us considerable annoyance and severe loss'. In 1822, by now the most important Indian ruler outside the British sphere of control, Ranjit Singh recruited several European officers. Two of them, both French, raised a model unit of regular infantry and cavalry, the Fauj-i-Khas, designed to act as a pattern for the rest of the army. By 1835, the regular army was organised on brigade lines and armed with flintlocks. At Ranjit's death in 1839, the army was about 150,000 strong, including 60–65,000 regulars. Many of the officers were Sikhs trained in European drill and tactics. Although defeated in the Anglo-Sikh Wars of 1845–6 and 1848–9, the Sikhs fought well, making effective use of their firearms and cannon.

In Persia, Crown Prince 'Abbas Mirza (d. 1833) developed a European-officered, armed and trained new army in response to Russian victories in the wars of 1804–13 and 1826–8. A Russian renegade named Yúsuf Khan, the Commander of Artillery in the 1810s of 'Abbas Mirza's eldest brother, established a foundry for casting brass cannon and a factory for manufacturing gunpowder. Aman-Allah Khan, the Vali of Ardalan (c. 1800–24), a powerful Kurdish leader, also tried to use European methods in the training of his troops, as did other provincial potentates. Success, however, was limited. The Russians were still victorious in 1826–8 and, in 1838, the Persian siege of

Herat was poorly handled and unsuccessful. The new units were regarded by observers as less impressive than traditional-style mounted levies led by Persian commanders. These continued to have a role in a military environment largely framed not by confrontation with Russia, but by the need to suppress regional risings, for example in 1832 and 1838, to overawe hostile royal princes and provincial governors, and to campaign against Türkmens, as in 1836.

After the death of 'Abbas Mirza, few attempts were made to continue Westernisation of the Persian armed forces. The army remained poorly organised and the sale of commands to unqualified individuals, who used positions for personal profit and took no interest in training, further weakened cohesion and quality. The government relied heavily on the powerful and well-armed tribal forces, that continued to focus on cavalry. This provided mobility in a country lacking roads and railways. Thus, the manipulation of tribal politics was seen as the route to domestic security, while, externally, there was an attempt to secure British protection against Russia. The Persian forces did not distinguish themselves in a brief conflict with Britain in 1856–7.

Nguyen Anh, who united Vietnam through conquest from 1788, ruling it as Gia-long (r. 1802–20), was interested in Western technology and he used it in developing his fleet. Square-rigged galleys constructed in the Western style were built. His successor, Minh-mang (r. 1820–41), took this further and tried to build steamships. Western models were borrowed for the uniform, arms and discipline of the Vietnamese army, as well as for fortifications. However, as with other instances of Westernisation, it proved difficult to translate form to substance. Tactically and technologically, the Vietnamese did not match leading-edge Western developments and, more seriously, did not embrace the process of continuous change that was increasingly powerful in European armies and navies. This difference owed something to cultural preferences, especially the conservative nature of Confucianism and its role in education, but even more to 'tasking'. The Vietnamese army was largely designed to cope with peasant uprisings; indeed, there were 307 uprisings during Minh-mang's reign. Vietnam proved vulnerable to Western attack: action against missionaries led to a Franco-Spanish expedition that seized Danang in 1858 and Saigon in 1859.

Westernisation of the military came later in Japan and China than in Egypt or the Punjab. Outside pressure, particularly from the American expedition of Commodore Matthew Perry in 1853–4, forced Japan to consider new ideas, although the domestic response was a crucial element: Western pressure on China was greater, but the domestic context there was less conducive to Westernisation. From 1867, the Tokugawa shōgunate in Japan began a serious effort to remodel its army along French lines. Already opposition domains, such as Choshu, had begun to introduce military reforms, and, as a consequence, the shōgunal army was defeated in 1866. This was followed in 1868 by civil war and the overthrow of the shōgunate in the so-called Meiji Restoration. Further, and yet more radical, military changes ensued. The domestic conflicts of the period demonstrated the superiority of Western weaponry, and the political shift of 1868 made it easier to advocate and introduce a new military order. The privileged, caste nature of military service monopolised by the samurai was replaced by conscription, which was introduced in 1872.

The two systems, one traditional, one Western and modern, were brought into conflict in 1877 with a samurai uprising in the south-western domain of Satsuma. This brought a substantial samurai force, armed with swords and matchlock muskets, into combat with the new mass army of conscripted peasants. In what was in some respects a repeat of the Ottoman and Napoleonic defeats of the Mamluks of Egypt in 1517 and 1798 respectively, individual military prowess and bravery succumbed to the organised, disciplined force of an army that, on an individual basis, was less proficient. Conscription was a crucial process in Japan, as well as in other states where it was introduced. It broke down the division still seen in the Ottoman, Persian and Chinese empires between a small, and sometimes Westernised, regular army, and very differently armed levies that were often tribal or clan-based in character.

Japanese military development was supported by policies of education and industrialisation, and was enhanced by the institutionalisation of planning. In 1874, the Sambókyoku, an office to develop plans and operations, was created within the Army Ministry. This became, first, the Staff Bureau and, subsequently, the General Staff Headquarters. The organisational transformation of the Japanese army was linked to an institutional professionalisation and, also, to the creation of a capacity for overseas operations. In the 1880s, not least due to the creation of a system of divisions, the army was transformed from a heavily armed internal security force, reliant on static garrison units, into a mobile force. Thanks to the progress of both army and navy, the Japanese developed an amphibious capability.

A European-style navy was also created, with a naval academy founded in 1871. By the end of the century, admission was on merit, an important step towards professionalism. While French and, later, German models and military missions influenced the Japanese army, the navy, in contrast, looked to Britain for warships and training. In 1871, Heihachiró Tógó, who was to defeat the Russian fleet at Tsushima in 1905, arrived in Britain for training, while in 1873, a British Royal Navy training mission arrived in Japan. Warships were also sent on training cruises to America or Europe. Power projection gathered pace, albeit, at first, in areas of traditional concern. In the 1870s and 1880s, effective sovereignty was established over the nearby Bonin, Kurile and Ryukyu (for long a tributary to China) Islands and the pace of colonisation in Hokkaido was stepped up, although an attempt to seize Taiwan from China in 1874 was unsuccessful and led to heavy losses of troops to disease.

Other non-Western powers did not make comparable progress. The Quajar Shahs of Persia devoted relatively little attention to improving the armed forces and, compared to Japan, the Ottoman empire and China made only limited attempts to Westernise their armies in the late nineteenth century. Instead, as in Ethiopia, the small regular army was greatly outnumbered by tribal forces that fought in a largely traditional fashion.

In Persia, there was a strong conservatism that restricted reform initiatives and, unlike in China, Ethiopia and the Ottoman empire, only limited conflict with foreign enemies. Nevertheless, visiting Russia in 1878, the ruler, Nasir al-Din Shah, was impressed by Russian Cossack forces and, thereafter, he used Russian officers to command and train the Persian Cossack Brigade founded in 1879. Similarly, the first modern police force in Teheran was established in 1879 with the advice of an Austrian officer. The Shah's oldest son, Zill al-Sultan, a provincial governor, built up a personal force of Western-trained troops in the 1880s and early 1890s. An instrument of Russian influence, 2,000 strong by the 1890s and the only well-trained force in the army, the Cossack Brigade was also a crucial support to the Shah, being used by Muhammad 'Ali Shah when he suppressed the popular national government in a royal coup in 1908. However, Tabriz, which had an effective popular guard, successfully resisted the army. In 1909, revolutionary and tribal forces advanced on Teheran and the Shah abdicated. Persia had been neither consulted nor informed when it was divided into regions of Russian and British influence and a neutral sphere in the Anglo-Russian Treaty of 1907.

In Siam (Thailand), under Rama IV (r. 1851–68) and, especially, Rama V (r. 1868–1910), a degree of modernisation included significant changes in the army, communications and finances. Siam also benefited from its location as a buffer state, being between spheres of British (Burma, Malaya) and French (Indo-China) expansion, although it lost territory to both powers. A Department of the Army was created in 1888, and conscription was introduced in 1902. The Siamese forces did not match those of Western powers, but they fought effectively against the French in Laos in 1893, and used modern weapons to suppress revolts that owed much to opposition to modernisation and centralisation policies. These revolts include the Raja of Pattani's rising in the south in 1902, and the Holy Man's Rebellion of the same year: a messianic rebellion that reflected regional opposition in the north-east.

While industrialisation was relatively localised in the period, the impact of industrial munitions production was more widespread as Western traders took their weapons to peoples and polities throughout the world. In New Zealand, the use of muskets was spread from the mid-1810s. Their value was such that in about 1820 one musket was worth 200 baskets of potatoes or fifteen pigs. Maori raiders armed with muskets became increasingly active in New Zealand from 1820. The Nga Puhi from the northern tip of the North Island raided to the southernmost tip of the island using their muskets to win victories, for example at Nauinaina in 1821 and Totara in 1822. These raids helped lead to a series of migrations and conflicts that were similar (although smaller in scale) to those in southern Africa in the period. The Ngai Toa tribe raided from the North to the South Island in 1830–1. The Maori sought to benefit from European settlement, but conflict with the British broke out in 1845. This Northern War (1845–6) indicated the ability of European empires to apply force from a distance: British power was asserted when troops were sent by sea from elsewhere in New Zealand and from Australia.

Several African rulers adopted a measure of European weaponry and methods. This was taken furthest by the Egyptian army, 60,000 strong in 1875 and equipped with modern weaponry: Remington rifles, Gatling machine-guns and 80-mm Krupp artillery. Egyptian forces took Equatoria (southern Sudan) in 1871, Darfur (western Sudan) in 1874, and Harrar (later British Somaliland) also in 1874. However, when, in 1875, the Egyptians pressed on into Ethiopia they were defeated at Gundet, providing the Ethiopians with the valuable booty of 2,000 modern rifles. The following year, another invasion was heavily defeated at Gura: inspired by talk of a holy war against Islam, the Ethiopians may have been able to field 100,000 men.

Holy war also played a major role in West Africa where the Islamic cleric al-Hajj 'Umar b. Sa'id (c. 1794–1864) had declared a *jihad* against all infidels in 1853. By 1862, he had conquered much of the upper Niger and upper Senegal region, although a rebellion in 1863 led to his death the following year. As a reminder of the continued variety of force structure and conflict in this period, that of al-Hajj 'Umar consisted of an élite of heavy cavalry, made up of his original disciples, complemented by infantry and by irregular auxiliary cavalry. It has been suggested that the standing army was about 12,000 strong but that, on occasion, as many as 30,000 men could be fielded. Weapons were a mixture of traditional arms and firearms, the best bought or seized from Europeans, although maintenance of the latter was not easy. This army clashed unsuccessfully with the French in the 1850s, being badly beaten in an unsuccessful attack on the French fort at Medine in 1857, and losing Guémon to French attack two years later. Disciplined French firepower was able to check brave, but poorly planned, frontal attacks. In 1893, the French defeated al-Hajj 'Umar's son and conquered the empire.

After the death of al-Hajj 'Umar, the major challenge to the French on the Upper Niger came from Samori Touré, the 'Napoleon of the Sudan', according to his French enemies. He relied on the sofas, professional troops trained along European lines and equipped with modern firearms, who were supported by a larger militia. The firearms were brought in part from British traders in Sierra Leone, but were also manufactured in Samori's own workshops: he had placed agents in the French arsenal in colonial Senegal to learn how to make rifles and cannon.

Further east, the Ethiopians developed a successful army thanks to the leadership of three emperors, Tewodros II, Yohannis IV and Menelik II. The army increased from fewer than 15,000 men in the 1860s to 150,000 in 1896, by when nearly half were armed with modern weapons. By 1880, a force of Ethiopian artillerymen had been trained, and in the 1890s French and Russian advisers improved the artillery, helping Ethiopia to a notable triumph over Italy at Adua in 1896. The Ethiopians used Hotchkiss machine-guns in the battle, although victory over the far smaller Italian army owed more to poor Italian tactics, not least the failure to coordinate operations.

In Madagascar, as in Ethiopia, there was a process of state formation. Andrianampoinimerina, ruler of Ambohimanga (r. c. 1783–c. 1810) in the centre of the island, used slaving to acquire guns and gunpowder from the coast where Europeans traded. Having conquered part of the interior, he left his son Radama (*c.* 1810–20) with the idea of extending the kingdom over the whole island. This proved a formidable task, not least because the army lacked adequate training, discipline and arms. Radama transformed it with the help of three sergeants who had served in Western armies. Drill, discipline and firearm proficiency was introduced in a smaller, 15,000-strong force, armed with modern European firearms. This force was far more effective than the spears and old guns that its rivals possessed, although disease, hunger and fatigue were major hindrances to operations, especially in the dry lands of the south. Much of the island was conquered in 1822–7, although rebellions inspired by demands for tribute and forced labour had to be suppressed.

The largest non-Western state, China, suffered defeat at the hands of Britain in the Opium War of 1839–42, as amphibious forces seized Amoy, Guangzhou (Canton), Shanghai and other coastal positions. The British made effective use of paddlewheel iron gunships which were able to sail up rivers, such as the Yangzi. Advancing to the walls of Nanjing, the British forced the Chinese to negotiate and to cede Hong Kong. In 1860, during the Arrow War, British and French forces fought their way to Beijing and captured the city, forcing the Chinese to accept greater Western commercial penetration; while, in 1884–5, China failed to block French ambitions in Vietnam.

The Taiping rebellion began in 1851, as a reaction against Manchu rule that included an attempt to create a new Han Chinese dynasty that would unite Christianity and Confucianism. Unlike the American Civil War, this was not a separatist struggle. Their ideological conviction made the Taipings formidable in battle, although the leadership was flawed and divided. Taiping numbers were also considerable. About three-quarters of a million troops took the major city of Nanjing in 1853: mines created breaches in the wall, through which the outer city was stormed, and human wave attacks carried the inner city's walls. That winter, a Taiping expedition advanced to within seventy miles of Beijing, but it was insufficiently supported, retreated in 1854, and was destroyed the following year. Their westward advance was also stopped after bitter fighting in 1854–5, while the Taiping were affected by civil war in 1856 and by the shift of foreign support to the Manchu in 1860: Taiping attempts to take Shanghai were blocked by Anglo-French firepower, then and in 1862. In 1860, the imperial siege of Nanjing was broken by the Taipings, but, in 1864, the city was captured, and in 1866 the last Taiping force was defeated. Rebellions elsewhere, especially in frontier areas, were suppressed in the late 1860s and 1870s, particularly in Yunnan in 1873 and Xinjiang in 1879.

In the second half of the century, some Chinese regional officials made a major effort to improve their forces. Western-officered units, especially the 'Foreign Rifle Company', which, in 1862, was renamed the Ever Victorious Army, were used against the Taiping in the early 1860s, and these forces served as an inspiration and a challenge to a number of Chinese leaders, encouraging the formation of Western-style armies towards the end of the century. Cannon production had been greatly influenced by European advisers in the seventeenth century. The first modern Chinese attempts to start military industries using Western technology were the 'self-strengthening enterprises' which began in about 1860. The initiative was taken by leading provincial officials, but their options were restricted by the determination to preserve unchanged traditional or Confucian Chinese culture and only bolt-on Western technology. The self-strengthening programme is frequently seen as a failure, not least because of deficiencies in particular enterprises, for example the insupportable cost of warship manufacture, because of the greater pace of Japanese progress, and because the Japanese defeated the Chinese in 1894–5. It was this latter defeat which compelled China to adopt industrial technology as well as a more modern, Western style of military training and ideology. The focus of this more broad-based reform was the so-called 'New Army' of the late 1890s.

In the war of 1894–5, the Japanese fleet won the battle of the Yalu river (1894) over the less speedy and manoeuvrable Chinese. Despite problems with logistics and transport, Japanese forces advanced speedily through Korea driving the Chinese before them, and then crossed the Yalu river into Manchuria and captured the major base of Port Arthur as well as Weihaiwei on China's north-east coast. Another force seized the Pescadores Islands. However, they were obliged to limit their gains owing to pressure from Russia, Germany and France. Japan kept Taiwan and the Pescadores, but was forced to return Port Arthur. This showed that industrial armaments and Western-style organisation and thought were not in themselves sufficient; the new scale of war and its geopolitical consequences gave a far greater weight to alliances.

A further instance, both of the strength of China's foreign opponents and of the capacity of their forces to mobilise quickly, was provided by the suppression of the Boxer movement in China. This anti-foreign movement began in 1897 and became nationally significant in 1900 when the Manchu Court increasingly aligned with the Boxers against foreign influence. Converts to Christianity were killed, hostilities between Boxers and foreign troops began, the government declared war on the foreign powers, and the foreign legations in Beijing were besieged.

Two international relief expeditions were organised. The first was blocked by the Chinese and forced to retreat to Tianjin, which was unsuccessfully besieged by the Boxers, whose swords and lances provided no protection against the firearms of the Western garrison. After Tianjin had been relieved, a second force was sent to Beijing, defeating Chinese opposition en route. Beijing's walls were breached and the legations rescued. The alliance of Western and Japanese troops paraded through the Forbidden City, a powerful sign of Chinese loss of face, as earlier was the failure of far larger forces to defeat the defenders of the legations in a siege of fifty-five days. The subsequent treaty with China, signed in 1901, decreed very large reparations, as well as twelve foreign garrisons between the coast and Beijing, and the prohibition of imports of foreign-made weapons for two years. The Boxer failure had made it clear that Western-type weapons were indeed required. Whereas earlier peoples might have boasted of their invulnerability to Western bullets, and been protected by the inaccuracy of firearms, now the Boxers had been made to pay for their trust in magic.

Conflict resumed in this volatile area in 1904. Japanese influence in Korea was challenged by that of Russia, and the confident and racialist Russians, unwilling to accept the Japanese as equals, refused to accept a Japanese offer of a recognition of Russian dominance in Manchuria in return for Japanese control of Korea. In the subsequent war of 1904–5, the Japanese were victorious not only at sea but also in defeating the Russians in the Liaotung peninsula and Manchuria, while a Japanese amphibious force landed in Sakhalin. The Japanese took heavy casualties in a conflict that showed the strength of entrenched positions supported by quick-firing artillery and machine-guns, and found it difficult to sustain the struggle, but, hampered by insurrection in European Russia, and operating at the end of very long supply lines, the Russians weakened first. In the subsequent peace, Japan gained Russian rights and privileges in south Manchuria, not least the lease on the Liaotung peninsula. Victory enabled the Japanese to create a protectorate over Korea in 1905. A rebellion there in 1908–10 was brutally suppressed, and in 1910 Korea was formally annexed, with a tough general becoming the first Governor General.

Korea did not provide the sole example of popular resistance to colonial control, nor of the brutal repression of such resistance. Having been ceded Taiwan by China in 1895, that year the Japanese suppressed a popular resistance movement; although, in the mountainous forests of the interior, tribesmen continued guerrilla resistance for over three decades. In the Philippines, the Americans beat the Spaniards easily in 1898, but then encountered bitter resistance from Filippinos, who also used guerrilla methods.

Conflict in the Far East had revealed that Western forces could be defeated (Russia 1904–5), but only by a non-Western state that adopted much of the Western method of conflict. Historically, the strongest non-Western state, China, had been humiliated by foreign powers and was overshadowed by their military effectiveness.

Western power, in the shape of British land and sea forces, had already heavily defeated Egypt in 1882, showing the gap between a Western military and a modernising, non-Western force. Anti-European action in Egypt led the British navy to bombard Alexandria, and British forces under General Wolseley then landed to restore their version of order. Following an all-night march, they launched a dawn attack on the Egyptian entrenchments at Tall al-Kabir, defeating their poorly trained opponents. The global impact of Western power was more wide-ranging and intensive than ever before.

Drawing attention to the degree to which certain states sought to Westernise at least aspects of their armed forces permits a focus on the most important military development of the period: the spread of Western imperial control over most of the world. This was different in character to the European impact across much of the Old World in the sixteenth and seventeenth centuries. Then, there had been attempts at conquest, for example in Morocco, but, in most of Africa and south and east Asia, European contact was essentially a matter of trade. Force might be involved, as with Portuguese conflict with Aceh and Mataram, but neither the Portuguese nor the Dutch, the other great European maritime force of the period, sought large-scale conquest. They lacked the manpower. For Portugal, Brazil proved a greater interest, while Dutch expansion was controlled by the East India Company, which essentially sought profit, not land.

In contrast, in the nineteenth century, particularly the last two decades, Western power was territorialised, as control over large tracts of the world and a significant portion of its population changed hands. Native polities were overthrown in a competitive rush by the Western states to gain land. This was seen as a source of prestige, a fulfilment of destiny, an area for missionary activity, and a valuable economic resource, providing both markets and resources, such as the tin of Malaya, the timber of Burma, and the cocoa of Ghana. Whereas, for centuries, the French had made little headway in Madagascar, where they had first established a position in 1643, the island was conquered in 1895.

There was also a determination to thwart or limit advances by other Western powers. For example, German interest in New Guinea led the British and Dutch to assert claims, so that, by 1895, boundaries had been settled. Spanish concern about British interest in the sultanate of Sulu in the southern Philippines led to a Spanish expedition to Sulu in the 1870s and to an agreement with Britain in 1885. The Americans were to take over the Spanish position when they conquered the Philippines in 1898 and also to use force to subjugate the sultanate.

The Russians advanced in both the Caucasus and central Asia. The centres of once great central Asian empires were brought under European control. Tashkent was captured in 1865 and Samarkand in 1868. The British feared that the Russians would press on to dominate Afghanistan and threaten India, and this encouraged their own intervention in Afghanistan. Lasting success there proved elusive. British support for an unpopular client ruler whom they installed in 1839, having captured Kandahar, Kabul and Ghazni, was swiftly challenged. However, a general revolt was mishandled and when the poorly led British force retreated from Kabul towards India in January 1842 it was delayed by snow and destroyed in the passes. A British army reoccupied Kabul that autumn, showing that the British had retained their ability to strike into Afghanistan, but it was deemed prudent to withdraw.

The British intervened in Afghanistan again in 1878–80. A successful advance on Kabul and Kandahar in 1878 was followed by the murder of the envoy in 1879, a fresh advance, and then, in 1880, the defeat of an outnumbered, outgunned and poorly commanded British force at Maiwand and the siege of the British garrison in Kandahar. A relief expedition from Kabul defeated the Afghans outside Kandahar, but, again, it was thought sensible to withdraw from Afghanistan. Both expeditions showed the difficulty of translating battlefield success into a lasting settlement. There was no lasting political solution on offer for the British bar withdrawal.

Western expansion owed much to an ability to exploit native divisions and win local support, as with the British use of their Indian army for operations in China, East Africa, south-western Asia (both Aden and the Persian Gulf), and on the lands seen by Britain as the North-West Frontier of India. From Algiers, which they had captured in

1830, the French expanded their power into the interior. In the 1840s, they sought to build up a network of favourable tribes, and when there was a major rebellion there in 1871 much of the population did not take part. Combined with the failure of those who did rebel to cooperate effectively, and with the arrival of French reinforcements after the end of the war with Prussia in 1871, this ensured that the rebellion was overcome by January 1872. The French used Senegalais troops to conquer much of West Africa in the 1890s, while at Omdurman in 1898, the decisive battle in which the Mahdist forces in Sudan were crushed, the British benefited from the assistance of Egyptian troops.

Whatever the use of local support, there was also the issue of the relative military capability of Western and non-Western forces. Technology definitely enhanced the former. This was a matter of weaponry, such as the mobile light artillery used by the French to blow in the gates of positions they attacked in West Africa, and, eventually, of machine-guns, although the early use of the latter was limited by their unreliability. In 1889, the British adopted a fully automatic machine-gun developed by Hiram Maxim that could fire 600 rounds per minute, using the recoil to eject the empty cartridge case, replace it, and fire. The British employed the Maxim in Gambia in 1887, the Matabele War of 1893–4, the Chitral campaign on the North-West Frontier in 1895, and at Omdurman, as a result of which the poet and, later, MP Hilaire Belloc wrote: 'Whatever happens we have got the Maxim gun and they have not.' The frontal assault of the Mahdists across flat ground greatly increased the impact of British defensive firepower. In Kenya in 1905, the field force sent to suppress resistance among the nomadic Nandi used its ten Maxims to cause heavy casualties. In a subsequent expedition, 407 Embu were killed, but only 2 among the field force.

At the same time, it is necessary to note the extent to which Western forces still closed with their opponents, particularly in storming positions. Furthermore, casualties could be heavy, especially in operations in the first half of the century. In 1807, the Bengal army of the British East India Company was rebuffed when it tried to storm the fortress of Kamonah in India. As one observer reported:

Out of 300 of the 17th Regiment which headed the storm, 145 are either killed or wounded. No men could behave more nobly than both Europeans and Sepoys [Indian troops in British employ], but no courage, no bravery could surmount the obstacles thrown in their way. The ditch was filled with bags of powder covered over with straw. The enemy awaited until our men had advanced within shot point blank. They then opened a most tremendous fire. Our men coolly advanced to the breach. Immediately the enemy set fire to the straw . . . as fast as our men mounted [ladders], they were either shot or scorched with powder bags thrown on them.[5]

There were similar scenes in the Peninsular War (1808–14) between Britain and France as the British stormed walled cities in Spain held by the French.

In addition to weapons, other aspects of Western technology were also important in aiding and encouraging imperial expansion. Communications had been enhanced by steamship, railway and telegraph. The first two speeded up, and made more predictable, the movement of troops and supplies. Thus the building of a railway was crucial to the logistics of Britain's campaign in Sudan. The telegraph offered a valuable enhancement to command and control, in particular to the strategic articulation of imperial systems.

In the field of medical science, critical to any army's success, some progress was made in understanding and counteracting tropical diseases. The British established the Royal Army Medical Corps in 1898, and in the (Second) Boer War (1899–1902), the death rates among non-battle casualties were lower than in earlier imperial operations; although, thanks to cholera, dysentery and typhoid, more British and imperial troops still died from disease than in battle.

These factors can all be seen in what is generally omitted from studies of Western imperialism, but was, in fact, one of its foremost instances, the conquest of the Native Americans. The consequences are still very much with us today, helping shape the USA, and thus the modern world. They are also irreversible and deserve particular attention, perhaps more so than other episodes of imperialism, such as the partition of Africa, that have been more ephemeral in their results (although disputed borders remain as legacies of Western colonialism).

The Native Americans suffered from being outnumbered and divided, as well as from an unhelpful international context. The demographic weight of the European-Americans and their willingness to migrate and force their way into regions already settled by Native Americans was crucial. Rapid European-American population growth led to significant levels of migration within America. Unlike many other cases of imperial expansion, the American advance was within areas whose sovereignty had already been ceded to America by other Western powers, although this was far less accepted by Native Americans. Unlike in Africa and south Asia, where Western rivalries acted as a prompt for expansion, there was, particularly after 1848, no danger from competing Western powers, and no need to pre-empt them within what was to become the USA. There was not the need to advance and fight in order to gain sovereignty that can be seen for example in European expansion in Africa in this period.

This made it easier for the Americans to achieve their goals of conquest at their own pace and without a major mobilisation of strength. At this stage, the Americans did not need to go overseas in order to fulfil what they saw as their national purpose and to make conquests. Instead, America's national and imperial boundaries coincided, helping encourage Americans to believe that their empire-building was different from that of Europeans. This was further encouraged by the thinly settled nature of the American West. The Americans faced no resistance from a large and resilient population comparable to that encountered by the French in Algeria or the Russians in central Asia.

In the late eighteenth century, it had been far from clear that it would be possible for the European Americans to advance even to the Mississippi, let alone the Pacific. At that time, the Natives were an important force, who had already proved their mettle against the British in the widespread series of risings collectively referred to as Pontiac's War (1763–4). The Natives were well suited to fighting in the back country, and were trained in the use of arms and in operating in units. Native military potential was considerable thanks to their hunter-warrior training and the, as yet, limited number of back-country Whites.

The Natives held their own in the American War of Independence (1775–83), but were not consulted in the subsequent peace treaty. Instead of a territorial settlement restricting the Americans to what they had conquered, the cession by the British of the 'Old Northwest' (modern Illinois, Indiana, Michigan, Ohio and Wisconsin) abandoned large numbers of Natives to American suzerainty; not unnaturally, the Natives did not accept the American view that they now ruled these lands by right of conquest and international treaty. However, the lessening of British support after American independence left Natives more vulnerable when the pace and pressure of American settlement accelerated, as it did after 1783. This settlement was seen by most Americans as a rightful response to the God-given opportunities for expansion, and this expansion as a recompense for their struggle for independence. In July 1787, Congress passed the Northwest Ordinance. This not only reasserted American sovereignty over the region, it also made it clear that this sovereignty was to be the prelude to settlement. The Ordinance provided for the establishment there of new states and thus for combining the advance of the frontier of settlement with a dynamic political structure.

Once the Natives had recovered from their demoralisation at British abandonment, from 1786 they responded to White American pressure with resistance. They were determined to protect their lands, lifestyle and fur trade from the Americans. Settler raids, in response, further exacerbated the situation and, in 1790, full-scale war broke out. For the settlers, pacification was construed in terms of the subjugation of the Natives followed by their resettlement beyond the bounds of American power or in reservations. This was a result of American ideology, as well as of the drive to create space for settlement by them.

There was no chance, however, that the large sections of America still occupied by Natives would be conquered rapidly by a tiny number of Americans. Although the ratio of conquerors to conquered was far less favourable to the Spaniards in what was to become Latin America in the sixteenth century, or to the British in India in 1750–1850, there was, in the latter two cases, no policy of clearing Natives from the land, and, partly as a result, both areas were subjugated more rapidly. In Latin America, Natives were required as the labour force, and in India, as also with most European colonies in the Tropics, there was no social revolution at the level of the cultivator of the soil. In contrast, in the United States, the expansion of American civilian settlement was a continuous process.

In 1790 and 1791, American expeditions into what became Ohio were defeated by a Native force under Little Turtle. Native skill, American command faults (not least underrating their opponents), and poor American fighting quality were all at issue. The American regulars were not prepared for frontier warfare. Their preference for muskets which could bear bayonets, over the slower-firing rifles, which could not, was inappropriate: in wooded terrain, it was accuracy, not rate of fire, that was important. The Natives fought in open, not close, order, in order to maximise their opportunity to deliver aimed fire and to minimise the target they offered.

However, from 1792, the Americans put an emphasis on training their regulars, creating the Legion of the United States, which was divided into four sub-legions, each a self-contained unit with dragoons, artillery, infantry and riflemen. As a microcosm, this offered the operational and tactical flexibility, specifically the combination of firepower and mobility, that the French were to use so effectively with their division and corp structures in the 1790s and 1800s. The value of this reform was clear at the battle of Fallen Timbers in 1794; the Natives were defeated.

This encouraged the forward drive of American expansion. Tennessee became a state in 1796, and Ohio in 1803, the year in which the Louisiana Purchase of lands from France led to an unprecedented westward extension of American sovereignty beyond the Mississippi. The Natives were unable to mount a coherent response for several years, but, from 1805, Native ideas of resistance received new direction from a stress on spiritual revival and a widespread rejection of accommodation, which was to lead to new conflict with the Americans.

Victories over the Shawnee at Tippecanoe (1811) and at the battle of the Thames (1813) reflected an improvement in American fighting quality. This was due to better training and tactical skill, and to a clearer understanding of Native techniques and their limitations. The building of forts was also important to the advance of American power. Natives were unwilling to mount frontal assaults, and lacked the heavy guns necessary to siegecraft. To the south, the Creek were defeated at Tallasahatchee (1813), Talladega (1813), and Horseshoe Bend (1814), the 800 Creek who died at the last being the largest Native number of fatalities in any battle with American forces. Debilitating Creek divisions also assisted the Americans, who were also actively supported by the Cherokee.

These American victories greatly weakened the Natives east of the Mississippi and helped ensure that they encountered only localised resistance over the following decades. Furthermore, the British settlement with the Americans in 1814, at the close of the War of 1812 between the two powers, ended the prospect of foreign support. A strengthening of anti-Native attitudes that stemmed from the warfare of the early 1810s led to the First Seminole War (1817–18), as the Americans invaded Florida, followed by the Second in 1835–42, as the Seminole rejected the government's attempt to move them west of the Mississippi. The Second War began in the Wahoo swamp, when 108 American regulars were ambushed and all but three were killed, a dramatic display of the vulnerability of regulars in unfamiliar terrain.

In the Second Seminole War, over 40,000 American troops were eventually deployed, while the Seminole were 5,000 men at the strongest. The numerical ratio of the two sides was different from that which generally prevailed in conflict between Western and non-Western forces, and was more favourable to the Americans. The latter attempted a three-pronged encirclement in 1838, but it proved impossible to apply the grand strategy of symmetrical warfare in Florida. The Americans were afflicted by the great difficulties of fighting in the waterlogged and humid terrain, and were hampered by disease, a lack of supplies, poorly trained troops, and the rivalries of officers. The Seminole generally avoided fighting in the open, and preferred guerrilla tactics. A system of forts provided an infrastructure for the American forces, but these forts could not prevent the Seminole from moving between them.

The labour that created the forts and the roads that linked them was symptomatic of a major characteristic of the Western military presence: its eagerness to build. Guerrilla conflict also forced a warfare of pursuit on the Americans, who transformed the struggle in 1838 when Negroes who abandoned the Seminole and joined the Americans were granted their freedom. This cost the Seminole their cooperation and they, plus captured Seminole, helped guide the small detachments increasingly used by the Americans to Seminole bases. The Americans were also effective in gaining operational mobility and in using the extensive waterways of the region. In 1841, they campaigned for the first time in the summer, a harsher environment but one that stopped the Seminole from raising their crops, and thus struck hard at their numbers. The few surviving Seminole eventually took shelter in the more inaccessible parts of the Everglades, where they were short of ammunition and food. The war was wound down, having cost the Americans over 1,500 men (although only 383 died in action) and $20 million. It showed that Natives could only preserve their independence in exceptional circumstances. The war can be paralleled elsewhere, for example in the Java War of 1825–30 in which the Dutch were initially thwarted by the mobility and guerrilla tactics of their opponents, but developed a network of fortified bases from which they sent out mobile columns.

East of the Mississippi, the Native presence in North America was dramatically lessened by the removal policy pursued from 1815 and, more explicitly, from 1830, when the Indian Removal Act was passed. Removal completed the total disruption of Native society, destroying any sense of identity with place. The defeat, in the Black Hawk War of 1832, of Black Hawk and his band of Sawk and Fox by regulars and Illinois militia underlined American dominance of the Mississippi valley.

The frontier of American control and settlement also moved west of the Mississippi, with expeditions followed by roadbuilding and the establishment of forts. Most activity, for example the expedition in 1834 into Comanche and Pawnee country, was peaceful, but it also reflected American military strength. Missouri became a state in 1821, followed by Arkansas (1836), Michigan (1837), Florida (1845), Iowa (1846), and Wisconsin (1848). The army introduced mounted regiments in 1833 and 1836 as it adapted to greater distances and to the advance beyond wooded terrain into the Great Plains. Cavalry was more expensive, but it permitted a lower density in fortifications than would otherwise have been necessary.

From the 1840s, the Americans were no longer interested in pushing the Native Americans back in a piecemeal fashion. Now the authorities in Washington sought total control of the whole of America. European America was seen as unbeatable, and as bringing civilisation to the Natives and to the lands of the West. This situation matched the trend throughout the West. Thus, in a similar vein in Argentina, Native peoples were brutally subjugated in the 'Conquest of the Desert' and then of Patagonia.

Success in war with Mexico in 1846–8 left the American state in control of extensive new territories stretching to the Pacific. Settlers began to enter the territories in substantial numbers, forcing the army to take up constabulary duties in the 1850s on an unprecedented scale. The depredations of migrating settlers on the bison herds that the Natives relied upon for food was a real threat to the livelihood of the latter. Widespread American military operations in the 1850s were characterised by the use of far more violence against women and children than in earlier conflicts, and there was also a greater willingness to massacre Natives. Then, and at other times, the Americans continued to benefit from rivalries between Natives. In particular, tribes such as the Lakota Sioux used the mobility given by their embracing of a nomadic horse culture to dominate and, at times, brutalise sedentary, agriculture tribes, such as the Pawnee, who had the horse, but had not become nomadic, encouraging many of the latter to look for aid to the Americans.

The railway played a major role in fostering American power, not only in speeding troops, but also in developing economic links between coastal and hinterland America and integrating the frontiers of settlement with the exigencies of the world economy. This was important in the spread of ranching, with the cattle being driven to railheads, and in the development of mining. Steamships also aided economic integration.

American advances were in part expressed through the building of forts. These could be bypassed by Native raiders, but they were difficult to take. The forts helped to control communication routes and were a solid sign of American power. Forts were built along the edges of settlements to deter raids, but strategic thinking developed in favour of using forts as bases for offensive campaigns against Native homelands.

After the Civil War, the American army developed techniques that focused on winter campaigning, and the coordination of independently operating columns advancing from different directions. Native villages were attacked, their crops and food stores destroyed, and their horses seized, crippling their mobility. Settlements were particularly vulnerable in the winter as those who escaped risked starvation and death by exposure. The killing of bison was also seen as a way to weaken the Natives. The totality of such methods can be compared to the devastation of parts of the Confederacy in 1864–5, but the wholesale devastation and persecution of the Natives in a series of quick and brutal campaigns was further justified by depicting them as pagan savages. The mobility of the regulars and their ability, through an effective logistical system, to stage winter campaigns indicated the potential of the army to adapt its military style and methods, and to develop an appropriate action–reaction routine.

The Natives could mount effective resistance, as in the war against the Bozeman Trail in 1865–8, and win battles, most famously Crazy Horse's triumph over Custer at Little Bighorn in 1876, but they could not match the inexorable American pressure. Crazy Horse surrendered in 1877, and Geronimo, the leader of resistance among the Apache, in 1886.

The American focus on mounted troops was not shared by all Western powers, but it was necessary in order to track down the mobile Natives. In contrast, most imperial forces pursued mobility through light infantry with only light artillery support; as in French campaigns in West Africa, and also in rapidly moving British columns. These were conflicts of rapid advances and where problems of supply encouraged the high-risk tactic of frontal assaults. There was not the time to bring up heavy artillery in order to attack fortified positions. These characteristics were also true of conflicts in Latin America, such as the War of the Pacific of 1879–83 in which Chile defeated Bolivia and Peru, in part thanks to amphibious operations.

The flexibility of Western military imperialism was both notable and necessary. Along with modern armaments and means of communication, it was important to be able to adapt to different physical and political environments. This linked the expansionism and warfare of the period with that of other imperial systems, such as imperial Rome, Mughal India and Manchu China.

Attitudes were important to Western conquest. Expansion was normative, an attitude that increasingly drew on triumphalism, racialism and cultural arrogance. What were believed to be divine purpose, natural right, geographical predestination, the appropriate use of natural resources, and the extension of the area of freedom and culture, all apparently combined. The sense of mission that underlay late nineteenth-century imperialism led to a determination to persist even in the event of setbacks. Translated to Europe this attitude was to lead to ferociously heavy casualties on the battlefields of the First World War.

7

FROM THE FIRST WORLD WAR TO THE PRESENT

In the West, the military history of the twentieth century appears clear-cut. It centres on the two world wars (1914–18, 1939–45), both seen as 'total' wars. Thereafter, the Cold War commands attention, not least because of its nuclear dimension. The 'hot' episodes of the Cold War are generally presented from an American perspective, with emphasis on the Cuban Missile Crisis and the Vietnam War. The latter leads on to American interest in the post-Cold War struggles in which they have been involved, particularly the Gulf War of 1990–1 and the intervention in Afghanistan in 2001–2. A different list would be offered in Western Europe, not least because of a greater emphasis in Britain and, in particular, France and Portugal on the wars of decolonisation. Nevertheless, the overall emphasis would essentially be the same.

All of these conflicts were indeed important in the international history of the period, but it is possible, with the hindsight of a new century, to suggest that the list requires expansion, and that the emphasis has to be shifted both chronologically and geographically. First, much that dominates attention – not least the two world wars – occurred in the first half of the century, and it may be asked how far it is still appropriate to use the developments and conflicts of that period to define modern warfare, and thus the process of becoming modern. The question is especially relevant because, in the light of the two world wars, modern warfare was defined as 'total', that is, demanding the mobilisation of all of the resources of society. This definition now appears less convincing. A war like the Falklands/Las Malvinas War between Britain and Argentina in 1982 did not involve hostilities in Britain itself, or a British attempt to conquer Argentina, and the impact in terms of civilian casualties or damage to the British economy was minimal.

Total war is difficult to define, as is 'limited' war. The totality of modern war can be one-sided, as the contrast between civilian casualties among the North Vietnamese or Afghans and the Americans in their separate conflicts might suggest. Both were different from the situation during the Second World War when all the major combatants, bar the Americans, were exposed to heavy civilian casualties.

Place and perspective as well as time are at issue. So far we have said nothing about China or India, the world's two most populous countries throughout the century. China played a major role in the Second World War, continuing the resistance to Japanese invasion that had begun in 1937, and absorbing a large percentage of Japanese military resources. As the most populous part of the British empire, India played a large role in both world wars, providing troops not only for operations close to its borders, especially against the Japanese in Burma in the Second World War, but also for more distant operations. In the First World War, 1.3 million men were sent to serve outside India, and nearly 48,000 of them were killed.

Yet the twentieth-century military history of both countries involved other significant conflicts. In the case of China, this was a case largely of domestic conflict, the civil war of 1946–9 continuing a pattern that had already been particularly intense in the 1920s and 1930s. This war ranks as the largest in number of combatants since the Second World War, but it has received insufficient attention from Western historians. For India, there were wars with Pakistan over disputed frontiers and regional predominance, and a border war with China in 1962.

The civil wars within China saw a mechanisation that echoed that in the West (although in a less intense fashion), with weaponry such as tanks and aircraft playing an increasing role. Throughout the non-Western world, this weaponry was supplied by Western powers or traders seeking influence or profit, a continuous process throughout the century. Thus, in the interwar period (1918–39), Afghanistan received aircraft from Italy and the Soviet Union, both seeking to challenge the British position in south Asia. In the 1930s, the Germans provided military support to the Nationalist Chinese, while, during the 1946–9 civil war, the Nationalists were armed by the Americans, the Communists receiving material from the Soviet Union (the Communist state created from the Russian empire).

This pattern of support became more widespread as decolonisation after the Second World War increased the number of states that sought weaponry; the Cold War, moreover, encouraged the major powers to compete in providing weapons and advisers. Thus, the struggle between Israel and its Arab neighbours owed much to the willingness of other powers to provide arms. The Israelis were initially helped by Czech and then French arms but, from the Six Day War of 1967, the Americans dominated arms supplies. In contrast, the Arab powers, particularly Egypt and Syria, were armed by the Soviet Union; having lost much weaponry in the wars of 1967 and 1973, they were extensively resupplied.

This might suggest that 'place' is of limited consequence, that the struggles outside the West essentially registered the same developments as those in Western warfare, because of the provision of Western weaponry and expertise, and that, partly linked to this, most struggles were inextricably part of a global military history driven by the great powers, most obviously as part of the Cold War. While correct in part, this approach fails to devote due weight to the autonomy of conflicts elsewhere and to their particular characteristics.

French Soldiers Resting, 1916, by C.R.W. Nevinson. The exhaustion of the conflict emerges clearly.
(Imperial War Museum)

Perspective is related to this issue. A Western perspective leads to a particular weighting, so that, for example, the role of conflict in China during the Second World War appears disproportionately small. More generally, the defeat of Germany's two attempts to win hegemony in Europe, and the establishment of the USA as the world's leading military power, are important themes in military history, but so also are the collapse of the European empires and the struggle for dominance in east Asia, a struggle that played a major role in igniting the Pacific War of 1941–5, but that also continued thereafter.

All of these struggles can be approached in terms of relative resources and of military operations. The two are not incompatible as accounts of what happened and why, but there is a difference of emphasis. For long, the resource interpretation, which puts an explanatory stress on the quantity and quality of resources, was dominant: thus, Germany had to lose the Second World War once it added the Soviet Union and the USA to its enemies in 1941, while Japan, with its lack of resources, was bound to lose to the USA. This approach has a number of flaws, not least its assumption of a set and unchanging political context for the conflict. However, its most serious weakness is that it tends to demilitarise military history by leading to an underrating of the extent to which factors involved in combat, aside from the quantity of manpower and weaponry, played a major role. In fact, resources alone did not suffice for victory. The French had more tanks than the Germans in 1940, but they used them with less effect. Similarly, the British had more troops in Malaya in 1941, but they were outmanoeuvred and outfought by the Japanese in a campaign in which the latter set the tempo.

In recent years, more emphasis has been placed on fighting quality as an explanation of success in war, with this taken to include factors such as unit cohesion, morale, command and control, all-arms coordination, leadership, tactical skill and operational flexibility. Thus, the defeat of German forces, both on the Western Front in 1918 and by Soviet armies in 1943–5, is ascribed not only to their being outnumbered, but also to their being outfought.

Prior to the outbreak of the First World War, the General Staffs of all the belligerents had pre-planned and executed manoeuvres on a massive scale in war games and staff rides. With these, staff officers convinced themselves that they could knock out their opponents before their own resources ran out. In the run-up to the war, the arms race escalated in Europe. Workshop space in Krupp's Essen works in Germany grew by an average of 5.2 acres (2.2 ha) per annum in the five years to 1908 and thereafter up to 1914 by 6.4 acres (2.66 ha) per annum. Even before the outbreak of war, Krupp was producing 150,000 shells of all calibres monthly, while in 1909 Hiram Maxim predicted raids on cities launched by 1,000 bombers.

In 1914, the Germans sought to repeat the successes of Napoleon and Moltke the Elder by mounting and winning a war of manoeuvre, although, owing to the alliance between France and Russia, there was now the need to plan for a two-front conflict. Moltke the Elder had adapted Napoleonic ideas of the continuous offensive to the practicalities of the industrial age, including railways. He had sought to destroy the cohesion of the enemy army and to envelop opposing forces, rather than relying on frontal attack. This was the strategy of first strike, and it underlay German planning prior to the First World War. Concerned about the ruinous consequences of a lengthy positional conflict, Count Alfred von Schlieffen, Chief of the General Staff from 1891 to 1906, left a plan for an attack on France through neutral Belgium, designed to permit flank attacks on the French, that was to be the basis of German strategy in 1914. However, he also excluded non-military problems from General Staff thinking, ensuring that planning failed to devote due weight to political consequences. Furthermore, Schlieffen failed to adapt his plan to changing circumstances, not least Russian recovery from defeat at the hands of Japan in 1904–5 and her build-up of an army that was more powerful than that of Germany's ally, Austria. His successor, Helmuth von Moltke (Moltke the Younger), and his colleagues in the General Staff, wanted war and, by emphasising future threats and stating that victory was still within grasp in 1914, helped to push civilian policymakers towards conflict. No alternative scenario to that of an all-out war was offered to the politicians. Moltke planned for a short and manageable war, but feared that it could be a long struggle, for which Germany was not prepared.

In the event, the 1914 campaign showed that German war-making, with its emphasis on surprise, speed, and overwhelming and dynamic force at the chosen point of contact, was not effective against a French defence that retained the capacity to use reserves by redeploying troops by rail during the course of operations. Aside from serious faults in German planning and execution, there were also problems with German equipment and discipline that qualify the usual historiographical picture of total German competence. The French success in stopping the Germans in the battle of the Marne in September 1914 ensured that there would be no speedy end to the war. France was saved, and Germany was thereafter committed to a two-front war. This made it difficult to shift forces to the east in order to defeat the Russians rapidly.

The First World War is recalled as a brutal struggle in which millions died in trench warfare with little apparent point. Casualty rates could indeed be very high. Of the 332,000 Australian troops who served overseas, 58,460 were killed and 212,000 were wounded. The stress in much discussion of the war is on impasse and indecisiveness; there are frequent complaints about incompetent commanders and foolish command cultures, and the abiding image is of machine-guns sweeping away lines of attackers. Battles such as Verdun (1916), the Somme (1916), and Passchendaele (1917) are seen as indictments of a particular way of war. In the end, the popular view gives credit to the invention of the tank by the British for helping overcome the impasse on the Western Front, while the Germans are seen as succumbing to domestic dissatisfaction and related problems that owed much to the socio-economic strains arising from the British blockade of Germany.

In fact, the terrible casualties of the war have made it appear more attritional than was the case (although there were specific engagements that were like this). Once the Germans lost the ability to mount a victorious campaign of manoeuvre, this does not mean that their opponents simply wore them down. Instead, like the Confederates in the American Civil War, they were outfought and defeated, both in offensive and in defensive warfare.

The heavy casualties owed much to the war being waged by well-armed industrial powers that were willing and able to deploy much of their young male populations. Despite the repeated failure of military operations on the Western Front to secure their objectives in 1914–17, and the heavy costs of the conflict, both sides showed the adaptability and endurance of modern industrial societies to continue a large-scale, long-term war.

Had the campaigns been waged in a different manner, been for example more manoeuvrist and less static, there is no reason to assume that casualties would have been lower. Instead, troops would have been more exposed to both offensive and defensive fire. Trench systems served to stabilise the line and protect troops, but, once they had been constructed, it proved difficult to regain mobility, although the

We Are Making a New World, 1918. The picture shows a devastated landscape created by the First World War. Paul Nash was an official war artist from 1917. *(Imperial War Museum)*

combatants sought to mount decisive attacks that would enable them to do so. In large part, the inability to do so was due not so much to the inherent strength of trench systems as to the force–space ratio on the Western Front. The same was true on the Isonzo front, where the Italians, as allies of Britain and France, launched eleven offensives in 1915–17, taking very heavy losses to push the Austrians back only six miles; and also at Gallipoli where, in 1915, British, Australian and New Zealand forces failed to break out from their landing zones in order to clear the Dardanelles and make possible an attack on Constantinople.

Where the force-space ratio was lower, it was harder to ensure concentration and mass, but, at the same time, it proved possible to achieve breakthroughs, to make major gains, and to achieve decisive results. This was particularly the case on the Eastern Front, for example with the German breakthrough at Gorlice–Tarnow in 1915, artillery and gas proving more effective than on the Western Front that year. Russia was knocked out of the war in 1917 as a consequence of the combination of defeat by the Germans and internal problems in sustaining the war; these interacted to create a crisis in support for Tsar Nicholas II and his replacement by a republican government. Under Kerensky, this sought to continue the war, but the Germans maintained their pressure and Kerensky was overthrown by the Communists in late 1917. The new leadership, under Lenin, negotiated the Peace of Brest-Litovsk with Germany the following year, accepting major territorial cessions. This hardly demonstrates the indecisiveness of conflict in this period; indeed, Russia had to accept territorial losses greater than those inflicted in any previous war.

Other powers were also knocked out in the war. Serbia was conquered by attacking Bulgarian, German and Austrian forces in 1915, as was Romania by the same powers in 1916. Italy was nearly knocked out by the Austro-German Carporetto offensive of 1917, and might well have fallen but for the dispatch of Allied reinforcements.

In turn, the Allies demonstrated their range with their successful overrunning of the German overseas empire. The one exception here was German East Africa, which proved an intractable problem. The war in Africa was very different from that in Europe. The ability to cope with disease was critical, while, given the distances and the nature of transport links, in Africa the movement of supplies played a major part. Operationally and tactically, manoeuvre and surprise were crucial in Africa. Firepower was less important than in Europe.

Mobility was also the characteristic of the conflict between the Ottomans (Turks) and their opponents: Britain in Mesopotamia and Palestine, the Arabs in Arabia, and the Russians in the western Caucasus. There were exceptions. The Allied landings in Gallipoli in 1915 and Salonica in 1916 led not to the rapid breakthroughs that had been anticipated, but to trench warfare and operational impasses. These, in turn, led to the abandonment of the Gallipoli attack after very heavy casualties. Yet there is no inherent reason why more attention should be devoted to these campaigns than to the others mentioned earlier in this paragraph.

The conflicts involving the Ottomans in part related to the German hope that it would be possible to destroy the empires of Germany's competitors. The German leadership planned through war, rebellion or revolution to extend the war, especially to Egypt, the Caucasus and India. This seemed the best way to threaten Britain's economic planning. The Ottomans were expected to fight both Russia and Britain and to provide the leadership for pan-Islamic revolts. In the words of the German diplomat Rudolph Nadolny, these were 'to light a torch from the Caucasus to Calcutta'.

In the event, the 270 million Muslims in the world did not respond. Within the Muslim world, Ottoman pan-Turkism was widely considered an unacceptable part of pan-Islamism. This was readily apparent in Egypt where German promises of independence required Ottoman troops and they, in turn, were repelled. By February

The most effective soldier-politician of the century, Mustafa Kemal (1881–1938), took a prominent role in the defence of Gallipoli (1915), and a crucial part in defeating Greek forces in Turkey (1921–2), before becoming a modernising first President of the Republic of Turkey from 1923 until his death.

Allied supplies on the beach at Gallipoli, 1915. The Allied attempt to force open the Dardanelles was thwarted by a well-conducted Turkish defence of the Gallipoli peninsula. The Allies failed to push initial advantages, and their advances were contained.

1915, Ottoman defeats further ensured that German hopes of a holy war directed against their opponents remained a dream. The Ottomans fought well in defence but were less effective on the offensive, in part because of poor leadership in the Caucasus by Enver Pasha.

On the Western Front, generals confronted the problems of the strength of the defensive. The available manpower made it possible to hold the front line with strength and to provide reserves, the classic need for all linear defence systems. For the offensive, generals faced the difficulty of devising an effective tactical system that would not only achieve breakthrough, but also then be able to sustain and develop it. This was far from easy, not least because of the problem of advancing across terrain badly damaged by shellfire, as well as the difficulties of providing reserves in the correct place, of maintaining the availability of shells for the all-crucial artillery, and of providing adequate information to commanders about developments. Deficiencies in

Turkish troops manning a trench in Palestine, where they were defeated by the British in 1917–18. The British achievement rested primarily on effective infantry–artillery coordination and a skilful strategy, although tanks and aeroplanes were also used, while cavalry played a major role in the breakthrough.

The Imperial Camel Corps Brigade marching into Beersheba in the Palestine campaign, November 1917. A month later, British forces under Allenby captured Jerusalem.

communications fed directly into command problems. From this perspective, it can be suggested that the actual length of time required to secure the defeat of one of the powers was understandable.

The length of the war arose in part from the time taken to develop tactics able to restore mobility to the Western Front, and in part from the time necessary to ensure the provision of sufficient munitions. The balance of resources was also important; the Germans ran out of reserves of troops in 1918, while the Allies had a fresh source of troops as a result of American entry into the war in 1917. Furthermore, unlike in the Second World War, there was no alternative sphere of commitment for the Americans in the Pacific or for the British in south-east and south Asia. Instead, Japan was already allied with Britain. The cover of the Royal Navy, the weakness of the Central Powers outside Europe, and the existence of poorly defended German territorial targets within striking distance gave Japan the security and opportunity to continue her pre-war aims at an accelerated pace.

The primary contribution of naval power to the result of the war stemmed from the ability of the Allies, principally the British, to retain control of shipping lines across the Atlantic; this gave them ongoing access to the resources of the American economy, while the Allied blockade undermined the German economy, and made it difficult for planners in Berlin to realise schemes for increased production. The blockade also increased the economic importance of Britain to the USA.

Nor did the principal challenge to the Allies come from the German High Seas Fleet. It spent most of the war off the high seas and, instead, in its bases, and rarely challenged the British navy in the North Sea. The major naval battle, Jutland in 1916, was to be the largest clash of battleships in history. Although outnumbered, the Germans inflicted heavier casualties, with more than 8,500 men killed on both sides in just one day. The British suffered from inadequate training, for example in destroyer torpedo attacks, and from command and communications flaws, but, in the big-gun exchange, they avoided the fate of the Russians at Tsushima and the damage inflicted on the Germans at Jutland, combined with the maintenance of British naval superiority, led the German surface fleet to take a very cautious position for the remainder of the war.

German squadrons and warships elsewhere in the world at the outset of the war were hunted down. By the end of 1914, foreshadowing events in the Second World War, the Allies, working in unusual concert, had cracked the three German naval codes. While the Germans seemed oblivious to this, the British navy repeatedly, through slovenliness or mistrust, failed to exploit this advantage to its full potential.

Instead, it was the submarine that posed the greatest challenge to the Allies, although the German shift to unrestricted submarine warfare helped the British by strengthening American support. Submarines had a tactical, operational and strategic impact. The risk from submarines served to discourage operations by surface ships. More seriously, the British had failed to take sufficient precautions to protect merchant shipping, and, by the spring of 1917, the Germans were inflicting very heavy losses on it. The German willingness to sink clearly marked hospital ships, as well as to open fire on survivors in the water, was all too typical of their way of waging war and serves, like the German atrocities against civilians in Belgium in 1914, as a reminder that there was a clear moral difference between the two sides.

It was very difficult to detect submerged submarines, and depth charges were only effective if they exploded close to the hulls. Finally, after much resistance from the British Admiralty, convoys were introduced from May 1917, leading to a dramatic reduction in losses. Convoys made it harder for the submarines to locate shipping, and the escorts were able to respond to attacks. By 1918, the rate of tonnage sunk per submarine lost had fallen. Crucially, American troops were able to cross the Atlantic to Europe in 1918.

The effectiveness of armies on the Western Front rose during the war, although the French were so affected by the costly failure of the Nivelle offensive of 1917 (which led some units to refuse to continue attacking), that they did not play a major role in offensive operations thereafter until the final advance on Germany in late 1918. The rise in effectiveness had two major components: first, the Germans developed stormtrooper techniques, using them with considerable success in their spring 1918 offensive. Indeed, German successes led the mark to rise by over a third on the New York exchange. These stormtrooper techniques relied on carefully planned surprise assaults employing infiltration, and focusing on opponents' strong points in order to destroy their cohesion. As a consequence, the Germans won tactical breakthrough, only to lose the advantage in part due to poor generalship by Ludendorff who could not exploit the success to operational effect. Furthermore, there were no realisable political goals to accompany the offensive. Instead, the Germans assumed they could use shock to force an Allied collapse. In practice, the offensive also led to heavy German losses and to a new extended front line that left them vulnerable to attack.

Second, the British focused on improving artillery firepower and accuracy and, more importantly, artillery–infantry coordination, so that they could dominate the three-dimensional battlefield and apply firepower more effectively than in earlier attacks. Their 1918 campaign was a great success in this respect.

Artillery played a greater role in the Allied success than tanks, although the Allies, unlike the Germans, appreciated the potential of the latter. Like other new weapons, tanks commanded attention, and indeed they had a capability that other weaponry lacked, especially for flattening barbed wire, the essential accompaniment to trenches. However, as was only to be expected of a weapon that had not had a long process of peacetime development and preparation, there were major problems with its reliability; these were exacerbated by the shell-damaged terrain across which tanks had to operate. Some of the statements subsequently made on behalf of the wartime impact of the tank, as of aircraft, reflected the competing claims about weapons systems made by their protagonists in the 1920s and 1930s, rather than an informed critical assessment of operations in the First World War.

"SWOOPING FROM THE WEST."

[It is the intention of our new Ally to assist us in the patrolling of the Atlantic.]

Wartime imagery. American readiness to act against German submarines as seen by *London* magazine.

American First World War enlistment poster stirs up hatred towards Germany. German forces were indeed responsible for atrocities in their advance across Belgium in 1914, while, more generally, the war's devastation owed much to German militarism.

The Allied offensive of 1918, especially that by British, Canadian and Australian forces, was not only effective, but also important to the development of modern warfare. In place of generalised firepower, there was systematic coordination, reflecting precise control of both infantry and massive artillery support, plus improved communications. The learning curve seen in the war was amply demonstrated, as was the deployment of greater resources: the British army had 440 heavy artillery batteries in November 1918, compared to six in 1914.

The war had profound political and social consequences. It led to the fall of the Austrian, German, Russian and Ottoman empires, and thus created long-term instability across much of Eurasia, as successor regimes sought to shape change to their benefit. Meanwhile, during the war, there were mobilisations of resources on a tremendous scale with inevitably serious economic and financial consequences. The number of Britons holding government securities rose to over 16 million, while 45 million Americans bought the first Liberty Loan. The costs of the war caused levels of inflation and government debt that challenged the middle classes, as well as the public finances; while social mores were affected by a decline of deference and by the rapidly shifting role of women in the militarised wartime societies; there was a major loss of confidence in political orders, Providence and the future of mankind. Anti-war feeling developed as just one of the far-reaching consequences, and it was more strongly marked in the 1920s than in the decade before the war.

As with the Second World War, which was followed by important conflicts in China, Indochina, the Dutch East Indies (now Indonesia), and Greece, the First World War led into a series of struggles. Some of these related to attempts to affect the peace terms or their implementation. One was the war between Greece and Turkey, which led to the victory of the latter. Others were of different origin, for example, the struggle between Irish republicanism and British forces. The civil war in Russia between the Communists and their opponents was the widest-ranging postwar struggle. It was complicated by international intervention against the Bolsheviks (Communists), particularly by the British and the French, but also by a range of powers, including the USA and Japan. Nevertheless, the war was won by the Bolsheviks. They benefited greatly from the divisions among their opponents and from the unpopularity of the 'White' or anti-Bolshevik cause with the peasantry, which saw scant reason to welcome counter-revolution. The Bolsheviks held Moscow and St Petersburg and, with them, the central position and the industrial centres and communication nodes, and the White generals failed to coordinate their attacks on them.

The Russian Civil War also entailed efforts by the Bolshevik government to regain control by force of regions where non-Russian ethnic groups had sought to win independence. Russian control was reimposed in the Caucasus, central Asia, and the Ukraine, but not in the Baltic states (Estonia, Latvia, Lithuania), nor in Poland. The Russo-Polish war demonstrated the characteristics of the warfare of the period. It was very mobile. This type of warfare was to be as common as the fronts and fixed sides that tend to dominate modern conceptions of twentieth-century warfare. In many cases in the conflicts after the First World War, the fluidity extended to political alignments.

The peace settlements that followed the war saw the European empires reach their territorial highpoint. Japan gained as mandated territories some of the German islands in the Pacific, but much of the Ottoman empire was allocated to Britain or France, albeit officially also as mandated territories; this meant that Japanese or European rule in these lands was answerable to the League of Nations, a permanent body for international arbitration set up in order to prevent wars. This distribution of territory reflected the determination of the victorious imperial powers to retain control of the colonial world, and it was intended as a closing stage to the process of territorial allocation that had reached a highpoint in the decades on either side of 1900. The German territories in Africa were also granted as mandates: to Britain, France, South Africa and Belgium.

In practice, it proved far harder than imagined to control the global situation. A conflation of already established anti-Western feeling with the spread of a new impulse of reaction against imperial authority affected large portions of the colonial world in the 1920s. This was particularly intense in the Muslim world. Opposition had varied causes and consequences, but it included hostility to British hegemony in Iraq, Egypt and Persia (Iran), a rising against French rule in Syria, the continuation of resistance in Libya to the rule Italy had sought to impose since 1911, an upsurge from 1921 in action against Spanish attempts to dominate the part of Morocco allocated to it (an opposition that spread into French Morocco), and the Turkish refusal to accept a peace settlement that included Greek rule over the Aegean coast and European troops in Constantinople.

Opposition, however, was not restricted to the Muslim world, nor did it begin only after the war. Indeed, there was a continuation of resistance to European imperialism that had begun in response to the original attempts to extend European control. This could be seen with the 1915–16 Volta–Bani War in modern Burkina Faso, then part of French West Africa; this was the largest military challenge the French faced in the region since they had first conquered it. Although lacking comparable firepower, with consequences seen in battles like Boho (1916), the rebels sought to develop tactics in order to weaken the French columns, to reduce support for the French, and to limit the impact of their firepower. The French themselves employed 'anti-societal' warfare, targeting their opponents' farms, herds, wells and families in order to destroy the human environment among which they operated. Once the rebels' centres had been subjugated, organised opposition ceased.

Britain, France, Spain, the Dutch, and Greece all sought to maintain their imperial position in the face of challenge after the First World War, and were willing to use considerable force to do so. The French shelled and bombed Damascus in 1926, while the British used the air power they had developed in the First World War to strike at opponents in Afghanistan, Iraq, South Yemen, and British Somaliland. Air attack was seen as a rapid response combining firepower and mobility; it did not entail the deployment of large forces.

In northern Morocco, the Spaniards responded to ferocious resistance in 1921–7 by using large quantities of mustard gas, dropped by air on civilians and fighters alike. Albeit after considerable difficulties, and largely due to French intervention, opposition to the Spaniards was brutally suppressed in 1925–7. So also was the anti-French rising in Syria, and that against the Dutch in Java. However, the Turks under Kemal Ataturk were able to impose their will after defeating the Greeks in 1922 and facing down the British the same year.

Britain, the world's leading imperial power, decided that it had exceeded its grasp. Commitments in Russia, Iraq, Persia, Egypt, Turkey, and over most of Ireland were all abandoned, and the British prepared for more self-government in India. This abandonment of aspirations and positions marked the start of the ebb of empire. As with many other important shifts in global power, this was a recognition of military capability, both absolute and relative, that did not essentially arise from the results of conflict, but that was as important as any war.

Ireland in 1921 provided an instructive example of the difficulty of suppressing a revolutionary movement. The Irish Republican Army (IRA) organised its active service units into flying columns that staged raids and ambushes in order to undermine the stability of British government. Assassinations and sabotage were also employed. The IRA was short of arms (many of which were gained by raids on the British) and was outnumbered by the army and the police, but it was able to take the initiative and to benefit from the limited options available to those trying to restore control. British reprisals against civilians sapped support for British rule within Ireland. After the Anglo-Irish treaty of December 1921, the IRA divided, leading to a civil war in the new Irish Free State that was won by the pro-treaty forces.

Emphasis on the weaknesses of imperial power in the interwar period serves as a valuable corrective to any focus on military developments within Europe. So also does a consideration of the scale of conflict in China in the 1920s and 1930s. As commander of the Guomindang (Chinese Nationalist) forces, Jiang Jieshi (Chiang Kai-shek), who had been trained in the Soviet Union, commanded the Northern Expedition: this was a drive north from Guangzhou (Canton) against independent Chinese warlords that began in 1926, and that benefited from Soviet military advisers, money and equipment. Jiang reached the Yangzi that year, defeating Wu Peifu in Hunan and Sun Chuanfang in Jiangxi. In 1927, he captured Nanjing and Shanghai, and defeated the Manchurian warlord, Zhang Zuolin. Jiang's forces occupied Beijing in 1928, agreed terms in Manchuria, and defeated two powerful warlords, Yan Xishan of Shanxi and Feng Yuxiang of Shaanxi, in 1929–30. However, this success depended on the cooperation of other warlords. Excluding Manchuria, most of China was now under the Guomindang. Japanese interventions against the Northern Expedition in 1927 and 1928, the two Shantung interventions, had failed to prevent this consolidation.

Like the Russian Civil War, warfare in China in this period indicated that mobility had not been lost due to increases in firepower. Purchasing modern weapons from Europe, especially France and Italy, the warlords had plenty of artillery and other arms, including aircraft, plus large armies: that of Wu Peifu was 170,000 strong in 1924, while, in 1928, Zhang Zuolin and his allies deployed 400,000 men against the Nationalists' 700,000. Combat was supplemented by negotiations, and the latter, especially defections by generals, played a major role in ensuring success. Thus it was necessary to create an impression of victory in order to win. The Soviet Union intervened militarily in 1929, sending forces into Manchuria in order to advance its own interests. The better-trained Soviets used modern artillery, tanks and, in particular, aeroplanes, and defeated Zhang Zuolin's son and successor, Zhang Xueliang, inflicting heavy casualties.

The role of the warlords, several of whom commanded powerful forces, is a reminder of the folly of considering modern warfare in terms of regular forces and states. Instead, the fissiparous tendencies seen in countries such as Lebanon and Angola towards the close of the twentieth century were also present earlier and helped to provoke civil conflict. The Chinese warlords were an echo of long-standing regionalism, especially tensions between north and south, as well as of developments before the Republican uprising of 1911–12 when regional units had gained greater autonomy. Tension with warlords continued: in 1936 the government suppressed those in the south-west.

China also witnessed the ideological conflict that was so important to the nature of war during the century. In 1927, the Communists formed the Red Army. Initially, it suffered from a policy of trying to capture and hold towns, which only provided the Nationalists with easy targets. In 1927, the Communists were swiftly driven out of the port of Shantou after they captured it, and were defeated when they attacked the city of Changsha. They captured the latter in 1930, only to be rapidly driven from it with heavy losses. The Red Army was more successful in resisting attack in rural areas. There it could trade space for time and harry its slower-moving opponent, especially as the Nationalists lacked peasant support. This led to the failure of Jiang Jieshi's 'bandit extermination campaigns', launched in December 1930, February and July 1931, and March 1933, to destroy the Communist control of much of Jiangxi province. These were major operations: in the fourth campaign, Jiang deployed 250,000 men. In 1933, he was persuaded to modify his strategy by German military advisers provided by Hitler. In place of the frontal attacks, which had proved so costly in the spring, there was a reliance on blockade in the fifth campaign, which began in October 1933. The Communists tried and failed to thwart this strategy by conventional warfare and, instead, in October 1934, decided to abandon Jiangxi in the famous Long March to Shaanxi in the north of China.

British imperial difficulties continued into the 1930s, not least with the Arab war in Palestine in 1936–8. Yet the British were able to deploy substantial forces, both there and in order to suppress opposition in Waziristan on the North-West Frontier of the British empire of India. The severe economic depression of the decade did not lead to the breakdown of imperial rule, although it did exacerbate strains, helping for example to cause a rebellion in the Irrawaddy delta region of Burma, based on a politico-religious rejection of British rule.

Signs of imperial vitality included the building of a major naval base at Singapore designed to provide a support for British power and influence in east Asian waters, and specifically to provide a check on Japanese naval strength. Far from empire being dead, the demands of imperial protection and policing helped determine the military tasking of the imperial powers and, therefore, their planning and force structures. Partly for that reason, subsequent criticism that not enough was done to prepare for a major war with another Western power is somewhat misplaced. In the 1920s, there appeared scant likelihood of this, and the major danger to Britain seemed the improbable one of the Soviets advancing through Afghanistan against India. In the early 1930s, the leading power that was most aggressive, Japan in Manchuria, was one that could only be influenced by Britain by naval pressure. In contrast, the British army took little role in planning for confrontation with Japan. It was not until the rise of Nazi Germany from the mid-1930s that the situation changed and the British focused on the possibility of another war in Europe.

The same was true of the USA. Having fought in the First World War, and intervened unsuccessfully in the Russian Civil War, the Americans deployed their power in the 1920s and early 1930s in order to further their interests in Central America and the West Indies. Neither task required the development of tank forces, nor did concern about Japan and, in particular, its potential challenge to the American position in the Philippines (seized from Spain in 1898). This was seen as best protected by naval strength, although air power played a part both in plans for the defence of the Philippines and in operations in the western hemisphere. The marines sent to support American interests in Nicaragua in 1928–33, in a struggle with rebels using guerrilla tactics, benefited from close air support, although it proved impossible to defeat the rebels.

Debate over the best force structure for armies was matched by concern about how best to develop and use naval and air power. Such debates were not new, but the range of options had increased with modern weapons. It was unclear how far air power had changed the situation at sea and, more specifically, whether it had made the battleship obsolete (as the Second World War was to suggest). In the interwar period, the USA and Japan made the greatest advances with naval aviation and aircraft carriers; more so than Britain, Italy, France or Germany, in all of which the stress remained on battleships. Improvements in aircraft, as well as more specific developments in carrier aviation, such as arrester hooks for landings, helped ensure that carriers, rather than seaplanes or airships, were seen as the way to apply air power at sea, and made it easier to envisage using carriers as the basis for operational and strategic tasks. In the 1920s, water-cooled aircraft engines were replaced by the lighter and more reliable air-cooled engine. The manoeuvrability, speed and range of carrier aircraft all improved. In 1927, the American fleet exercises included a carrier attack on Pearl Harbor, its own main Pacific Fleet base. The Japanese, meanwhile, had completed an experimental carrier in 1922. They established a separate aviation bureau; in the 1930s, their aircraft industry produced very effective planes.

Nevertheless, battleships remained central to American and Japanese naval thinking. This left the proponents of other weaponry having to explain how their recommendations, such as carriers and submarines, would effectively combine with battleships. Big battleships continued to be built, laid down and projected, including by Japan and the USA. Under the Marusan Programme of 1937, the Japanese began to build the *Yamato* and *Musashi*, which were to be the most powerful battleships in the world. In the USA, keels were laid for four comparable 45,000-ton battleships in 1941, and seven were projected at over 60,000 tons each.

The use of submarines also excited considerable interest among naval planners in the interwar period, and there were major developments in the range of torpedoes. The size, speed and range of submarines improved. For example, the American S class of 1918–21, with a range of 5,000–8,000 miles at a surface speed of 10 knots, was replaced by the B class (12,000 miles at 11 knots), and then by the P-boats of 1933–6, the first American submarines with a totally diesel-electric propulsion; followed by the Gato class introduced in 1940: double-hulled, all-welded-hull submarines with a range of 11,800 miles and a surface speed of 20–5 knots. By the time of the Japanese attack on Pearl Harbor in 1941, the American navy had 111 submarines in commission, while the Japanese had 63 ocean-going submarines.

Advocates for air power on land claimed that it had dramatically changed the nature of war and that bombers could be employed not merely to influence the flow of battle and campaign, but also, as a strategic arm, to attack enemy industry, and to sway an opponent's domestic opinion by bombing its cities. These arguments were pushed hard by those, particularly in Britain, who supported a separate service organisation for air power. This emphasis led to a downplaying of close air support as a goal. In the USA, the stress was on strategic bombers, and this led to confidence, even complacency, that deploying B-17s in the Philippines would give a vital advantage in the event of war with Japan in the western Pacific.

Such debates were pushed to the fore from the mid-1930s. The catalyst was the rise of Adolf Hitler to power in Germany (1933), and his proclaimed determination (in 1935) to ensure a wholesale overthrow of the peace settlement at the close of the First World War. This led to fears of a coming major war, that were accentuated by the aggressive policies and bellicosity of Japan, as well as of Fascist Italy under Benito Mussolini. These powers expanded their armed forces, although in different ways. Despite sharing the Nazi language of progress and strength through mechanisation, the Italians lacked the industrial base to make comparable progress, while their conquest of first Libya and then Ethiopia led to a stress on an appropriate force structure for these tasks that did not match the requirements of conflict between European states.

The Germans made much of their commitment to mechanisation and created the first three Panzer (armoured) divisions in 1935. These were designed to give effect to the doctrine of armoured warfare that was developed in Germany, in particular by Heinz Guderian. Initially drawing heavily on Britain's use of tanks in the First World War, and on subsequent British thought, the Germans developed their own distinctive ideas in the late 1930s. The Germans planned to use tanks in mass in order to achieve a deep breakthrough, rather than employing them, as the French did, as a form of mobile artillery in support of infantry. The Panzer divisions were to seize the initiative, to move swiftly, and to be made more effective by being combined arms units incorporating artillery and infantry. Indeed, tanks were to be the cutting-edge of their successful 'lightning strike' blitzkrieg operations in 1939–40.

In practice, however, the German army did not match the claims made for it by propagandists, and was less of a war 'machine' than they suggested. The mechanisation of its infantry was limited and its logistics were overly dependent on horse transport. Nevertheless, the German army was streets ahead of its Italian counterpart; this was to be revealed when the Italian army proved unable to match technology, command quality, and doctrine to its large numbers of troops, many of whom were captured by the British in successful invasions of Libya and Ethiopia in 1940–1.

The Soviet army had also developed an interest in mechanisation, but this was cruelly interrupted when Stalin, the paranoid Soviet leader, turned on his officer corps in 1937, following doubts over their loyalty. His purges led to a brutal wasting of talent that also stymied innovative thought. The consequences were seen in the very poor showing of the Red Army when it attacked the tiny state of Finland in 1939–40; although Soviet forces were more successful against the Japanese in border clashes at Zhanggufeng (1938) and Nomonhan (1939).

Response to these new possibilities, specifically the build-up of new military forces, was not restricted to the major industrial powers. It could also be seen in independent states elsewhere, although the nature of the resulting forces varied, as indeed did the challenges they met. In Persia in 1921, Riza Khan, a Russian-trained colonel in the Persian Cossack Brigade, suppressed internal rebellions and seized power. He created a new and disciplined national army, 40,000 men strong, the loyalty of which he gained by better equipment, regular pay and success, and used it to crush opposition. Campaigns in 1922–5 spread governmental power throughout Persia. Dissidence in Mashhad, Tabriz, Gilan and Kurdistan was crushed. Khuzistan in the south-west was occupied in 1924. The disunited tribes had been defeated and Riza Khan was crowned Shah in 1926. Thereafter, the position of the tribes was further weakened by disarming them and forcibly introducing taxation and conscription, so that tribesmen could be used against other tribesmen. With these advantages, major tribal rebellions were crushed in 1929 and 1932. The tribesmen suffered heavily from the improved mobility of their opponents. Armoured cars and lorries operated on new roads and were supported by the automatic weapons and observation planes of government forces.

Inside neighbouring Iraq, army expansion was supported by nationalists as a way to integrate the new state. In 1933, the tribes had about 100,000 rifles, the army only 15,000, but conscription was introduced in 1934, and the army was able to break the military power of its disunited opponents. In 1933, the Assyrians (Nestorian Christians) were defeated, and in 1935 tribal uprisings were suppressed.

In the late 1930s, the Afghan air force used British-supplied light bombers to help ground forces suppress rebellions. In Ethiopia, a tank was employed to help thwart a coup in 1928 while, the following year, bombing runs with a triplane flown by a Frenchman over a terrified rebel army helped to cause it to flee in disorder. In Saudi Arabia, Chevrolet trucks equipped with machine-guns were used to provide mobile firepower.

The Japanese showed in China that it was not necessary to introduce mass-mechanisation in order to conquer large tracts of territory. Japan was technologically behind the European powers in various aspects of military innovation, such as the use of tanks. This led in Japan to a greater stress on 'spirit' over material, for example with an emphasis on the use of bayonets and swords in attack. The Japanese army developed Manchukuo (Manchuria), which it seized in a five-month campaign in 1931–2, as a military and industrial base effectively outside civilian control; it then used this territory to support expansionism in China and to strengthen Japan in the event of war with the Soviet Union, a possibility greatly feared (and anticipated) in Japanese army circles. The greater understanding outside the West (compared to previous centuries) of the need for industrial capacity as a basis for war-making, led to the Japanese development of coal- and iron-based heavy industry in Manchuria, which served as the basis of a powerful military-industrial complex (ironically much of this was to be seized by Soviet forces at the time of Japan's surrender in 1945).

Helped by this, as well as by the absence of hostile foreign intervention, and the lack of other conflicts to absorb their attention, the Japanese made further advances in China. Rehe (Jehol) was overrun in 1935, and in 1937 the Japanese launched what became an all-out war of conquest, although it was formally termed an incident, and had begun as an unexpected clash at the Marco Polo Bridge near Beijing when Japanese night manoeuvres were fired upon. Unlike in 1931, the Nanjing government responded to subsequent Japanese moves, ensuring that full-scale war broke out. Beijing, Shanghai and then Nanjing were captured that year, Canton and, against sustained resistance, Wuhan in 1938, and the island of Hainan in 1939.

However, despite expanding their army from 408,000 troops in 1937 to 2.08 million in 1941, and stationing over 1.5 million of these troops in China and Manchuria, the Japanese lacked the manpower to seize all of China and, even within occupied areas, their control outside the cities was limited. Japanese military leaders were surprised by their failure to impose victory. It was far easier to destroy the Chinese navy in 1937 and to deploy overwhelming force against cities, the nodes of the transportation system, than it was to fight in rural areas. There, the ratio of strength and space told against the Japanese, particularly when their opponents, most notably the Communists, employed guerrilla tactics and hit Japanese communications.

As with European expansion in Asia and Africa in the sixteenth, seventeenth and eighteenth centuries, it was easier for Japan to develop island bases in the Pacific, such as Truk, Kwajalevin and Saipan, and to hold coastal positions in China, than it was to conquer a large area of mainland. The Japanese also failed to incorporate local élites into their imperial system on any large scale. Japanese conquests in China indicated a lesson that Hitler would have done well to consider before attacking the Soviet Union in 1941: that such high-visibility gains did not necessarily lead to overall victory.

Japanese policies, such as the 'kill all, loot all, burn all' campaign launched in China in 1941, also showed that brutality did not work, a lesson that their racialism prevented both Japan and Nazi Germany from learning. Earlier, the massacre by Japanese forces of large numbers of civilians after the capture of Nanjing, including, for example, using people for bayonet practice, did not break Chinese morale and, instead, testified to an emerging immoral and callous attitude within the Japanese military. Operations in China continued during the Second World War, with Changsha falling to the Japanese in 1944 in Operation Ichigo: this was designed to overrun airfields near Guilin used by American planes in their bombing of Japan.

The Second World War began with a series of swift German successes against Poland in 1939, Denmark, Norway, the Netherlands, Belgium and France in 1940, and Yugoslavia and Greece in early 1941. These led Hitler to a conviction of his own ineluctable success, and that of the Wehrmacht under his leadership. In practice, German war-making was actively helped by poor strategic and operational choices by his opponents. A failure by their opponents to retain sufficient reserves, seen in both the Polish and the French campaigns, ensured that the Germans were able to retain the initiative they gained by first launching the attack. The extended perimeter of opposing forces in Poland in 1939, France and the Low Countries in 1940, and Yugoslavia in 1941 also gave the Germans major advantages. So did their ability to win and use air superiority, to retain the tempo of armoured advances, both of which disoriented their opponents and sapped their will to fight, and to operate in terrain their opponents considered impassable or very difficult, which they did to decisive effect in the Ardennes in 1940 and in the Balkans the following year. However, the campaigns also revealed difficulties with German operations. There were serious problems with moving the infantry and supplies forward with sufficient speed.

When Hitler attacked the Soviet Union in 1941, these problems were to be compounded by the vastness of the territory that had to be conquered if he was to achieve his goals (he did not want only a triumph near the frontiers), as well as by the availability of massive Soviet reserves. Lulled by over-confidence in the value of a swift offensive, the Germans had not planned or prepared adequately for the conflict. Soviet doctrine, with its emphasis on defence in depth and its stress on artillery, proved effective once the initial shock and surprise of the German attack had been absorbed, although the Red Army suffered heavy defeats at the outset and, in initial counter-attacks, lost large quantities of men, tanks and aircraft. More generally, the war showed that employing tanks to try to revolutionise conflict was of limited value in the face of 'counter-tank' practices, such as the use of anti-tank weapons and the employment of tanks in mobile defence.

In the Soviet Union in 1941, the need to advance on a broad front slowed the impetus of the German attack. The Red Army was able to hold the assault on Moscow when the Germans resumed it after clearing their flanks. The Soviets also proved better at operating in the difficult winter conditions that followed the onset of winter.

Once their advances had been held in late 1941, and, again, in late 1942, the Germans suffered from the absence of sufficient manpower, artillery and supplies. They lacked strong operational reserves to cope with Soviet counter-attacks, and were badly hampered by Hitler's maladroit interventions, although the same was also true of Stalin's role. Nevertheless, the Soviet ability to mount a counter-attack in late 1941 indicated the continued resilience of their centralised and authoritarian governmental system, and its ability to mobilise resources.

Stabilising, let alone advancing, the front proved an enormous strain on German resources. The 1942 offensive – Operation 'Blue' – was jeopardised by a poorly conceived and executed plan. In this, the Germans planned the seizure of the Caucasian oil fields in order better to prepare for the lengthy struggle that American entry into the war appeared to make inevitable. However, they underestimated Soviet strength, and failed to make sufficient logistical preparations. Furthermore, there were serious flaws in the development of the operation, specifically in the decision to attack simultaneously towards the Volga as well as the Caucasus. Hitler's conviction that Stalingrad, on the Volga, had to be captured, foolishly substituted a political goal for operational flexibility. At Stalingrad in late 1942, the attacking Germans were fought to a standstill despite a massive commitment of resources. When the Soviets counter-attacked, Hitler again failed to respond with the necessary flexibility and forbade a retreat from Stalingrad by the Sixth Army before it was encircled.

The dismal outcome of Operation 'Blue' was an important stage in the war, although it had been the German failure before Moscow in December 1941 that had been the real turning point in the war in the east. More generally, Stalingrad was not the decisive moment in the war, if that implies that the Germans could have won up to then: the viability of Hitler's plan to attack in the east in order to destroy the Soviet Union is unclear, while the German decision to declare war on the USA on 11 December 1941 had dramatically changed the situation.

After Stalingrad, the Second World War reverted to a prolonged struggle of attrition, although there was usually much more obvious movement than in the First World War. The Germans proved formidable foes on the defensive, and succeeded in stabilising the front after the loss of Stalingrad, in part thanks to Field Marshal Manstein's skilled employment of counter-attacks. However, the Germans were outnumbered and outfought thereafter, and their attempt to regain the initiative with the Kursk offensive of 1943 was defeated.

The Soviet Red Army proved increasingly successful in attack, adept at developing cooperation between armour, artillery and infantry, and at making the latter two mobile. It achieved what has been seen as its own blitzkrieg. This was especially so in the breakthrough attacks in March and April 1944, which drove the Germans back across the Bug, Dniester and Pruth, and those in June–September 1944, which overran Belorussia (White Russia) and took the Soviets close to Warsaw, in the process destroying much of the German Army Group Centre and causing over a half a million casualties. The Germans were outgeneralled and outfought, although the Soviets suffered from the extent to which so much of their industrial base had been overrun by the Germans in 1941.

In less than two and a half years' fighting, the Red Army drove the Germans from the Volga to the Elbe, a distance greater than that achieved by any European force for over a century, and one that showed that a war of fronts did not preclude one of a frequent movement of those fronts. This was not simply an advance on one axis but one across much of Eastern Europe. Soviet operational art towards the end of the war stressed firepower, but also employed mobile tank warfare: attrition and manoeuvre were combined in a coordinated sequence of attacks. Once broken through, mobility allowed the Soviets to prevent their opponents from falling back in order. They also used deception measures effectively.

Although the Red Army absorbed the bulk of the German forces, the latter also fought the Western Allies, principally Britain and (from December 1941) the USA. The Americans mobilised their resources far more speedily and extensively than they had done in the First World War. By 1943–4, the USA was producing about 40 per cent of the world's total output of munitions, thanks, in part, to an increase in the country's overall productive capacity by about 50 per cent between 1939 and 1944. Furthermore, unlike with Russia in 1917, the Germans were unable to benefit from knocking out a major opponent militarily, while, in addition, in the Second World War they were unable to use political pressure and approaches in order to limit the number of fronts on which they had to fight.

The Germans and Italians were defeated in North Africa in 1942–3, fatally weakening Italy, and Italy was invaded by Anglo-American forces in September 1943. Amphibious power and air support allowed the Allies to seize the initiative, but a rapid German response gave them control of central and northern Italy, and a series of hard-fought offensives were required to surmount successive defensive lines. However, the German units sent to Italy were obviously not available to fight the Soviets nor to resist the Allies in France.

On 6 June 1944, Anglo-American forces landed in Normandy and the Germans were outfought over the following three months. The Allied breakout was followed by a deep exploitation, much of it by American mechanised forces, that drove the Germans out of France and Belgium. After being held near the German frontier that winter, and put under considerable pressure by a German counter-attack in the battle of the Bulge, the Allies resumed the advance. They fought their way to, and across, the Rhine and joined the Red Army in forcing unconditional surrender on the Germans, a war goal announced at the Casablanca summit conference in January 1943.

The Germans had also been battered by an air offensive of hitherto unprecedented fury. Ground-support operations were very important to the advancing Allied armies, particularly to Anglo-American forces, for example in Normandy in 1944. Strategic bombing also had an impact, not least by leading the Germans to devote resources, particularly of aircraft, to resisting it. It was particularly difficult for the Germans to replace pilots, as they had failed to increase their training programmes.

Despite the limited precision of high-flying planes dropping free-fall bombs, such bombardment disrupted German (and Italian) industrial production and communications. For example, the impact of bombing delayed the construction of a new faster class of German submarine so that this did not become operational until too late to challenge Allied command of the sea. In addition, strategic bombing seemed a necessary demonstration of Anglo-American commitment and resolve, and thus an important contribution to keeping the Soviet Union in the war, in the absence of the Second Front invasion of France that Stalin pressed for, and which the Western Allies were not ready to mount until June 1944.

However, the impact, and morality, of bombing civilians have been more controversial. The destruction of much of Dresden in February 1945, with 130,000 civilian casualties, is a cause of particular anger. At the time, though, when contemporaries could vividly recall the terror of German bombing attacks, for example on Warsaw in 1939, Rotterdam and London in 1940, and Belgrade (with 17,000 people killed) in 1941, and of German unpiloted missile attacks on London in 1944–5, there was less concern about the ethos of the policy. The extent to which bombing affected German morale is unclear.

At sea, as in the First World War, the Germans were more effective in submarine than surface warfare. Surface ships made some damaging attacks on Allied merchant shipping in pursuit of a strategy of disrupting the British commercial system and diverting British warships from home waters. This culminated with the dispatch of the battleship *Bismarck* into the Atlantic in May 1941. However, the *Bismarck* was soon shadowed by British warships with modern radar equipment. Having sunk the *Hood*, the largest warship in the world, on 24 May south-west of Iceland, the *Bismarck* faced a massive deployment of British warships, including five battleships, two battle cruisers, thirteen other cruisers, and two aircraft carriers. Disabled after a hit on the rudder by an aircraft-launched torpedo on 26 May, the *Bismarck* was sunk by torpedoes from the cruiser *Dorsetshire* after she had been pummelled by battleship fire. German auxiliary cruisers inflicted important damage to Allied merchant shipping, but the last was sunk in October 1943.

Once France had been conquered in 1940, German submarines were better able to attack Allied shipping, especially in Atlantic waters, which, again, were a vital supply route for Britain. However, it was not until 1943 that the Germans devoted enough emphasis to submarine construction. As a result, they had insufficient submarines to achieve their objectives. The German submarines also lacked air support. Nevertheless, the development of 'wolf pack' tactics for attacks on convoys, and improvements in submarine specifications, particularly the 'snorkel', which allowed the underwater starting of diesel engines, increased their military effectiveness. The Allies, in turn, were helped by the rapid adoption of convoys, the extension of air cover, and the improvement of radar, as well as by their ability to intercept and decipher German naval codes. At the same time, it is salutary to be reminded that technology frequently did not operate as anticipated. Admiral Sir John Power of the

British navy complained in 1943, 'It was painfully obvious immediately that V/S [visual signal] and W/T [wireless telegraphy] communications within the squadron were quite hopeless. The EG frigates owned up that they never used anything but R/T [radio telephone], and, as the three destroyers could not use R/T, we had to start off at scratch teaching elementary signal procedure.'[1]

The building of far more merchant shipping from 1942, particularly by the Americans, was very important to Allied victory, as was the availability of more escort vessels and their improved armaments. The battle of the Atlantic was won by the Allies in the spring of 1943, although it continued to be a serious struggle until the end of the war. In May 1943, when forty-one submarines were lost, the Germans ordered a halt to attacks on convoys in the north Atlantic and the withdrawal of submarines to areas where there was less Allied air power. In the battle of the Atlantic there were heavy casualties on both sides; 28,000 of the 42,000 men who served in the German submarine service, a centre of Nazi fervour, were killed.

The Japanese had also been unable to sustain the early success won by their aggressive seizure of the initiative and initial skill. On 7 December 1941, they attacked the major American Pacific base at Pearl Harbor without any prior declaration of war. Thanks in part to total radar silence, they were undetected on their journey. Flying from six aircraft carriers, the 353 planes in the Japanese strike force found battleships, two of which they totally destroyed, rather than the aircraft carriers, which were not in harbour. The loss of these battleships, and damage to three others, forced an important shift in American naval planning away from an emphasis on capital ships and, instead, towards carriers.

The ability of the Japanese in the early stages of the war to mount successful attacks, to gain great swathes of territory, in the face of weak and poorly led opponents, and to establish an apparent stranglehold on the Far East, did not deter the Americans, as the Japanese had hoped, from the long-term effort of driving back and destroying their opponents. The American government and American public opinion were not interested in the idea of a compromise peace with the power that had attacked Pearl Harbor.

By the end of May 1942, the Japanese had overrun Hong Kong, Guam, the Philippines, the Dutch East Indies, Burma, Malaya, and Singapore: the last of these fell on 15 February, and was a terrible blow to British prestige in Asia. Japanese forces benefited from outfighting their opponents, from air superiority, from the operational flexibility of their plans, and from the combat quality and determination of their units. This was particularly seen in Malaya where the Japanese were outnumbered. The Dutch, British and American units in the region were weak, poorly prepared, and suffered from the vastness of the area they had to cover. There were also serious operational lapses, as in the failure to provide adequate air cover to the *Prince of Wales* and the *Repulse*, the two British capital ships sunk off Malaya on 10 December, and with the loss of most of the American planes in the Philippines on the ground two days earlier. In April 1942, a Japanese naval raid on Ceylon (Sri Lanka) led to heavy damage to shore installations and the sinking of British warships inadequately protected from dive-bombers.

However, the Japanese found it impossible to maintain their hold on success. Their move towards Port Moresby in New Guinea, which would have increased the threat of an attack on Australia, was postponed as a result of the battle of the Coral Sea on 4–8 May, the first battle entirely between carrier groups. The turning point was the American victory on 4 June 1942 over a Japanese fleet seeking both to capture Midway Island and defeat the Americans in a decisive battle. At Midway the sinking of four heavy Japanese carriers and the loss of many aircraft and pilots shifted the naval balance in the Pacific, as the initiative and the arithmetic of carrier power thereafter moved rapidly against the Japanese. They lost their offensive capacity, and that at a time when the Germans were still taking the initiative in Russia and North Africa. The rallying of much Indian opinion behind Britain, especially the increase of the Indian army to become a million strong in 1942, the largest volunteer army in history, helped ensure that the Japanese were held in south Asia. Having conquered Burma, they were unable to advance into India.

In geopolitical terms, the loss of Japanese offensive capability made thoughts of joint action with the Germans against the British in south-west Asia even more implausible. Germany and Japan were unable to create a military partnership, or obtain economic assistance that to any extent matched that of the Allies. Despite having large, long-range submarines, the Japanese also did not carry the war against America's lines of communications in the eastern Pacific.

The extent of Japanese conquests strained the capacity of their military to hold them, but in the Midway operation the Japanese had been hit by flawed preparation. This contrasted with the more effective repair effort that had returned damaged American aircraft carriers to service, and with the American ability to intercept and decipher Japanese radio messages. Aside from their losses, Japanese confidence was badly hit. Midway showed the power of carriers, but also their vulnerability. They were a first-strike weapon, and required a tactical doctrine similar to that later developed for nuclear confrontation. This vulnerability led to a continued stress on battleships and cruisers, both of which were also very important for shore bombardment in support of amphibious operations. Air power in the Pacific was seen as a preliminary to the latter, rather than a war-winning tool in its own right; this was to change, however, with the advent of the atom bomb.

In November 1942, American naval successes compromised the ability of the Japanese to support their forces on Guadalcanal, from which they were evacuated in February 1943: this was a breaching of the Japanese defensive perimeter that reflected the American ability to apply their strength. Heavy Japanese losses of aircraft and crew in the struggle over Guadalcanal helped the Americans to seize the initiative in 1943 as they began a process of island hopping in the Solomon Islands. Covering a landing on Bougainville in the Solomons in November 1943, a force of American cruisers and destroyers beat off an attack by a Japanese counterpart with losses to the latter in the first battle fought entirely by radar. Radar was also to help carriers defend themselves against air attack.

Carriers played a major role in the island hopping, and the ability to deploy them both in the south-west and central Pacific reflected the extent to which superior American resources permitted the simultaneous pursuit of more than one offensive strategy. During the war, the Americans deployed nearly 100 carriers of all sorts in the Pacific. As a result, air power could be applied from the sea as never before. The Japanese also continued building warships, but they could not match the Americans and were now particularly short of trained pilots. The vast extent of the Pacific created unprecedented problems of war-making and infrastructure. Substantial fleets had to operate over great distances and needed mobile support and maintenance. The scale of planning was substantial. In August 1943, the Combined Staff Planners outlined a schedule culminating in an invasion or siege of Japan in 1947.

Aside from carriers, the securing of airfields was also important to the American advance. In the central Pacific, the Americans opened up a new axis of advance, directed at the Philippines, and captured key atolls in the Gilbert Islands in November 1943. This was only after difficult assaults on well-prepared and highly motivated defenders, but it paved the way for successful operations against the Marshall Islands in January–April 1944.

Without air superiority, Japanese naval units were highly vulnerable. The Americans could decide where to attack and could neutralise bases, such as Rabaul, that they chose to leapfrog. This lessened the extent of hard, slogging conflict and helped the Americans maintain the pace of their advance. In June 1944, the American Task Force 58, with over 900 planes, covered an amphibious attack on the Marianas – Saipan, Tinian and Guam – leading to a struggle with the Japanese First Mobile Fleet and its 400 planes. Japanese attacks, launched on 19 June, were shot down by American fighters with no damage to the American carriers. The Japanese also lost two carriers to American submarines. The Americans were even more successful next day, sinking or damaging Japanese carriers with a long-range air attack in the failing light. Aside from providing a forward logistical base, the Marianas gave the Americans the opportunity to bomb Japan with B-29 heavy bombers. This battle led to the resignation of the Japanese cabinet on 18 July.

The Philippines were attacked that October, and the Japanese fleet comprehensively destroyed in the battle of Leyte Gulf. On land, the Japanese fought to the end, a sacrificial policy perhaps emerging out of the earlier stress on 'spirit' that matched the use of *kamikaze* (suicide) planes against American warships. Such attacks were a response to an organisational defect in the Japanese naval air arm that made an air group integral to its ship with no reserve air groups to replace the strike element of carrier task forces. It proved near impossible to train pilots fast enough to replace losses.

In Burma, the Japanese were outfought on the ground. The simplicity of their determined offensive tactics was no longer adequate against British and Commonwealth troops with improved training, and benefiting from high unit quality, plus superior logistics, air power and artillery. Having heavily defeated a Japanese invasion of north-eastern India in March–July 1944, the British invaded Burma that December.

In the Pacific, the Americans could choose where to land, but the fighting and logistical problems of operations on shore both remained formidable. Early in 1945, the Americans seized the islands of Iwo Jima and Okinawa in order to provide air bases for an attack on Japan. The overcoming of the well-positioned and determined Japanese forces was slow and involved heavy casualties. This led to fears about the casualties that an invasion of Japan would entail. Instead, the two deliverable atomic bombs were dropped by American aircraft on the Japanese cities of Hiroshima and Nagasaki in August 1945. Over 280,000 people died, either at once, or eventually, through radiation poisoning. The Japanese surrendered unconditionally: the atom bombs had exposed the inability of their armed forces to protect the nation, although the earlier firebombing of Japanese cities, the destruction of their merchant shipping, and the declaration of war on Japan in August 1945 by the Soviet Union all contributed to the surrender. The use of the bombs prevented not only the heavy cost to both sides of an invasion but also, probably, a resort by both sides, in that event, to chemical and biological weapons. The dropping of the atomic bombs followed a period of intensive area bombing of Japanese cities with devastating effects, particularly due to the use of incendiaries.

The Second World War was swiftly succeeded by the retreat from empire on the part of the European colonial powers and by a Cold War between the Soviet-led Communist bloc and their American-led counterpart. The two processes were intertwined, not least in the decolonisation struggles that helped to undermine support in the West for the maintenance of imperial power. This was particularly so for France. After bitter struggles in 1946–54 and 1954–62, the French abandoned Indochina and Algeria.

In some respects, the first prefigured America's later failure in Vietnam. The French forces had superior technology and held the urban centres, but were vulnerable to the guerrilla tactics of the Communist and nationalist Viet Minh. French reliance on the road system to link their positions led to a vulnerability that the Americans later were better able to avoid thanks to their vastly greater air transport capability. By the end of 1950, the French had been driven from most of their outposts, and this helped the Communist Chinese to supply munitions to their Viet Minh allies. However, in 1951, a more vigorous French command led to the outfighting of the Viet Minh when the latter attacked well-defended fortified bases where the French were able finally to employ their conventional forces and air power, which used napalm among other weapons.

The strategy of fortified bases failed, however, at Dien Bien Phu, as the Viet Minh, now equipped by the Chinese, were able to counteract France's modest air power and to overrun poorly chosen and outgunned positions. The French, who suffered from growing domestic criticism of the war, then withdrew. Their army had shown an ability to learn during the conflict, and had developed counter-insurgency tactics, but it could not respond adequately to the Viet Minh's dynamic synergy of guerrilla and conventional warfare, a synergy that reflected their organisational and doctrinal flexibility, and their successful logistics. The Americans provided massive quantities of military equipment to the French, but this could not sway the struggle.

The Cold War played a major role in the independence struggles in Portugal's African territories, which culminated in the colonies gaining independence in 1975. Communist countries had provided arms and training for the guerrilla movements. Having made a major military effort in south Asia in the Second World War, Britain had already granted India independence in 1947, and Burma in 1948, and most of the rest of her empire followed rapidly from the late 1950s, including Sudan in 1956, Malaya and Ghana in 1957, Nigeria in 1960, Cyprus and Kenya in 1963, and Zambia and Malta in 1964.

The Cold War also led to a build-up and enhancement of conventional forces, as well as a quest for nuclear superiority, as the atomic was followed by the hydrogen bomb, first exploded by the Americans in 1951 (the Soviets followed in 1953), and as land- and submarine-based intercontinental missiles, capable of delivering atomic warheads, were developed. These super-weapons helped keep the peace and limit war. Not using nuclear weapons was more important than using them, and this goal helped dictate military options in relations between the great powers.

In addition, there were open conflicts involving the forces of at least one of the major powers. In the Korean War (1950–3), an American-led United Nations (UN) coalition fought a Communist coalition, eventually ensuring a partition of Korea. The Americans were the largest contingent in the UN forces, and the British the second largest. The Chinese, who intervened in support of the North Koreans and against the UN forces from late 1950, proved better able to take advantage of the terrain and outmanoeuvred opponents who were more closely tied to road links, although, at the tactical level, Chinese human-wave frontal attacks fell victim to American firepower. At the same time, the Chinese had made a full transition to a conventional army with tanks, heavy artillery, and aircraft. As a result, the war in Korea did not prefigure the guerrilla conflict that was to be seen in Vietnam.

The Korean War followed on from the Chinese Civil War (1946–9), in which the Communists under Mao Zedong made the successful transfer from guerrilla warfare to large-scale conventional warfare. The Communists won the war despite the greater size (initially) of the Nationalist forces, their superiority in the air, and extensive American support for the Nationalist cause. When Japan suddenly surrendered in August 1945, the Communists had liberated much of the north, capturing Japanese weapons. Negotiations with the Nationalists broke down, as the Communists were determined to retain control of the north. In 1946, the Nationalists occupied the major cities in Manchuria, but most of the rest of the region was held by the Communists. The following year, Communist guerrilla tactics had an increasing impact in the north. In 1948, as the Communists switched to conventional, but mobile, operations, the Nationalist forces in Manchuria were isolated and then destroyed, and the Communists conquered most of central China. Much of the rest of China, including Beijing, Nanjing and Shanghai, was overrun the following year. Beijing fell in January at the close of a campaign in which about 890,000 Communist troops had successfully advanced out of Manchuria against an enemy force of about 600,000 Nationalist troops. In the same period, forces 600,000 strong on both sides fought over the route to Nanjing, a struggle won by the Communists, who crossed the Yangzi in April 1949. The rapid overrunning of much of southern China over the following six months testified not only to the potential speed of operations, but also to the impact of success in winning over support. In 1950, Tibet was conquered by the Communists.

Technology did not triumph in the Chinese Civil War: despite Soviet help, the Communists were inferior in weaponry and, in particular, lacked air and sea power, but their strategic conceptions, tactical skill, army morale and political leadership were all superior. The Nationalist cause was weakened by poor civilian and military leadership, severe economic problems and inept strategy, and, as the war went badly, by poor morale. The Nationalists were left only with Taiwan, where they were protected by American naval power and by the limited aerial and naval capability of their opponents.

The weakness of the Nationalist regime in China looked towards that of the government in South Vietnam that was faced, from 1959, by a Communist rebellion led by the Viet Cong and supported from the North. In the Vietnam War, which escalated from 1964, American-led support for South Vietnam was wrongly based on the assumption that unacceptable losses could be inflicted on the North Vietnamese in the same way that they could on the Americans: this was the standard Western assumption of a threshold of loss beyond which any society would withdraw its support for war.

In fact, as the Americans deployed far more troops in 1966 and inflicted heavy losses, the North Vietnamese only sent more men south. The Americans cracked first, after attrition had led to stalemate, and been replaced by unsuccessful American attempts to control the countryside; by contrast, their opponent's morale was sustained, despite heavy casualties in mass attacks on American strong points, particularly during the Tet offensive of 1968. Although they held on to the major urban areas, the Americans could not deny control of the countryside to their opponents. American units suffered from a lack of accurate intelligence and this helped to lead them into ambushes. General Vo Nguyen Giap, the North Vietnamese commander, was an effective leader, who developed logistical capability to give effect to his strategy of denying his opponents (first France and then the USA) control over territory and his maintenance of operational pressure. Giap was less successful when he turned to positional warfare and to mass attacks against opposing forces in reasonable positions, as in 1951 against the French, and in 1968 and 1972 against the South Vietnamese, but his military strategy and the political determination of the North Vietnamese government did not depend on continual success.

The jungle nature of the Vietnamese terrain limited the options for American airpower. This was applied for both strategic and tactical goals and, in the latter case, played an important role in helping army units under attack. Over half the $200 billion the USA spent on the war went on air operations, and nearly 8 million tons of bombs were dropped on Vietnam, Laos and Cambodia; South Vietnam became the most heavily bombed country in the history of warfare. There were also major American bombing offensives against North Vietnam, designed both to limit Northern support for the war in the South and to affect policy in the North. These attacks faced serious opposition from anti-aircraft fire as well as from aircraft.

As an indication of the difficulty of assessing military history, controversy continues over the extent to which a more determined (less restricted) and persistent air campaign would have ensured American support. The proponents of air power claim that had Operation Rolling Thunder (the bombing of the North) continued instead of ending in October 1968, it would have led the North to yield; but it had certainly not stopped the Tet offensive.

Air power also played a major role in the unsuccessful attempt to block Viet Cong supply routes, as well as the more successful endeavour to provide tactical and supply support for American troops on the ground. Tactical support led to the use of slow-flying gunships able to apply massive firepower. Helicopters were extensively used, not least in applying the doctrine of air mobility. Airlifted troops brought mobility and helped take the war to the enemy. As an example of the scale of conflict, the Americans flew about 36,125,000 helicopter sorties during the war, including 7,547,000 assault sorties, in which machine-guns and rockets were used, plus 3,932,000 attack sorties. Over 2,000 helicopters were lost to hostile causes (and many others to accidents), but heavier losses had been anticipated.

As the war became increasingly unpopular in America, the USA disengaged, finally leaving in 1973. This left South Vietnam vulnerable and, in 1975, it was overrun from the north in a conventional campaign in which the North Vietnamese made good use of tanks and ably integrated them with infantry and artillery. South Vietnamese forces in the Highlands were pushed back. The North Vietnamese then advanced on Saigon, and it was attacked from a number of directions, while the regime's morale and cohesion collapsed. The conventional offensive was more effective because it was supported by guerrilla forces.

The following decade, the Soviet Union was also involved in an unsuccessful counter-insurgency campaign, although there were important differences as well as similarities. The Soviets were able to overthrow the Afghan government in 1979, in part by the use of airborne troops. The new regime then 'invited' a permanent military presence. Thereafter, however, the Soviets found it impossible to crush guerrilla resistance and finally withdrew in 1989. The bellicose nature of its society, and the fragmented nature of its politics, made Afghanistan difficult to control, and the Soviets held little more than the major towns. The Soviet forces were poorly trained, their doctrine and tactics were those for war in Europe, and they had inadequate air support. Without that, the infantry was vulnerable. In addition, relations between the Soviet and Afghan armies were poor. As in Vietnam, 'hearts and mind' did not work. Driving the population off land that could not be controlled was the strategy followed from 1983, but this did not win support, and Soviet sweeps or operations, such as the relief of Khost in late 1987, were followed by a return to base that brought no permanent benefit. The Soviets were unable to force large-scale battle on their opponents. The guerrillas benefited from ample foreign support, including American ground-to-air Stinger missiles which brought down Soviet helicopter gunships. They also used the Soviet RP6-7 anti-tank grenade launcher, which proved effective against all Soviet vehicles. Technology was useful to the Soviets, particularly with aerial resupply, but it could not bring victory. Soviet air-assault forces were effective, but were not employed with sufficient frequency. The Russian General Staff Study of the war noted that it posed unfamiliar problems:

> combat was conducted throughout the country, since there were no clearly defined frontlines. . . . The war in Afghanistan gave the Soviet forces their first significant experience in the preparation and conduct of operations and combat against irregular guerrilla formations on mountain-desert terrain . . . the peculiarities of counter-guerrilla war and the rugged terrain determined the Soviet tactics in Afghanistan, where it was impossible to conduct classic offensive and defensive warfare. In Afghanistan, the principal forms of combat were the raid, block and sweep, ambush and those actions connected with convoy escort and convoy security.[2]

The Chinese were more successful when, in 1979, they attacked Vietnam, in part because their goals were far more limited. In this campaign they sent eventually about 120,000 troops to confront an equal number of Vietnamese. The Chinese captured three provincial capitals, but were knocked off balance by the Vietnamese decision to turn to guerrilla tactics. Affected by poor logistics, inadequate equipment and failures in command and control, the Chinese withdrew with maybe 63,000 casualties. Nevertheless, they had shown that they would not be deterred by Soviet–Vietnamese links, and their invasion testified to growing Soviet weakness.

The Cold War also saw intervention by the major powers in regional struggles, as well as a rush to arm and train allies and protégés. When Soviet-armed Somalia attacked Ethiopia in 1977 with weapons including MiG fighters and Ilyushin-28 bombers, the Soviet Union offered arms to Ethiopia if it abandoned its American alliance, which it did. By March 1978, 11,000 Cuban and 4,000 South Yemeni soldiers had arrived to help Ethiopia. The Cubans were necessary in order to man the tanks, armoured personnel carriers and artillery provided by the Soviets. More generally, the Cubans displayed a high level of competence in supporting indigenous armies in Africa. In Ethiopia, the Soviets also provided air reconnaissance, signal intercepts, and a commander, General Petrov. He ably adapted cutting-edge weaponry and operational systems devised for war in Europe to the exigencies of Africa, although he was helped by the nature of the terrain, much of which was relatively flat and lacking dense vegetation. Having gained air dominance and used it, in January 1978, to attack Somali supply routes, Petrov launched assaults spearheaded by tanks and rocket-launchers and supported by air attacks. Firm resistance near Jijiga led to the use of airborne attacks with parachutists assisted by helicopter troops. These enabled the attackers to overcome the tactical strengths of the Somali position and victory at Jijiga was followed by the reoccupation of the disputed Ogaden region. This campaign was one of the most impressive of the decade and showed how what the Americans termed 'AirLand Battle' could be waged and won.

Decolonisation led to a far greater number of independent states in Africa and Asia, and many of these became involved in conflict. Border disputes arising from the departure of colonial powers were responsible for many struggles, for example between India and Pakistan in 1947–8 and 1965, and, at a far smaller scale, Mali and Burkina Faso in 1995, as well as for China's successful attack on the Indian border in 1962, a limited operation in which prospects for exploitation were gravely limited by logistical factors.

Such border clashes were sometimes intertwined with insurrectionary movements. Libya intervened in Chad in the 1980s both in order to pursue a territorial claim to a northern strip of the country and in order to support protégés seeking to control the entire country. Overt Libyan military intervention in 1983 with about 6,000 men led to a military response by France and Zaire, who enjoyed the benefit of intelligence provided by American aerial surveillance. The Libyan advance was reliant on Soviet doctrine and training, but this was not going to be a conflict decided by armoured vehicles and related tactics. Instead, the Chad forces opposed to Libya benefited from light vehicles and a raiders' search for mobility, and used mortars and anti-tank rockets in order to inflict heavy casualties on the Libyans. These tactics were employed again in the 'Toyota War' of March 1987, with the Libyans losing over 3,000 troops as they were driven from much of the north of Chad. French aircraft were used against Libyan ground forces on a number of occasions. However, the French did not act at the close of 1990 when a new faction invaded Chad from Sudan and overthrew the government. Attempted coups, rebellions, and ethnic clashes continued there for years.

Foreign intervention could lead to the overthrow of governments, as with the Vietnamese conquest of Cambodia in 1978–9 and the Tanzanian overthrow of President Amin of Uganda in 1979. The latter campaign was typical of many in Africa. The fighting quality of the Ugandan army varied greatly, élite units mounting a resistance that most of the demoralised army was unwilling to do. Tactical mobility was crucial in clashes, helping ensure that light anti-tank weapons put paid to armoured personnel carriers which were largely road-bound. Libyan intervention on behalf of Amin could not sway the struggle.

More generally, the removal of the constraints of Western control or hegemony led states to pursue regional territorial and political interests, often using force to that end. Thus, India sent troops into Kashmir in 1947, overran the princely state of Hyderabad in 1948, occupied the Portuguese possessions of Diu and Goa in 1961, conquered East Pakistan in 1971, creating the state of Bangladesh, annexed Sikkim in 1975, sent 100,000 troops to help Sri Lanka against Tamil insurgents in 1987, and intimidated Nepal in 1995. Indian operations revealed the growing capability of

'Third World' military systems. In 1947, the Indians sent troops by air to Kashmir. In 1961, India used 71,000 troops to overrun Goa, which had a garrison of only 4,000 men, in one day. Although allied to Portugal in NATO, the Americans refused appeals for help. Some 160,000 Indian troops were sent into East Pakistan in 1971, while, at the same time, other Indian units fought Pakistani forces in West Pakistan. In 1984, the Indian army stormed the Golden Temple of Amritsar, the leading Sikh shrine, which had become a major terrorist base. In 1998, India carried out a nuclear test.

Other would-be regional powers also mounted attacks. Egypt sent up to 60,000 troops to help the republicans in the civil war in Yemen in 1962–70. Syria unsuccessfully invaded Jordan in 1970 in support of Palestinian guerrilla forces, while Turkey invaded Cyprus in 1974, partitioning the island. Iraq invaded Iran in 1980, launching a struggle that lasted until 1988 and that involved more combatants (probably over 2.5 million by 1988) than other conflicts of the period. The Iranians outnumbered the Iraqis, but international isolation made it difficult to keep their equipment maintained (always a major problem with foreign sources of supply), and the Iraqis benefited from assistance from most other Arab states as well as from powers fearful of Iran. The Iraqis used gas against Iranian attacks, and both sides employed missiles, targeting opposing capitals.

Another would-be regional power, Argentina, engaged in an arms race and naval confrontations with Chile, with which it had a territorial dispute, and in 1982 provoked war with Britain over an island group in the south Atlantic. The Falklands had been under British control from 1833, but were claimed, as the Malvinas, by the Argentinians, whose ruling military junta was convinced that the British government was uncertain of the desirability of holding on to the colony. On 2 April 1982, the virtually undefended islands were successfully invaded. In Britain, the Thatcher government decided to respond with an expeditionary force, dispatched on 5 April, that included most of the navy, and rejected American mediation attempts that would have left the Argentinians in control. The British lacked a large aircraft carrier, and therefore airborne early warning, but had two anti-submarine carriers equipped with Sea Harrier short take-off fighter-bombers. On 25 April, the British recaptured the subsidiary territory of South Georgia, and on 2 May large-scale hostilities began when a British nuclear-powered submarine sank the Argentine cruiser, *General Belgrano*. This was crucial to the struggle for command of the sea. Exocet missiles fired by Argentinian aircraft subsequently led to the loss of a number of British warships (showing that modern anti-aircraft missile systems were not necessarily a match for manned aircraft), but not the two carriers which provided vital air support (but not superiority) for both sea and land operations. The Argentinians on the Falklands outnumbered the British force and also had both aircraft and helicopters, while the British were short of ammunition because they had underestimated requirements. Landing on 21 May, British troops advanced on the capital, Port Stanley, fighting some bitter engagements on the nearby hills, and forcing the isolated, demoralised and beaten Argentinians to surrender on 14 June. American logistical and intelligence support aided the British, but, in the end, it was a matter of bravely executed attacks, the careful integration of infantry with artillery support, and the ability to continue without air control. In contrast, Britain peacefully handed Hong Kong to China in 1997 after a negotiated settlement.

In the Middle East, there was a series of wars between Israel and Arab neighbours (1948–9, 1956, 1967, 1973 and 1982). The Arabs proved unwilling to accept the culmination of the Zionist movement in the form of an independent Israel, and this ensured a high level of tension in the region. Israel was able to establish its independence in the face of poorly coordinated and badly prepared attacks by neighbouring Arab states in 1948–9. In 1956, Israel attacked Egypt in concert with Britain and France, overrunning the Sinai peninsula, but withdrew in the face of American and Soviet pressure. The weak resistance put up by the Egyptians reflected Israeli success in gaining the initiative, as well as the poorly trained nature of the Egyptian army and its inability effectively to use weapons it had received.

In 1967, rising regional tension led to a pre-emptive Israeli attack on Egypt, which began with the destruction of 298 planes, and, as the war spread, to the conquest not only of the Gaza Strip and Sinai from Egypt, but also of the West Bank section of Jordan and the Golan Heights in Syria. In Sinai, Soviet T54 and T55 tanks used by the Egyptians were beaten by American Patton and British Centurion tanks used by the Israelis who showed greater operational flexibility. Having broken through into the Egyptian rear, the Israelis ably exploited the situation, and they also benefited from the destruction of the Egyptian air force at the outset of the war. The war also indicated the role of field maintenance and repair in mobile warfare: the Israelis proved more effective than the Egyptians. More generally, overnight repair of equipment and its return to the battle line is a key element in the war-making ability of a modern army. Non-battle losses through mechanical failure are apt to be more costly than battle losses.

Israel remained in occupation of the regions conquered in 1967, ensuring that it now controlled a large Arab population. Over 600,000 Arab refugees were based in neighbouring Arab states, where they challenged the stability of Jordan, and helped overthrow that of an already divided Lebanon which moved into full-scale civil war from 1975. In the long term, the presence of a large Arab population within Israel and in Israeli-occupied territories was also to challenge the stability of Israel.

Meanwhile, in 1973, in the Yom Kippur War, Egypt and Syria failed, in a surprise attack, to drive Israel from its conquests. The Israelis were equipped with American M48 and M60 tanks, which had double the rate and range of fire of the Soviet T55 and T62 tanks, but Israeli aeroplanes and tanks proved vulnerable to ground-to-air and air-to-ground missiles. The Israelis, nevertheless, were able to drive the Syrians back and to advance across the Suez Canal, encircling Egyptian forces before a ceasefire ended the war. As in 1967, the failure of Arab armies demonstrated the vulnerability of forces with a lower rate of activity, the problems arising from losing the initiative, and the need for a flexible defence. In this war, there was large-scale use of

Despite launching a surprise attack on the Israelis, Egyptian success in the Yom Kippur War of 1973 was to be shortlived. The Israelis swiftly regained the initiative and displayed their superiority at manoeuvre warfare.

tanks: Egypt and Syria lost about 2,250 tanks, the Israelis 400. Tank attacks, such as the Syrian advance with 800 tanks through the Israeli lines, and one by Egypt on 14 October, in which the Egyptians lost about 250 tanks, were clashes for which there was planning but scant experience.

The 1973 war was mostly waged on land and in the air, but, at sea, both sides deployed missile boats, the Israelis sinking at least nine Egyptian and Syrian ships and driving their navies back to harbour. As with aircraft carriers, the emphasis was on an accurate first strike, but, compared to the Second World War, all ships now depended, at least in part, on the use of electronic countermeasures to block missile attacks.

The USA tried to ease regional pressures, which threatened the world economy because of the concentration there of oil production and reserves. It helped arrange a peace settlement between Egypt and Israel (1979). However, Israel's determination to act as a regional power and its concern about instability on its borders led, in Operation Litani, to its invasion of southern Lebanon in 1978 and the destruction of the Palestine Liberation Organisation's infrastructure before it retired; Syria already had occupied much of the country in 1976 in order to prevent the civil war between Christians and Palestinian refugees from producing an unwelcome result. In June 1982, the Israelis again invaded southern Lebanon, hitting the Syrians hard and, this time, advancing as far as Beirut, which they occupied in September. However, it proved impossible to 'stabilise' the local situation in Israel's interests.

More generally, conflict in Lebanon demonstrated the limitations of advanced weapons. In September 1983, the American Sixth Fleet bombarded Druze militia positions on the hills near Beirut in support of the Lebanese army, firing shells the size of small cars; yet, the following month, neither the Americans nor the French could prevent the destruction of their headquarters in Beirut by lorries full of high explosive driven by suicidal guerrillas. As a result of their losses, and of a more general sense of political impotence, the American marines sent to Lebanon in 1982 were withdrawn in 1984. Subsequently, the Israelis had to withdraw from the bulk of Lebanon (1985) and eventually to abandon the Security Zone established along the frontier with Israel: they faced a guerrilla force, the Hizbullah, willing to take casualties, enjoying foreign support, and able to respond tactically (for example with surface-to-air missiles) to such Israeli advantages as air power, while still maintaining pressure on Israel.

In 1987, the *Intifada*, a rebellion against Israeli rule in occupied Arab territories, began with stone-throwing crowds challenging Israeli authority. It was to underline the weakness of imposed political settlements in the Middle East where the bulk of any population felt alienated, and also to expose the limitation of regular troops in the face of popular resistance. The Israeli High Command found it very difficult to deal with what was to them a novel form of warfare. The Oslo Agreement of 1993 and the subsequent creation of a Palestinian autonomous territory under Yasser Arafat failed to prevent an increased escalation of conflict between Israel and Palestine from the late 1990s.

Aside from anti-imperialist movements and wars between states, there was also conflict as governments faced rebellions, many of which were separatist in origin. These occurred with increasing regularity after 1945. In 1946, the Shah led the Persian army into Tabriz, producing a bloodbath that cowed Azerbaijani separatism, while in 1959 the Chinese army defeated an uprising by Tibetans. Attempts by the Pakistani army, dominated by troops from the Punjab in West Pakistan, to suppress the Bengali nationalism of East Pakistan, provoked a rebellion in 1970. The Pakistani army was more successful in quelling a tribal uprising in Baluchistan in 1972–6 that arose from attempts to limit autonomy and tribal power. In Syria, the Alawite-dominated regime and army brutally crushed a rising by Sunni Muslims at Hama in 1982.

The Indonesian army suppressed Communist and Islamic opposition, including the Darul Islam (House of Islam) in west Java in the 1950s, as well as the Republic of the South Moluccas in 1952, and rebellion in Sumatra and Sulawesi in 1957–8. The latter was backed by CIA aircraft. The Indonesians also unsuccessfully sought to overthrow Brunei in 1962, by fomenting a rebellion, and to conquer north Borneo from British-supported Malaysia in 1963–5. They also annexed western New Guinea (as West Irian) in 1963, invaded East Timor in 1975, and brutally resisted demands for independence by the Fretilin movement in East Timor and the Free Papua Movement in Irian; only over time did international pressure eventually lead the Indonesians to leave East Timor in 1999.

In the Nigerian Civil War of 1967–70, the Nigerian government felt no hesitation in using starvation to help destroy the attempt by the Ibos to create an independent state of Biafra. The federal forces benefited from overwhelming numerical superiority and from the availability of British and Soviet weaponry. The Nigerian navy was crucial, both in imposing a debilitating blockade and in enabling the Nigerians to seize ports and coastal positions. Although there were some able commanders and some brave troops on both sides, operations and fighting in the war showed the problems of rapidly expanding armies with untrained men. The application of force proved difficult: air attacks were frequently ineffective and artillery was often poorly aimed. Infantry weaponry was more important in the fighting, while the Nigerian army also made good use of armoured personnel carriers. However, the role of ethnic and factional considerations weakened the army's fighting competence. Logistical support in the difficult terrain was not improved by chaotic command and organisational systems characterised by corruption.

This was the first major war in sub-Saharan Africa fought to a resolution with modern weapons, in which all the commanders were African. The Nigerian army subsequently came in the 1990s to play a regional role in peacekeeping in Liberia and Sierra Leone that reflected its own regional agenda. Poorly trained for the role, the Nigerians tended to use firepower as a substitute for policing, although, in both cases, the situation was very difficult: drug-taking adolescent fighters operating on behalf of factions had reduced both countries to a form of gangland chaos, and this made it difficult for regulars to identify opponents who could be defeated.

Many other rebellions were small-scale, for example the unsuccessful attempts in 1966 by the kingdom of Buganda to secede from Uganda, and the Shifta war of 1963–7, when Somalis in north-east Kenya unsuccessfully sought to break away to join Somalia. Such struggles, nevertheless, were important to the history of individual states and, in aggregate terms, made up much of the military history of the world.

International relations appeared to stabilise in the mid-1970s, with American–Soviet strategic arms limitation talks leading to agreements in 1974 and 1976, the West German Ostpolitik normalising relations with Communist countries, the end of the Vietnam War, the Helsinki treaty of 1975 recognising the position and interests of the Eastern bloc, and the Camp David summit of 1978 leading to an Egyptian–Israeli peace treaty the following year. Tension was to revive in the 1980s, with the Soviet invasion of Afghanistan and the deployment of new missiles by the USA and the Soviet Union, but the Soviets were affected by increasing economic problems that, in part, stemmed from high levels of military expenditure.

There was also a decline in the Soviet willingness to use force. Reformist Communist movements had been suppressed in Hungary in 1956 and Czechoslovakia in 1968. In each case, there had been a large-scale deployment of Soviet forces. The determined use of armour, backed up by air attacks and helicopters, crushed popular opposition in Hungary in 1956. Twelve years later, about 250,000 Soviet troops, supported by Bulgarian, Hungarian and Polish contingents, invaded Czechoslovakia. Heavily outnumbered, fearful of the consequences for domestic opinion, and without any prospect of Western support, the Czech government did not offer armed resistance, and the invasion was far less violent than that of 1956. Non-violent protest, such as demonstrating in front of tanks, did not, however, preserve Czech resistance.

In contrast, in 1981, it was decided in Moscow not to send Soviet forces to Poland to prevent a probable democratic takeover by the Solidarity movement. In the event, Solidarity was suppressed by the Polish army, but it is clear that a major cultural shift against the use of force had occurred among the Soviet leadership.

The end of the Cold War with the collapse, as a result of domestic pressures, of the Soviet Union (dissolved in 1991) did not lead to the 'end of history' foretold by some of the more superficial commentators who believed all too readily that it represented a triumph for American-led democratic capitalism, and that there would be no future clash of ideologies to destabilise the world. However, the Western powers, led by the USA, were now able to intervene more frequently against states that earlier would otherwise have looked for Soviet support. In February 1991, Iraq was driven from Kuwait (which it had invaded with overwhelming force the previous August) in a swift campaign in which the Iraqis were outgeneralled and outfought by American-led coalition forces that benefited not only from superior technology, but also from their ability to maintain a high-tempo offensive in executing a well-conceived plan that combined air and land forces. Allied fighting quality, unit cohesion, leadership and planning all played a major role in ensuring victory. The Iraqis had surrendered mobility and the initiative by entrenching themselves to protect their conquest of Kuwait. They were defeated with heavy casualties, including over 80,000 prisoners, while their opponents lost 44 men killed. Winning air superiority ensured that the Iraqis were short of supplies. In addition, their command and control system had been heavily disrupted, their morale was low, and they could not 'understand' the battle.

The doctrine of AirLand Battle, nevertheless, proved more difficult to execute in practice than to advance in theory, and to train for, not least because of the problems of synchronising air and land forces under fast-moving combat conditions. However, compared to earlier conflicts, target acquisition and accuracy were effective, even if some of the high-tech weaponry, such as the Patriot missile, did less well than was claimed at the time.

Although it was smaller-scale, and was to be overshadowed by the Gulf War, the Americans had already shown in December 1989, in Operation 'Just Cause', that airborne forces could play a major role in overthrowing the government of General Noriega in Panama. Overwhelming force brought rapid success with limited casualties.

The following years, however, indicated weaknesses in the military policies of the major powers. In 1992, the Americans sent troops to bring stability to Somalia, but, in October

1993, a Somali ambush of an American Ranger force, leading to the death of eighteen soldiers, was rapidly followed by the abandonment of aggressive operations by the American troops in Somalia. American intervention ensured that Somalia in the 1990s rated a mention in global military history, but this intervention was in fact tangential to a bitter and lengthy period of conflict. Following Somalia's failure in the Ogaden war with Ethiopia in 1977–8, a weaker President Barré had faced growing opposition from clans who, increasingly, obtained heavier arms. The Somali National Movement mounted a serious challenge from 1978, although, in 1988, the government was able to drive them from the northern towns they had seized, albeit causing heavy civilian casualties in the process. In 1989–90, other resistance movements further eroded Barré's position, and he fled into exile in January 1991, mounting unsuccessful attempts to return that April, as well as in April and September 1992.

Somalia was split into areas controlled by clan-factions, each of which deployed artillery and armoured vehicles, as well as the light lorries carrying heavy machine-guns which were a distinctive feature of Somali warfare, and several of which made use of child fighters. The United Nations intervened in 1992, in order to bring humanitarian relief, although also, if necessary, to disarm the factions. The UN forces were inadequate to the latter task, and the ambiguity of the mission helped to lead to chaos. The Americans were determined to remove Mohamed Aideed, whose faction dominated the capital Mogadishu. Having mishandled this, the Americans resorted to attacks from the air that killed many, mostly civilians, to no real benefit. The United Nations forces withdrew in March 1994. Faction fighting continued and the number of factions increased, as did civilian casualties.

Meanwhile, the Russians had encountered serious problems in the Caucasus, where Islamic independence movements were able to rely on considerable popular support, as well as on the mountainous terrain. The Russians responded by invading the rebellious region of Chechnya in December 1994, capturing the capital, Grozny, in 1995 after a lengthy siege in which they employed devastating firepower. Thereafter, success in crushing resistance proved elusive and in 1996 the Russians withdrew under a peace agreement. The 1994–6 campaigns revealed the deficiencies of the badly led, ill-equipped, undertrained, poorly motivated, and below-strength Russian forces. Not least among these deficiencies was Russian counter-insurgency warfare, although it is also necessary to emphasise large Chechen numbers. The renewed Russian attack in 1999–2000 led to the fall of Grozny, but revealed similar military deficiencies.

The British, meanwhile, had failed to suppress IRA terrorism in Northern Ireland, although they had contained the situation sufficiently to allow negotiations that produced a peace settlement in 1998. British troops had been deployed on local streets from 1969 in order to maintain control in the face of serious rioting, but IRA terrorism proved impossible to suppress. Given the difficulties of their task, the British army maintained a high level of professionalism, but that did not protect them from criticism from many who seemed less willing to condemn the deliberate terrorist policy of murder of civilians and military employed by the IRA. In 1972 alone, there were 1,853 bomb incidents, although, that year, the army also successfully regained control of 'no-go areas' of Londonderry and Belfast hitherto controlled by the IRA. This led the IRA to follow the course of terrorism, rather than that of waging guerrilla warfare. The British made heavy use of helicopters to supply fortified posts, as roads were vulnerable to mines, and used intelligence-gathering in order to strike at terrorists, but there was a limit to what could be achieved. At the same time, the terrorists were unable to drive the army out of Northern Ireland. Of all modern forms of warfare, that of insurgency and counter-insurgency seems most likely to lead to a war of attrition.

While the fall of the Soviet Union led to conflict in the Caucasus, the disintegration of Yugoslavia in 1991 had the same effect in the Balkans. In 1992, the Serbs tried to prevent Croatia from gaining independence, and this war spilled over into Bosnia. Western settlements were eventually imposed in Bosnia in 1995 and in Kosovo in 1999 at the expense of the expansionism and ethnic aggression of a Serbian regime that unsuccessfully looked for Russian sponsorship. The brutal slaughter of civilians by the Serbs (and, to a lesser extent, by their opponents) was an all-too-familiar feature of the conflict in much of the modern world, and reflected the extent to which ethnic groups were seen as the units of political strength and thus as targets. In 1995, the Bosnian Serbs murdered about 7,000 unarmed Muslim males in Srebrenica. The Serbs used the same tactics in Kosovo against its majority Albanian population. The Western response over Kosovo, a bombing and cruise-missile campaign by American, British and French forces, caused far less damage to the Serb military than was claimed, but did help lead to the Serb withdrawal.

In 2001, Russia lent diplomatic support to the American air offensive against the Taliban regime in Afghanistan. The fall of the regime was seen as a success for air power, which included B-52 and B-1 'stealth' bombers, Tomahawk cruise missiles, AC-130 gunships, unpiloted drones, and CBU-130 'Combined Effects Munitions' which spread cluster bombs. However, the Taliban ultimately had to be overcome on the ground by rival Afghan forces, particularly the so-called Northern Alliance. Furthermore, the lack of coherence of the Taliban regime and the porosity of alignments in Afghanistan were both important to the war's outcome. Warlords switched allegiance, and the Taliban position collapsed on 9–12 November, with the fall of Mazar-e Sharif, Herat and Kabul. American air power and Afghan ground attack combined to ensure the fall of more firmly defeated Kunduz on 26 November.

The example of Afghanistan underlines the extent to which debate over the effectiveness of strategic bombing has overshadowed the success of aircraft, including helicopters, gliders, and aircraft for transport and for parachutists, in other roles. These have included being an effective supplement to artillery; an operational tool for the isolation of battlefields, sometimes effective (Normandy 1944), and sometimes a failure (Korean War: Operation 'Strangle'); an element in manoeuvre, with long-range helicopters carrying American marines in 2001 to seize Kandahar airfield from an aircraft carrier base 450 miles away; and as a means of providing strategic lift, moving American troops and equipment from the USA to the Persian Gulf in days.

It is appropriate to close with Afghanistan as it serves as a reminder of the variety of military circumstances, force structures, taskings, and fighting methods across the world. Conflict there continues in 2002, as it also does for example in Kashmir, Sri Lanka, Chechnya, Palestine and Xinjiang, while 'cold wars' remain important, as between China and Taiwan, or North and South Korea. Despite the fascination of many observers with weaponry, it is the very varied uses to which it is put that is more notable. One prediction is safe: the bodies of the killed will mock claims that war has no future.

8

CONCLUSIONS

In 1922, the Chief of the General Staff of the British Forces in Iraq wrote, in a report on part of Mesopotamia: 'Aeroplanes by themselves are unable to compel the surrender or defeat of hostile tribes.' That view, like the approach of military historians, with their necessary emphasis on the past, may appear to have been made redundant by the march of technology. Certainly historians who warned about the difficulty of winning recent conflicts, especially those over Kosovo and Afghanistan, by the use of air power have been mocked. Yet, examined carefully, these conflicts suggest the need for caution before affirming technological triumphalism. In 1999, George Robertson, the British Secretary of State for Defence, publicly scorned historians who warned about the difficulty of winning the Kosovo conflict by air power alone, and also about the contrast between output (bomb and missile damage) and outcome. In fact, the subsequent Serbian withdrawal from Kosovo revealed that NATO estimates of the damage inflicted by air attack, for example to Serb tanks, had been considerably exaggerated. The Serb withdrawal appears to have owed much more to a conviction that a NATO land attack was imminent, as well as to the withdrawal of Russian support, than to the air offensive. These were not, however, totally separate. The threat to the Serbs on the ground from a NATO invasion made their forces vulnerable to air attack as it made dispersal, rather than concentration, a less viable proposition.

As another instance of the limited ability of technology alone to determine developments, in Afghanistan in 2001 the Taliban position was broken by the combination of air attack and ground assault. The air attack helped switch the local political balance, but the victorious campaign did not lead to the clear-cut pro-American triumph that had been hoped for. Instead, it became readily apparent that the war had provoked a regrouping and realignment of factions. Far better than nothing, but not forcing opponents to accept the will of the victor.

Indeed, the history of recent decades indicates the limitations of military power as a tool of policy, and also of advanced technology as the war-winning element. This might appear a surprising view given America's existence as the sole superpower. It is often argued that the so-called Revolution in Military Affairs, based in particular on information warfare capability, enables the most technologically advanced powers, especially the USA, to overcome both distance and resistance in order to secure victory with minimal casualties.

This is, in fact, another version of the mechanisation of the military imagination that has been so potent since the advent of the aeroplane and the tank, and probably had earlier anticipations with the chariot and gunpowder. It is obviously important to seize and develop every advantage that new weaponry can bring, but it is mistaken to imagine that a technological edge guarantees victory at low cost, or, indeed, victory. To be sure, advantages in weaponry are valuable in symmetrical warfare, i.e. between opposing forces that operate in a similar fashion; but, even then, a host of other factors intrude, including strategy, tactics, leadership, unit cohesion and morale, as well as contextual issues, such as the respective determination of the powers engaged.

In asymmetrical warfare, by contrast, the advantages conferred by superior weaponry are severely curtailed. Compare, for instance, the frustration of American forces in the asymmetrical Vietnam War with contemporaneous Israeli success in the symmetrical and short Six Day War of 1967, and then look to the intractable difficulties facing the Israeli military as it struggled to resist the impact of suicide bombers and fighters in the early 2000s.

Finally, technological advantage in both types of conflict inevitably inspires the development of countermeasures involving weapons, tactics, or strategy. Thus, the impact of air power has been greatly lessened by the development of anti-aircraft weapons whose cost-benefit payoff is immense compared to that of a state-of-the-art aircraft. There is no reason to imagine that this process will cease. There will remain military limits to effective force projection, and skilful policy-making will continue to require a shrewd understanding of capability and limits.

This process is not new. Former great powers also struggled to learn and adjust to their capabilities and limits. The Mongols could not conquer Japan or Java, the Ming could not dominate the steppes, and the Manchu failed in Burma. Under Philip II, Spanish power reached across the Pacific but could not suppress the Dutch revolt. Between 1775 and 1842, Britain, the strongest military power in the world, still lost hold of thirteen North American colonies, intervened unsuccessfully in Argentina and Egypt, and suffered defeat in Afghanistan. In historical terms, it is logical to suppose that while American power will dominate the twenty-first century, it will also encounter its limits. This apparent contradiction will provide an important element of the military history of the century, and an understanding of it is important if the American public and policy-makers are to be brought to appreciate what the USA can and cannot reasonably do in the world.

The technological sweep of current American power is awesome, and will become even more so in the future. Aircraft that can fly from the USA to bomb targets halfway round the world, refuelling in mid-air, are different from what Britain and even Russia could throw at Afghanistan in the past, as is the degree of aerial surveillance: indeed the weaponry would have been the stuff of fantasy for earlier generations. For example, the Afghan war showed that unmanned aircraft, hitherto used for surveillance, could be employed to fire missiles. This was not so much a robotic weapon as a sophisticated firing platform controlled from a distance, but it offered a marked enhancement of capability at the intersection of artillery and air power.

The spread of technology, however, has not lessened the need for considered planning and the appropriate use of force. The range of industrial technology, especially with air power, means that two combatants can be fighting much more contrasting wars than ever before. This does not ensure that a technological superiority is decisive. Industrial technology allows for greater mobility (speed and distance) and thus expands the potential area for conflict. The role of 'contact points', where societies with very different technologies interact, remains an important aspect of relative military capability, and thus of military history, but now the 'points' cover the entire surface of the world. The quickening of mobility through technology, however, does not necessarily mean that wars are quicker, faster, briefer or more successful than pre-industrial conflicts.

Mention of Afghanistan provides a further historical resonance. It is possible to point to the earlier difficulties in operating there experienced by outside forces, such as the armies of Alexander the Great or, more recently, the Mughals in 1646–7 and 1672–4. In both cases, armies whose force structure and doctrine made them battle-winning found it difficult to prevail against opponents who did not choose to engage in battle. The ability to force a way along particular routes and to gain control of individual sites did not mean the subjugation of a society.

Whatever the technology available, this has remained the case across the span of human conflict. This situation should encourage attention to the social, political, economic and cultural factors that make it more or less likely that military strength and success will have consequences. As with warfare itself, this leads us to focus on the varied cultural 'landscapes' of the world and their interaction.

It is clear that the willingness to accommodate, and indeed to acculturate to, the more powerful, especially conquerors, has been far from constant across history. In general, the availability of syncretic options, for example the assimilation of local religious cults by the conqueror's religion, and the co-option of local élites, have been the most important means of success. In the modern world, it is unclear how far capitalism will lead to an accommodation with American power, both through a desire to benefit in economic terms, by means of trade and investment, and because of the prestige of the USA as the leading economic power and the source of the themes, modes and goods of the global culture of Hollywood and consumerism. Aside from the rejection of this culture by particular groups, most prominently the range of opinions somewhat misleadingly simplified as radical Islam, there is also the prospect that force will be employed against Western hegemony in order to alter the availability and terms of transactions within this world, as states and social groups seek to gain more resources or to retain control of their own. Pressure for water and oil lends specific intensity to what may also be a more generalised competition for living standards and jobs. While these factors may seem the product of economic change, population growth, and environmental degradation in the modern world, they in fact look back across the ages to competition over watering holes, grazing lands, and the most fertile soil. The modes of conflict change greatly, as do their political, social, economic and cultural contexts, but the root causes appear inherent to human society.

One theme that can be traced back is the impact on the conduct of war of human pressure on the environment. The clearance of trees for agriculture, the most important aspect of this pressure, was of great importance, as was the alteration of natural drainage patterns. The creation of settlements and, over the last century, the urbanisation of society also transformed the topography of war. As yet, there has been no systematic study of the impact on force structure, doctrine and tasking of environmental change across history, but it repays attention, not least because it challenges the ahistorical assumption that the battlefield as well as the face of battle and the experience of war are somehow unchanging.

The availability today of real-time, look-down, multi-sensor surveillance is an important aspect of the way in which the environment of war has changed, and also a reminder that the distribution of state-of-the-art weaponry is, as ever, restricted. Similarly, in the late twentieth century, infrared viewing devices altered the night, defoliation chemicals, such as the Agent Orange used by the Americans in the Vietnam War, changed vegetation cover, while experiments with lasers and nerve gases threatened to change the sensory nature of combat and to add new dimensions of vulnerability.

Today, the capability of a high-tech military to deliver a hard punch is formidable, particularly in symmetrical conflict, but the problems of dealing with intractable local opposition remain, whether the conflict is defined as a war, or as peace-keeping, or as a police action. Both political and religious ideologies serve to prepare groups or societies for long conflicts. Major-General John 'Boney' Fuller, a leading British thinker on military affairs, wrote to an American correspondent in July 1965: 'Today your government and its military advisors appear to have accepted the concept that the way to defeat Communism in Vietnam is by bombing when clearly the precepts garnered from World War Two should have told them that ideas cannot be dislodged by bombs.'[1]

The course of the Vietnam War amply demonstrated Fuller's argument. Air attack brought important tactical and operational benefits, but it proved to have only limited value as a strategic tool, and was certainly not war-winning. Fuller's reference to the Second World War might appear misleading, as the use of atomic bombs led to the surrender of Japan, but by 1965 there were powerful constraints on such use, most particularly possession of atomic bombs by the USA's Communist rivals. Furthermore, cultural constraints played a role in discussion of 'anti-societal' strategies. Mao Zedong claimed that the loss of many million Chinese in a nuclear attack would not prevent the others from fighting on. To wipe out much of society by the use of such weapons appeared the equivalent of the race warfare known later as 'ethnic cleansing' or indeed of genocide: a means that was unacceptable, however potentially effective it might be as a way to destroy the ideas referred to by Fuller. This did not prevent planning for atomic confrontation and war, but it was generally done as a means to deter or repel threats and aggression, and not as a means to launch wars of aggression. It is possible that this may change, and that the deterrence provided by fears of mutual destruction will ebb. If so, this may usher in a new age in human impact on the environment and in the character of conflict.

The future prospects of sustained successful global military interventionism by the USA are questionable. However much the USA (whether or not supported by allies) might dominate at the high end of the power spectrum, the cost of trying and failing to control a rogue state, such as North Korea, is likely to remain at a level that rewards caution, and military leaderships are apt to encourage such prudence. On the other hand, as the experience of the Vietnam War suggests, politicians lacking knowledge of military affairs listen only to the advice they want to hear and often manipulate promotions to ensure that they hear it, and politicians can usually find, within the military, officers willing to tell them what they want in order to advance or protect their own careers. Thus, it is possible that the imperatives of political commitments may override military prudence in a crisis. US attacks are more likely to succeed in destroying opposing forces, or at least their infrastructures, than in creating lasting political solutions.

The nature of American force structure is also important. An emphasis on preparation for great power symmetrical warfare, first with the Soviet Union and then with China, affected the ability of the USA to engage in other conflicts successfully. This emphasis led to a stress on air power and long-range missiles. In the 1950s, jet aircraft carrying nuclear bombs appeared to be the best response to overwhelming Soviet conventional superiority. This doctrine and force structure, in turn, led to an emphasis first on submarine and land-based intercontinental ballistic missiles and, later, on space-based weapons.

This emphasis led to a relative shift of resources away from conventional forces, especially the army, and downplayed the multiple-tasking of forces and preparation demanded by the range of commitments the USA might face. The result became clear in the Vietnam War where courage and can-do spirit could not compensate for the lack of adequate training and doctrine in counter-insurgency warfare on the ground and in close-support air operations. In particular, the effective coordination of air and ground forces in the Vietnam War was affected by the independence of the air force. The doctrine and structure of air power emphasised its capacity to deliver decisive victory independently, rather than through support of land and sea operations.

The risk that war will not conform to the high-tech model that is anticipated and sought remains. Aggregate military capability is not the same as capability or success in any particular scenario. The specific danger the USA faces is the conviction that the technological edge known by the shorthand of the Revolution in Military Affairs can substitute for the political willingness to commit troops and risk heavy casualties, and can also ensure that those who are beaten accept that they have lost and are willing to heed US wishes. The latter is a particular problem with global interventionism. The ability to project strength and win the battle does not mean that the war, more

A Wessex helicopter hovering over HMS *Antelope* burning fiercely and sinking in Ajax Bay, 5 July 1982. This frigate sank as a result of the accidental detonation of an unexploded Argentinian bomb during a defusing attempt. The Falklands War showed the vulnerability of sea power to air attack. Air-launched missiles were responsible for the loss of the destroyer *Sheffield* and bombs for that of the destroyer *Coventry* and the frigate *Ardent*.

specifically the war to force changes in policy and attitude, has been won. To be sure, it is better to be prepared for the wrong war than not to be prepared at all – but only marginally so. It is likely that long-term, low-intensity operations with casualties throughout will be required if the USA is to sustain its hegemony.

More generally, the US military, like that of other powers, are affected by the extent to which small-unit deployment for battle has not changed greatly since 1918. High-quality manpower, training, motivation, discipline and leadership are still essential at the small-unit level. Closing with the enemy remains difficult and costly on the battlefield. Weaponry is rarely the key and, historically, not for long when a large technological advance is made.

The dominant note on which to conclude when surveying the character of modern war is that of variety. Major powers have to be ready for a range of military possibilities, and force structures and doctrines have to be developed accordingly.

At the start of the new millennium, planning for total war between the major powers became less pertinent than at any time for over a century. This reflected the dominant role of the USA within the West, the degree to which other Western states could not wage war without US consent and cooperation (as the British discovered, negatively, over Suez in 1956 and, positively, in the Falklands War in 1982), and the decline of Soviet, and then Russian, power. According to the International Institute for Strategic Studies, in 2000 the USA spent $295 billion on its military budget, Russia $59 billion, China $41 billion, and the seventeen NATO European powers $162.5 billion. By 2001, US military spending had risen to $310 billion, more than the next nine largest national military budgets combined. For 2002, the sum was due to rise by $36 billion, to about 40 per cent of the world's total military spending; although costs for items, such as pay and social benefits, varied greatly across the world, as did expectations about food and accommodation.

This contrast in expenditure between the USA and other powers owed much to US wealth, but also reflected the impact of the 11 September 2001 suicide attacks on New York and Washington by Islamic terrorists, in a jet-fuelled jihad, and the consequent political consensus behind an enormous arms build-up. Other priorities, such as social welfare, played a far larger role in many, although not all, of the poorer and economically weaker states that were second-rank military powers, particularly the NATO European powers.

The resulting contrast in military capability is likely to continue and be accentuated by the very large military and military-industrial investment on research and development in the USA. The results are very apparent in the use of satellites and related high-speed technology. The US satellite-based global positioning system, employed for surveillance and targeting, is not matched elsewhere, and is being strengthened as the USA invests in a new network of spy satellites, contributing to the militarisation of space.

Like other hegemonies in history, that of the USA partly rests on force, and is therefore inherently unstable. The USA benefits from the absence of insurrectionary movements and political breakdown in North America, but the global pretensions of its power, the far-flung nature of its economic, political and strategic interests, and the nature of domestic assumptions makes it vulnerable to feeling that it has to act in areas where it will be difficult to enforce its will and to avoid long-term entanglements. This is particularly true in Latin America and the Middle East.

Aside from the USA, only China is able to act as a threatening great power, but its military is weaker, Furthermore, China's challenge is restricted by the circumspection of its military projection: there are US forces in east Asia, not Chinese forces in the West Indies. Since 1950, China has clashed with the USA in the Korean War, and with India, North Vietnam and the Soviet Union, but all, bar the Korean War, were short-term conflicts, and the Chinese were, and are, wary of military, and indeed diplomatic, commitments further afield. Despite this, China and the USA have clashing interests in east Asia, especially over Taiwan, and also a powerful distrust between the two states that reflects their very different political cultures.

At the close of the book it is appropriate to mention China, the world's most populous country, and one with a very long and important military history, alongside the USA, currently, and likely long to remain, the world's leading economic and military power. If they define great-power politics at present, there are also a host of other military forces, both states and non-state agencies, particularly guerrilla movements. Between them, they have kept much of the world at war or unstable for the last decade, and it is all too likely that this will continue. There is little sign in many countries that a sense of shared humanity exists sufficient to discourage the use of force as the means of politics.

NOTES

CHAPTER 5

1. BL, Add. 57313, f. 13.
2. M.H. Fisher (ed.), *The Travels of Dean Mahomet. An Eighteenth-Century Journey Through India* (Berkeley, 1997), p. 55.

CHAPTER 6

1. Sheridan, 4 Ap. 1797, W. Cobbett (ed.), *Parliamentary History of England vol. 33* (1818), cols 226–7.
2. BL, Add. 56088, f. 5.
3. BL, Add. 54483, f. 22.
4. Quoted in T. Ballard, 'Army After-Action Reports, Circa 1860s', *Army History*, No. 30 (1994), p. 37.
5. I. Gordon, *Soldier of the Raj* (Barnsley, 2001), pp. 92–3.

CHAPTER 7

1. BL, Add. 56097, f. 145.
2. *The Russian General Staff, The Soviet–Afghan War. How a Superpower Fought and Lost,* translated and edited by L.W. Grau and M.A. Gress (Lawrence, Kansas, 2002), pp. 305–6.

CHAPTER 8

1. London, King's College, Liddell Hart Archive, Fuller Papers 4/6/24/2.

FURTHER READING

For reasons of space, the focus is on recent works. Earlier literature can be pursued via the bibliographies and footnotes of these works.

GENERAL

S.E. Alcock, T.N. D'Altroy, K.D. Morrison and C.M. Sinopoli (eds), *Empires. Perspectives from Archaeology and History* (2001).

J.M. Black, *War. Past, Present and Future* (2000).

N. Di Cosmo (ed.), *Warfare in Inner Asian History, 500–1800* (2002).

A. Crosby, *Throwing Fire: Projectile Technology through History* (2002).

D.A. Graff and R. Higham (eds), *A Military History of China* (2002).

F.W. Kagan and R. Higham (eds), *The Military History of Tsarist Russia* (2002).

J. Keegan, *A History of Warfare* (1993).

W.H. McNeill, *The Pursuit of Power: Technology, Armed Force and Society since AD 1000* (1983).

G. Parker (ed.), *The Cambridge Illustrated History of Warfare* (1995).

CHAPTER 1

R. Amitai-Preiss, *Monguls and Mamluks: The Maluk-Ilkhanid War, 1260–281* (1995).

J. Carman and A. Harding (eds), *Ancient Warfare* (1999).

A. Ferrill, *The Origins of War* (1985).

D. Graff, *Medieval Chinese Warfare, 300–900* (2001).

V.D. Hanson, *The Western Way of War: Infantry Battle in Classical Greece* (1989).

L.H. Keeley, *War before Civilisation: The Myth of the Peaceful Savage* (1996).

CHAPTER 2

B.S. Bachrach, *Early Carolingian Warfare. Prelude to Empire* (2001).

W.W. Farris, *Heavenly Warriors. The Evolution of Japan's Military, 500–1300* (1992).

J. France, *Western Warfare in the Age of the Crusades, 1000–1300* (1999).

J. Haldon, *Warfare, State and Society in the Byzantine World 560–1204* (1999).

N. Hooper and M. Bennett, *The Cambridge Illustrated Atlas of Warfare. The Middle Ages, 768–1487* (1996).

H. Kennedy, *The Armies of the Caliphs. Military and Society in the Early Islamic State* (2001).

Y. Lev (ed.), *War and Society in the Eastern Mediterranean. 7th–15th Centuries* (1997).

L. Levathes, *When China Ruled the Seas. The Treasure Fleet of the Dragon Throne 1405–1433* (1994).

S. Morillo, *The Battle of Hastings: Sources and Interpretations* (1996).

D. Nicolle, *Arms and Armour of the Crusading Era 1050–1350* (1988).

S. Rose, *Medieval Naval Warfare, 1000–1500* (2001).

P. Varley, *Warriors of Japan as Portrayed in the War Tales* (1994).

CHAPTERS 3 AND 4

T.J. Barfield, *The Perilous Frontier: Nomadic Empires and China* (1989).

J.M. Black, *European Warfare 1494–1660* (2002).

P. Brummett, *Ottoman Seapower and Levantine Diplomacy in the Age of Discovery* (1994).

M.C. Fissel, *English Warfare, 1511–1642* (2001).

J. Glete, *Warfare at Sea, 1500–1650* (1999).

J. Glete, *War and the State in Early Modern Europe* (2001).

J. Gommans, *Mughal Warfare* (2002).

J.R. Hale, *War and Society in Renaissance Europe, 1450–1620* (1985).

J.A. Lynn, *The Wars of Louis XIV 1667–1714* (1999).

R. Murphey, *Ottoman Warfare, 1815–1914* (2000).

G. Parker, *The Military Revolution: Military Innovation and the Rise of the West, 1500–1800* (2nd edn, 1996).

D. Parrott, *Richelieu's Army. War, Government and Society in France, 1624–1642* (2001).

A.J.R. Russell-Wood, *The Portuguese Empire, 1415–1808* (1998).

J.K. Thornton, *Warfare in Atlantic Africa, 1500–1800* (1999).

S. Turnbull, *The Samurai: A Military History* (1977).

——, *Samurai Invasion* (2002).

J.S. Wheeler, *The Irish and British Wars 1637–1654* (2002).

CHAPTER 5

J.M. Black, *European Warfare, 1660–1815* (1994).

A. Gat, *The Origins of Military Thought* (1989).

R. Harding, *Seapower and Naval Warfare, 1650–1830* (1999).

A. Starkey, *European and Native American Warfare 1675–1815* (1998).

H.M. Ward, *The War of Independence and the Transformation of American Society* (1999).

P. Wilson, *German Armies. War and German Society, 1648–1806* (1998).

CHAPTER 6

J.M. Black, *Western Warfare 1775–1882* (2001).

B. Bond, *The Pursuit of Victory: From Napoleon to Saddam Hussein* (1996).

B.A. Elleman, *Modern Chinese Warfare, 1795–1989* (2001).

G. Rothenberg, *The Napoleonic Wars* (1999).

I.R. Smith, *The Origins of the South African War, 1899–1902* (1996).

L. Sondhaus, *Naval Warfare, 1815–1914* (2000).

B. Vandervort, *Wars of Imperial Conquest in Africa, 1830–1914* (1998).

G. Wawro, *Warfare and Society in Europe, 1792–1914* (1999).

CHAPTER 7

G.W. Baer, *One Hundred Years of Sea Power. The U.S. Navy, 1890–1990* (1993).

O. Bartov, *Hitler's Army: Soldiers, Nazis and War in the Third Reich* (1992).

I.F. Beckett, *Modern Insurgencies and Counter-Insurgencies* (2001).

J.M. Black, *Warfare in the Western World 1882–1975* (2002).

A. Bregman, *Israel's Wars, 1947–1993* (2000).

J. Buckley, *Air Power in the Age of Total War* (1998).

A. Clayton, *Frontiersmen. Warfare in Africa Since 1950* (1998).

E.J. Erickson, *Ordered to Die: A History of the Ottoman Army in the First World War* (2001).

N. Ferguson, *The Pity of War* (1999).

R.C. Hall, *The Balkan Wars 1912–1913* (2000).

M. Howard, *The First World War* (2002).

R. Reese, *The Soviet Military Experience* (1999).

S. Sandler, *The Korean War* (1999).

M. Sherry, *The Rise of American Air Power: The Creation of Armageddon* (1987).

R. Spector, *At War. At Sea. Sailors and Naval Warfare in the Twentieth Century* (2001).

H. Strachan, *The First World War. I. To Arms* (2001).

S. Tucker, *The Great War, 1914–1918* (1997).

——, *Vietnam* (1998).

J. Verhey, *The Spirit of 1914: Militarism, Myth and Mobilisation in Germany* (2000).

INDEX